D1035698

Educated Women

Higher Education,
Culture,
and
Professionalism
1850–1950

*A twelve volume series of
never-before-published
anthologies and dissertations*

Edited by
Barbara Miller Solomon
Harvard University

A GARLAND SERIES

Titles in this Series

BLACK WOMEN
IN HIGHER EDUCATION

An Anthology of
Essays, Studies,
and Documents

Elizabeth L. Ihle, editor

Garland Publishing, Inc.
New York & London 1992

Library of Congress Cataloging–in–Publication Data

Black women in higher education / edited by Elizabeth L. Ihle.
        p.   cm. — (Educated women)
    Includes bibliographical references.
    ISBN 0–8240–6840–8
    1. Afro-American women—Education (Higher)—History—
Sources. 2. Afro-American college students—History—Sources.
I. Ihle, Elizabeth L. II. Series.
LC2781.B474 1992
378'.0089'96073—dc20   92-7240
                                                            CIP

Printed on acid-free, 250-year-life paper
Manufactured in the United States of America

To

John, Blair, and Beth

CONTENTS

A NEW CENTURY OPENS: RULES AND POLICIES

BREAKING AWAY: HIGHER EDUCATION IN THE 60S AND BEYOND

PREFACE

Black Women in Higher Education offers a collection of documents that illustrate the wide range of experiences in African-American women's pursuit of higher education from the nineteenth century to the present. The publication of this anthology affirms the growing interest of scholars and students in both African-American and women's history.

What higher education means has always varied according to the historical time and context. African-American women's higher education begins before the Civil War at Oberlin College. Before delving into those beginnings for Black women at colleges, one must have some understanding of the broader historical context of higher education in America.

Both before and after the Civil War, many schools and colleges offered a combination of liberal arts and practical training. In the late nineteenth century, the growth of private secondary schools and the establishment of public high schools paved the way for more advanced collegiate study. The term "higher education" often applied to any studies beyond the elementary level, although the rate of educational development varied from region to region. For example, southerners in the 1880s labelled as higher education what we now consider to be high school education, and even that education was a privilege only available to relatively few people. During the same time period, however, other parts of the country were experiencing a significant expansion in the number of public high schools. When substantial populations of students were receiving a high school education, then colleges could raise their academic standards. As a result, the term "higher education" became equated with what might be considered at least two years of college today and, before long, four years. This historical anthology reflects these evolving definitions of higher education in the context of African-American women's lives.

Not only do the documents presented here speak to changing definitions of education, but they also examine Black women's higher education from a variety of perspectives. The authors came from a wide range of economic backgrounds. Some students had no financial worries, but many more women described the efforts and sacrifices that they and their families made to achieve the goal of higher education. Some pieces are written in the first person, and others are more formal essays. Still other selections offer information from student publications, administrative sources, professional associations, community organizations, and oral histories. Whatever the source, all these documents share a commonality: they speak to the persistent determination of African-American women—in the face of many obstacles—to gain knowledge and empowerment through formal education at colleges and universities.

THE BEGINNING: LATE NINETEENTH CENTURY

The African-American women who pursued college work in the nineteenth century truly were pioneers, as the desirability of college education for women of any race was still a debatable matter in many circles. As schools and, later, colleges for Blacks opened in the decades following the Civil War, what the goals and content of women's collegiate education ought to be were frequently discussed.

"Lists of Antebellum Black Women Students at Oberlin," "A Black Oberlin Woman in the 1860s" (Fanny Jackson Coppin), and "A Black Oberlin Woman in the 1880s" (Mary Church Terrell) all underscore Oberlin College's important role in the history of women's education. It was the first institution to admit both African-Americans and women. In 1862 it bestowed the first baccalaureate degree on an African-American woman, Mary Jane Patterson. Included here are lists naming Black women who went to Oberlin before the Civil War and two memoirs of personal experiences.

Significantly, the lists identify women enrolled in other programs as well as baccalaureate recipients. Nineteenth-century colleges often offered a variety of curricula below the baccalaureate level, thereby placing students in less demanding programs. At this time, students who completed bachelor's degrees were exceptional; elementary teaching, the career ambition of many college women, did not require such a degree. Those who did earn bachelor's degrees, such as Mary Jane Patterson, were high achievers in college and often thereafter. The Oberlin student memoirs, by Coppin and Terrell, are indeed expressions by exceptional women.

The memoir by Fanny Jackson Coppin describes her experiences at Oberlin. Her humble origins, extraordinary efforts to educate herself, satisfaction in being an Oberlin student, and subsequent career as an outstanding educator fit the profile of many Oberlin graduates. The observations she offers about the eagerness of freedmen and women to learn are corroborated by many other observers. Coppin's pride in being a symbol of her race was typical of other Black students at Oberlin.

Mary Church Terrell, author of the 1880s Oberlin memoir, is less typical. Daughter of a successful Memphis businessman, she escaped the financial struggle of many students and completed both the institution's college preparatory program and a baccalaureate degree. (Both Terrell and Coppin had been discouraged by the Oberlin administration from entering the baccalaureate program because of gender, but they pushed forward nevertheless.) Terrell later became a nationally known figure through her many civic activities; she was a founder of the National Association of Colored Women and eventually received honorary doctorates from Oberlin, Wilberforce, and Howard.

The great concern for morality is used to justify Black women's education, as can be seen in the following section of five documents, "Moral Training for Black Women: Selected Excerpts." In the late nineteenth and early twentieth centuries a commonly held idea, particularly among whites, assumed that African-American women tended to be promiscuous, a view that conveniently disregarded and distorted the tradition from slave days of white men's sexually assaulting Black women with impunity. Such a stereotype was clearly an affront to the moral reputation of Black women. Whether or not they believed in this negative label, educators of Blacks used the myth as a compelling argument for the further schooling of women. Moreover, as is evident in the following excerpts, the stereotype was consciously combatted in the strict day-to-day school policies governing student life.

"Black Women's Higher Education: A Man's Perspective from the 1880s" (William T. Alexander) embraces the widely accepted nineteenth-century belief that women are the key to the moral improvement of the human race through their influence in family life and therefore should be educated with this idea in mind. Alexander, however, offers no specifics as to the content of their higher education. Also, he makes no references to the necessity of preparing African-American women to work outside the home, unlike other educators of the time.

The next selection, "A Report Concerning the Colored Women of the South" (Mrs. E.C. Hobson and Mrs. C.E. Hopkins), was an 1896 report presented to the John F. Slater Fund, one of several philanthropic organizations that supplied funds for African-American education in the postwar South. The next brief excerpt, "Sophia Packard to J. D. Rockefeller—December 29, 1883," is taken from a letter written by Packard, one of the founders of Spelman College. The last two excerpts, taken from "*The New Negro on Campus: Black College Rebellions of the 1920*" (Raymond Wolters) and "*The Negro Woman's College Education*" (Jeanne L. Noble), are comments on the very strict rules for women at Black colleges. All these educators were determined to prove the high moral standards of African-American women.

"Virginia State University: A Woman's Recollection of 1887–1889" (Ruth Brown Hucles) adds another dimension to the picture of college life for Black women in the nineteenth century. Virginia was one of three southern states to fund college education for African-Americans before 1890; the other states that took advantage of the Morrill Land Grant Act of 1862 were Mississippi and South Carolina. Most colleges for African-Americans in the postwar South had been initiated through private missionary societies. When funds from the North dwindled, many schools closed, leaving some private institutions and the three state institutions. Hucles's autobiographical essay, "Virginia State College as I Knew It as a Student and Worker," gives insight into the experiences of a Black woman at a public institution.

"Higher Education for African-American Women: A Justification" is an excerpt from a piece by Anna Julia Cooper, a well-known educator in Washington, D.C. She maintains that Black males got attention and encouragement to complete a higher education far in excess of that given to females. She uses some of her own experiences in college preparation courses to illustrate her point.

"Women Students at Atlanta University, 1894: Report, Rules, and Photo" gives another glimpse of college life in the nineteenth century. Among the existing centers of college education, Atlanta, Georgia, ranked high. Not surprisingly, private institutions that had continued for Blacks were in cities or areas with large Black populations. Fisk, for example, was located in Nashville, Tennessee; it had awarded its first degree in 1875 and continued to produce sizable numbers of college-trained graduates. Atlanta, however, had numerous colleges for African-Americans: Spelman College for women, Morehouse College for men, Morris Brown College, Clark University, and Atlanta University. Through this selection—a photograph of the 1894 graduating class, a follow-up report on their activities in the year since graduation, and a dress code—one can attain a slight sense of being a student in Atlanta at the end of the nineteenth century.

A NEW CENTURY OPENS: RULES AND POLICIES

The beginnings of the twentieth century witnessed both retrenchment and growth in African-American higher education. While the popularity of Booker T. Washington's industrial education served as a deterrent to the growth of academic public high schools for Blacks and college-level courses at Black state institutions, private high schools and colleges continued to grow to meet the demands of their African-American clientele who wanted a solid liberal arts education. The establishment of college alumnae clubs, references to problems facing college-educated women, and more numerous accounts of women's collegiate experiences attest to the increasing number of female African-American college graduates.

"Atlanta University Student Life c. 1900" (Bazoline E. Usher) opens this section on the twentieth century, as our understanding of issues relevant to African-American students' lives at Atlanta University expands. Usher went to Atlanta University, worked for 40 years in the Atlanta public school system, and eventually became supervisor for Black education. She was interviewed under the auspices of Radcliffe's Black Women's Oral History Project, where she discusses her life as a student around the turn of the century. The interview illustrates the economic class differences among African-American students. Generally, the economic level that African-Americans considered to be middle class, white Americans would have probably considered to be somewhat lower. The interview also implies that rules at coeducational Atlanta University were somewhat more lenient than those at nearby Spelman.

While a number of the private institutions of higher education for African-Americans were becoming more advanced in the early 1900s, their public counterparts were experiencing mixed progress. Some southern states established specialized schools for African-Americans when the 1890 renewal of the Morrill Act specified that funds had to be used for both races. Although the names of most of these schools referred to their agricultural, technical, or industrial natures, a number of them originally offered some college-level work, primarily as a means of preparing teachers. Around the turn of the century, however, some states even dropped these few college courses and justified their actions on the grounds that African-Americans were not qualified to take advantage of collegiate levels of schooling.

Most of these public institutions were coeducational, and the decision whether or not African-Americans were offered a collegiate curriculum usually did not relate to gender. Instances did occur, however, when women were barred as students simultaneously with the elimination of college courses for Blacks. "The 1901 Decision to Bar Women from North Carolina A & T" (Carrye Hill Kelley)describes such an instance. It documents reasons for removing women from North Carolina A & T; they were not readmitted until 1926.

"Defense of Black Women's College Education" (Mary Church Terrell) illustrates that racism and sexism were not solely southern phenomena. Her 1901 letter to the *New York City Independent* plainly indicates that African-American women, despite obstacles, were participating in college courses in coeducational, integrated institutions throughout the country. These women of the North or the Middle West were more likely to be the daughters of middle- or upper-class families than those of poor ones who could not afford to go far from home for schooling. Poverty often limited mobility.

"Women's Life at Tuskegee, 1911–1915" (Hattie Simmons Kelly) brings up another issue in the education of African-Americans—an issue particularly applicable perhaps to those struggling with poverty. Many white Americans of the early 1900's considered the education offered at Booker T. Washington's Tuskegee Institute

in Alabama to be ideal for African-Americans.[1] Its philosophy was to train Black people in low-level, economically useful occupations. Such education would give them practical tools, ways to earn a living, and the respect of white southerners. Although Washington's philosophy has been criticized as being too accommodating to the southern white power structure and to the northern philanthropists who financed southern education as a means of improving the South's economic productivity, it was highly influential at the time. Hattie Simmons Kelly, a student at Tuskegee from 1911 to 1915, describes her student life there in this piece. She later served at Tuskegee as dean of education and later as dean of women.

By 1915, African-American women had been at colleges long enough to be establishing systems of support and aid for themselves and others. The existence of role models, alumnae associations, and clubs were all structures that were useful to the African-American aspiring college woman. The four selections in this section show the impact of role models, the efforts of college graduates to socialize with each other, and speculations about what the African-American woman should do with her education.

"Mary McLeod Bethune in 1915: A Student's Perspective" (Lucy Miller Mitchell) gives a rare glimpse of an indefatigable educator and her influence on a younger Black woman. Bethune, who later in life became a national figure as the first African-American woman to be a high-ranking federal administrator, began her career by founding a school for African-American women in 1904. It became coeducational when it merges in 1923 with Cookman Institute for Boys (founded in 1872) and moved to Daytona Beach, Florida. At Bethune-Cookman College she became the first African-American woman college president, serving until 1947. She also served in President Franklin Delano Roosevelt's administration from 1936 to 1944 as director of the Division of Negro Affairs of the National Youth Administration. Educated at Scotia Seminary in North Carolina (at that time a school for only African-American women), Bethune worked tirelessly throughout her life for the cause of education and a fair deal for African-Americans. Lucy Miller Mitchell's comments and memories provide some insight into the impact of this charismatic leader on one of her students. Mitchell later achieved prominence for her work in early childhood education and child day care.

"A Home for Black Women at the University of Iowa, 1908–1929" demonstrates conscious efforts by college graduates to provide concrete help as well as to serve as role models to younger Black women. The late 1800s and early 1900s had witnessed the development and growth of African-American women's clubs in many cities across the nation. These associations generally attracted women from the middle and upper classes, many of whom had received some higher education. The clubs served largely the same functions that their white counterparts did, offering continuing education for their members, undertaking projects to improve their community, and providing a social outlet for their members and their families. Clubs founded by African-American women, however, sometimes undertook the additional responsibility of meliorating the effects of racism. This document shows how one such club helped African-American women at the University of Iowa, where housing was not provided for them. The club purchased and maintained a home where the college women could live.

"The College Alumnae Club: An Early History" provides another example of organizational support for African-American college-educated women. Strictly for college women, the College Alumnae Club began in Washington, D.C., in 1910, with Mary Church Terrell as its first president. The selection included here, a history of its early years, lists the many colleges and universities nationwide where African-American women had graduated by that time. The fact that the club was established in Washington D.C. is indicative of the high degree of cultured life available to African-American's in the nation's capital.

"Opportunities for the Educated Black Woman in the 1920's" (Eva D. Bowles) shifts focus from African-American women's helping of each other to questioning the future. The Black woman struggled with many of the same problems that her white sister did. One of those dilemmas, what to do with her college education, is the theme of this article. Teaching had provided the original justification for higher education, and a majority of women taught at some point in their lives; but the twentieth century opened other possibilities. Social work and school administration became options, with a few rarer possibilities in law, medicine, and business.

Economic class remained an important factor in determining the outcome of a student's college experience. Poorer students tended to go to public institutions near their homes, which was often the least expensive way of pursuing a higher education. "Working One's Way Through College: A Kentucky Woman's Experience in the 1920s" (Alice Allison Dunnigan) offers the reader a vision of college life as seen through the eyes of a very poor student. She also indirectly tells the reader about administrative problems (and very likely underfunding) in a segregated public institution and about levels of education necessary for a teaching certificate. (Baccalaureate degrees were not required of elementary teachers in a majority of the states until the 1950s.) For the poorer student such as Dunnigan, teaching was still the future path after college.

The next two selections, "A Black Woman at the University of Cincinnati, 1918" (Lena Beatrice Morton) and "The University of California at Berkeley in the 1920's" (Ida L. Jackson), specifically provide examples of racism and sexism in integrated colleges. Although the authors cite racial discrimination in a number of forms, it appears in both accounts in swimming class incidents. Physical education, perhaps because of its potential for more physical contact and bodily awareness, was a particularly vulnerable area for manifestations of discrimination and prejudice. At the University of Cincinnati, Morton decides whether principle or graduation was more important. At the University of California at Berkeley, not having many African-American classmates, Jackson tells of being aided by white mentors.

Also striking in these two articles is the commitment of African-American families to education, for both authors speak of their families moving in order to improve the daughters' opportunities for education. The glimpse into college life in the late 1920s and early 1930s gained here brings to light one more aspect of student life—that of African-American Greek organizations that began to form in the first decades of the twentieth century. These include three sororities founded at Howard (Alpha Kappa Alpha in 1908, Delta Sigma Theta in 1912, and Zeta Phi Beta in 1920) and Sigma Gamma Rho founded at Butler University in 1922.

Racism was no respecter of economic class. "A Black Woman's Experience at Wellesley" (Jane Bolin Offutt) is a reminiscence of a privileged student at Wellesley College, one of the prestigious Seven Sister institutions. As in a number of other firsthand accounts, racist attitudes extended to the faculty. Offutt's experience of being discouraged in pursuing law school because of her sex as well as her race is ironic in a women's college known for promoting the ambitions of its students. The fact that the author became the first African-American woman judge in the United States in 1931 demonstrates the potential loss to society caused by arbitrary distinctions based on race and sex.

The problems of African-Americans at traditionally white institutions caught the attention of the National Association of College Women, which had emerged from the College Alumnae Club. "A Call for Interracial Cooperation from the 1928 National Association of College Women" documents the concern and support of African-American alumnae for students such as Offutt.

Not surprisingly, sex stereotyping was also present in African-American institutions of the 1920s as the next four selections demonstrate. "Requisites for a Dean of Women: 1927" (Tossie P.F. Whiting) describes the duties of a dean of girls (in secondary school) or women (in college). This position emerged in African-American schools in the 1910s and 1920s as a result of the influx of adolescent girls into the newly established high schools as well as colleges for African-Americans. The dean became an important shaper of school policy and the creator of many rules students had to follow. Tossie Whiting's reference to the female student's need for more adequate safeguarding illustrates African-American institutions' awareness of the need to uphold moral and behavioral standards that were beyond reproach in the surrounding community. Whiting was dean of women at what was then called the Virginia Normal and Industrial Institute, the state's land grant institution for African-Americans.

Fisk University, one of the most prestigious of the private African-American institutions, gives the reader the next two examples of sex stereotyping within African-American institutions, public or private.[2] "Standards of Fisk Women—The 1928–1929 Fisk Handbook" perhaps written by a dean of women, is Fisk University's statement of womanhood taken from a 1928 student handbook. "Collegiate Womanhood: The Double Bind of Race and Sex" (Majorie L. Baltimore) appeared in the institution's alumni journal in 1930, endorsing the traditional concept of female nature while supporting women's movement into civic life and condemning women's radicalism. Baltimore is the first author of those collected in this anthology to refer specifically to the dual burden of sex and race faced by African-American women.

"The Women at Tennessee State from a 1927 Male Perspective" (Ozaana Vineyard) indicates that students were also adept at sex stereotyping. Although highly complimentary of the Tennessee State female students' beauty and character, the male speakers in the dialogue say nothing about the women's intellectual ability or desire for knowledge, the most obvious reasons for pursuing a higher education.

MID-CENTURY: DISCRIMINATION BY RACE AND SEX

As African-American college-educated women moved into the mid-twentieth century, they continued to voice articulately their concerns and opinions. They cited discrimination when they saw it in various forms.

They spoke both of their own needs and satisfactions and of changing issues and lasting questions for the Black woman pursuing higher education. They began to produce leaders in higher education.

"Mary Elizabeth Branch: Black College President" describes the second African-American woman to head a college and also brings up a more general issue for educators—coeducation versus the woman's college. Two articles are presented here about this woman who served as president of Tillotson College in Austin, Texas, from 1930 until her death in 1944. At the beginning of Branch's presidency, Tillotson (along with Spelman and Bennett colleges) was a women's institution. Tillotson, however, began accepting men in 1935, most likely as a means of increasing enrollment. The first article describes Branch from the perspective of her alma mater, Virginia State College, and the second, from the perspective of an observer who watched Tillotson grow. The institution survives today as the coeducational Huston-Tillotson College.

The next document turns back to all too familiar questions of discrimination. "Pay Inequity: One Woman's Experience" (Eva B. Dykes) points out that even the most educated African-American women suffered because of their gender and illustrates economic discrimination against female educators. In elementary and secondary schools, a differential in salary was often justified on the grounds that males had to take care of discipline. That rationale did not apply in higher education. At all levels, the differential also was justified by the fact that men had to support families, but few thought of women who were widowed with children or who, though single, supported aging parents or perhaps nieces or nephews. A salary gap between men and women still exists in a number of higher educational institutions today, though certainly in not so blatant a form as Eva Dykes relates.

"Black Women's College Curriculum: Needed Reforms" (Lucy B. Slowe) argues that Black colleges and families must take more responsibility for ensuring that women students receive the tools needed to be successful in the world. Enormously influential in African-American women's higher education, Slowe was a founding member of Alpha Kappa Alpha sorority, a charter member of the District of Columbia College Alumnae Club, a founding member of the National Association of Deans of Women and Advisors To Girls in Negro Schools, and the dean of women at Howard University from 1923 until her death in 1937. In the essay included here, she criticizes the tendency of many African-American colleges and families to restrict women and urges a more solid education both in and outside the classroom to prepare women for greater participation in the economic, social, and political aspects of their communities.

"Student Life in the 1930s: Tennessee State" gives us the voice of a student who, of course, has her own perspective. This 1935 Tennessee State graduate's concern with social life provides a contrast with Slowe's recommendations for improving African-American women's higher education. Despite the repressive rules in place in many African-American colleges, this interviewee indicates that students still managed to have fun.

"Defense of the Women's College" (Florence M. Read) returns to the perspective of the college administrator and introduces another influential educator within African-American institutions. Florence Read was a white woman who served as president of Spelman College from 1927 to 1953. She would

probably have agreed with Lucy Slowe's assessment. Read goes further, however, returning to the single sex issue and arguing that such an educational setting offers special advantages to African-American women.

"White Staff Life at Spelman" (Dorothy K. Clark) draws from the unpublished autobiography of Read's white secretary at Spelman in the late 1930s. Clark's reminiscences provide another viewpoint on Black college life as well as illustrate the restrictive racial mores in place in Atlanta at that time.

"Bennett College: Another Black Woman's College" (Constance H. Marteena) gives a description in 1938 of the only other historically African-American college for women besides Spelman still in existence. The picture of this North Carolina college underscores Bennett's active role in the life of the surrounding community, a focus in the education of many African-American women.

Despite the influence of Spelman and Bennett, coeducation moved forward, as can be seen in "Bethune-Cookman College in the 1930s" (Ward N. Madison). Ward N. Madison, a staff member of the General Education Board (GEB), a philanthropy largely funded by the Rockefellers, wrote this memo about a visit to Bethune-Cookman College in 1938, after Mrs. McLeod had taken a position with the Roosevelt administration and while Dr. Abram Simpson was serving as acting president. The selection makes clear that, even at this institution quite well known and possibly better financed than others of a similar nature, funding was still precarious. It also shows that, at least in the minds of its leaders, a clear distinction had not been made between higher education and vocational education. Furthermore, although rules at many historically African-American colleges had been re-

laxed, the long class days at Bethune-Cookman demonstrate that students were still not trusted to use discretionary time effectively.

Another aspect of African-American higher education brought to light by Madison's memo is the power of philanthropy to shape higher education, especially in institutions as financially needy as Black colleges. Throughout the first half of the twentieth century the GEB and other philanthropies molded such institutions by giving them funds to start or improve aspects of their programs that the philanthropy approved. On the one hand, the millions of dollars that the GEB and other philanthropies gave to improve education at all levels and for both races in the South obviously had a positive impact. Yet critics charge, perhaps justifiably, that the philanthropists' main interests were developing more efficient workers and content second-class citizens as a means of making the region economically progressive and socially stable. The GEB selected the institutions it aided with great deliberation and care; Bethune, for instance, began seeking the GEB's help in 1905 but was not seriously considered until the 1930s.

"A Black Student at a White Institution: 1940s Perspective" (Edythe Hargrave) returns to the theme of prejudice as experienced by the individual student. Hargrave indicates that prejudice was still especially strong in physical education classes and in extracurricular life and also suggests that Blacks graduating from this college were highly respected for their scholastic ability.

Following this personal view is the researched view of another student, "The Black College Woman in the 1940's" (Marion Vera Cuthbert). This selection is a chapter from the first dissertation written about college-

educated African-American women. Cuthbert completed this work in 1942 at Columbia University. In a number of states, particularly in the South, segregation laws prohibited African-Americans' admission to in-state graduate schools, and so qualified African-Americans were given scholarships to study elsewhere. A popular choice was Columbia, which ironically probably provided a better graduate education than did many of the public universities of the South. Cuthbert makes some interesting points about the reasons why African-American women went to college and why more men than women graduated. She also faced a problem still encountered by today's historians of African-American women's higher education—a lack of previous studies. Most of her data related to all African-Americans' education, and she had to extrapolate what she could that applied to women.

At the time of Cuthbert's publication, World War II gave a new focus to educators of women. "Problems in Black Women's College Education" (Flemmie P. Kittrell) analyzes the needs of African-American college women in relation to the war. Flemmie Kittrell, a home economist who served both at Bennett College and Howard University, believed that African-American colleges were equipped to prepare women for the upheavals caused by war. She thought, however, that women needed more training in integrating their professional and domestic lives.

"The Effect of World War II on Black College Women, 1944" is an excerpt from the minutes of the fifteenth annual meeting of the National Association of Deans of Women and Advisers To Girls in Negro Schools founded earlier by Lucy D. Slowe. Kittrell presided over this meeting. Its main topic was the effect of the war on the girls and women in the

members' charge. Additionally, how to control relations between servicemen and the Black female students apparently attracted much discussion.

"The Double Barrier of Race and Sex: A Voice from the 1940s" (Willa B. Player) voices observations and analysis of a more serious nature but from the same time period. Player later served as president of Bennett College from 1955 to 1969. (Bennett College succeeded in electing a woman president more than three decades before Spelman did.) Coming from earlier in her career, this essay discusses the limitations of career choice for the college educated African-American woman in the segregated South.

Women's colleges such as Bennett and Spelman clearly invoked great loyalty in their graduates. "Spelman in the 1950s," an interview with a 1956 graduate, is pervaded by the pride that the unnamed interviewee took in Spelman. Having attended a public African-American institution before transferring to Spelman, she was in a position to state differences between the publicly segregated institution and the private African-American college for women.

From the 1930s on, the National Association for the Advancement of Colored People (NAACP) had supported a series of court cases to integrate American education. It directed its first efforts toward professional and graduate education because a number of states kept their graduate and professional schools segregated by establishing similar (but inferior) facilities in African-American institutions or in providing tuition grants that enabled African-Americans to be trained out of state.

These practices were largely stopped through a series of court decisions: Black students were admitted to the University of Maryland law school via the

Murray case in 1935, to the University of Missouri law school via the *Gaines* case in 1938 (although the plaintiff Gaines disappeared and was never seen again), and the University of Oklahoma law school via the *Sipuel* case in 1947. Finally in *Sweatt v. Painter,* in 1949 the Supreme Court decreed that once a student was admitted, he or she could not be discriminated against, for example, by being forced to sit in a certain part of the classroom or cafeteria.[3] After these victories, the NAACP then turned to desegregating public elementary and secondary schools, its efforts culminating in the famous B*rown* decision of 1954.

The next educational focus of the NAACP was undergraduate collegiate education. "Autherine Lucy and the University of Alabama, 1956" (Nora Sayre) describes the NAACP's early efforts in Alabama to desegregate undergraduate education with the help of Autherine Lucy who had applied to the University of Alabama to pursue a library science degree, which was unavailable in the public African-American institutions of the state. The description of her experiences and the subsequent interview with her are riveting.

"Black College Women's Education in the 1950s: A Survey" (Jeanne L. Noble) provides an overview rather than the intensity of individual experience. Author of *The Negro Women's College Education*, Noble conducted a survey of college women who were members of Delta Sigma Theta sorority, and the results are reported here. Noble served as president of the Deltas from 1958 to 1963 and had been active at the national level before her election. Since her sorority, like the other African-American sororities, tended to attract the more affluent of African-American students, the survey may not accurately reflect the concerns of the whole spectrum of college alumnae. The results of her survey, however, are interesting. For instance, graduates of traditionally white institutions were more liberal arts minded than their peers at historically African-American institutions.

BREAKING AWAY: HIGHER EDUCATION IN THE 60'S AND BEYOND

The 1960s was indeed a time of "breaking away" for African-Americans in the United States as the activism of the civil rights movement intensified and forced white power structures to adapt to demands for equal treatment. The field of higher education and African-American students themselves all felt catalytic changes, ones of attitude as much as of concrete privileges gained. This section introduces a smattering of experiences, thoughts, and descriptions reflective of Black women in higher education from the civil rights era on.

"Angela Davis at Brandeis, 1961–1964," taken from her autobiography, describes her undergraduate years in the early 1960s. One receives an overwhelmingly strong impression of an international awareness not seen in earlier students' writings. Davis links racial oppression in the United States with struggles for freedom throughout the world. Coming from the prep school Elizabeth Irwin, Davis attended Brandeis University on scholarship and used her four years there to increase her global awareness through extensive reading, friendships with foreign students, and travel. Her perspective was also shaped by the Cuban missile crisis, the bombing deaths of four girls in a Birmingham church, and President John F. Kennedy's assassination. Davis later joined the Communist party and remains a political activist, as well as a teacher and writer.

"Nikki Giovanni at Fisk, 1959–1967" presents a different autobiographical reflection on college experiences during the 1960s. Poet Giovanni entored Fisk at age 16 in a special program for gifted students but was soon released for going home at Thanksgiving without permission. Later, as she relates in the more recent interview, she returned to Fisk and graduated. Her own political awareness seems to have developed more fully in her post-undergraduate years. A widely published poet and author, Giovanni currently teaches at Virginia Polytechnic Institute and State University in the mountains of southwestern Virginia.

"Women and Men: The Balance of Power on College Campuses" (Yvonne R. Chappelle) shifts away from personal accounts of undergraduate years to an educator's statement of a perceived critical imbalance. Her focus on the dearth of African-American males in college settings seems almost prescient, for that concern is frequently voiced in the 1990s. She offers a number of suggestions to help increase male leadership in student, faculty, administrative, and staff roles. However, she offers no details of how to do so without discriminating against females.

The next two articles were especially written for this anthology by African-American faculty members at James Madison University. "The Graduate Experience" (Joanne V. Gabbin) eloquently recounts her experiences as a graduate student in 1969–1970 at the University of Chicago (the only report of graduate school included here). Like Davis, Gabbin refers to the impact on national events on her own life. Gabbin currently directs the honors program at James Madison University.

"A Black Woman on a White Campus: 1970's Perspective" (Daphyne Saunders Thomas) is the second essay from a James Madison faculty member. Thomas repeats a familiar theme from a more modern perspective, as she paints a picture of her life as an undergraduate at the predominantly white Virginia Polytechnic Institute and State University. Thomas is an assistant professor in the Department of Finance and Business Law at James Madison University.

"Spelman: Riding High in the 1980s" (Paula Giddings) records a triumph long in the making at one of the enduring African-American colleges. Johnnetta Cole made history in 1987 as she became the first African-American woman to serve as president of Spelman College. Two articles, one shortly before her inauguration in the fall and the other after her first semester, portray a scholar-administrator with caring concern for students.

"Black Women's Studies Has Come of Age" concludes this anthology, affirming African-American women, higher education, and a newly recognized field of scholarship. The editorial pages reproduced here come from *SAGE*, a scholarly journal about African-American women, founded in 1983 by Patricia Bell-Scott and Beverly Guy-Sheftall. Housed at Spelman College, the journal has given increased recognition to the emerging field of African-American women's studies and provided an outlet for the increasing number of scholars examining its various aspects.

This anthology has offered the reader a sampler of the dreams, obstacles, disappointments, and achievements in the history of African-American women's higher education. Progress at many times was slow and occasionally nonexistent, disheartening to all but the very determined. Yet the nearly 130 years since Mary Jane Patterson graduated from Oberlin

shows an overall pattern of advancement brought about by the courage and tenacity of women who valued the collegiate experience. May they serve as examples to today's women of all races as the struggle for equity in higher education continues.

NOTES

1. See James Anderson's fine study *The Education of Blacks in the South, 1860–1935* (Chapel Hill: University of North Carolina Press, 1988), which offers a critique of Washington's philosophy and its impact on African-American education. He says little, however, about African-American women's education.

2. Fisk and a number of other African-American universities underwent student rebellion in the mid-1920s. See Raymond Wolters's book *The New Negro on Campus: Black College Rebellions of the 1920s* (Princeton: Princeton University Press, 1975). Wolters describes campus unrest at Fisk, Howard, Tuskegee, Hampton, Wilberforce, Florida A & M, and Lincoln (Mo.).

3. Mark V. Tushnet's *The NAACP's Strategy Against Segregated Education, 1925–1950* (Chapel Hill: University of North Carolina Press, 1987) and Richard Kluger's *Simple Justice: The History of Brown v. Board of Education and Black America's Struggle for Equality* (New York: Knopf, 1976) describe these cases in more detail.

ACKNOWLEDGMENTS

This anthology gives me the opportunity to share a number of documents that I have collected over the years in my research in the history of African-American women's higher education. It also allows me to thank publicly a number of institutions and individuals who have assisted me with the collection and assembling process. These groups and individuals deserve my deepest thanks.

My original research on the topic was funded by a summer grant from the James Madison University Foundation in the early 1980s; the task of putting this anthology together was made easier through an educational development leave from the foundation in the 1989–1990 academic year. In the meantime, a federal grant from the Women's Educational Equity Act provided me with additional time to do research and some travel. The Rockefeller Archive Center gave me funds to look at their invaluable collection of materials from the General Education Board and photographic archives.

Over the years numerous librarians and other helpful individuals assisted me in research at their respective institutions. These people include Tom Rosenbaum at the Rockefeller Archive Center in North Tarrytown, New York; Ednita Bullock at Bennett College and Glenda Campbell at the F. D. Bluford Library at North Carolina A & T, both in Greensboro, North Carolina; Wilson Flemister and other staff members at the Robert C. Woodruff Library of the Atlanta University complex; Ann Allen Shockley in Manuscript Collections at Fisk University and Georgiana Cumberbatch in the Special Collections

Room at Tennessee State University, both in Nashville, Tennessee; Esme Bahn in the Moorland-Spingarn Collection and Maricia Battle in the photographic archives at Howard University in Washington, D.C.; the staff of the Southern Historical Collection at the University of North Carolina at Chapel Hill; and the staff at the Schomburg Center for Black Culture of the New York City Public Library.

A number of other scholars also assisted me. My thanks goes to Joyce Antler of Brandeis who suggested this project. Patricia Bell-Scott at the University of Georgia made a number of helpful suggestions and sent me potential material. Faustine Jones-Wilson of Howard University housed me while I did research at Howard and set a wonderful role model of scholarship and efficiency. Nikki Giovanni at Virginia Polytechnic Institute and State University generously consented to an interview and returned the typescript promptly. Barbara Miller Solomon, who was the general editor of the series of books of which this one is a part, was unfailingly supportive. Maida Solomon gave valuable assistance in editing the introductory essay. The editors at Garland, first Mary Ross and then Anita Vanca, were always encouraging and supportive.

My colleagues at James Madison University were also helpful. I am grateful to the staff at the Carrier Library, particularly Barbara Miller and Gordon Miller, for their unfailingly professional skills and support. Much of the material was assembled on a microcomputer lent by James Wilson in Academic Computing Services. Professors Daphyne Thomas and Joanne Gabbin generously agreed to write articles about their experiences as African-American women in the university setting. Student assistant Jill Haessler was extremely helpful in organizing and copying material. I deeply appreciate Joan Frederick's reading the manuscript and offering comments.

The book could never have been completed without the support and tolerance of my family—John, Blair, and Beth. For their understanding when I slipped away to work at odd hours I am most grateful.

College Class. Huston-Tillotson College

(GEB records.1054.849 Annual Report, 1952.
Courtesy Rockefeller Archive Center)

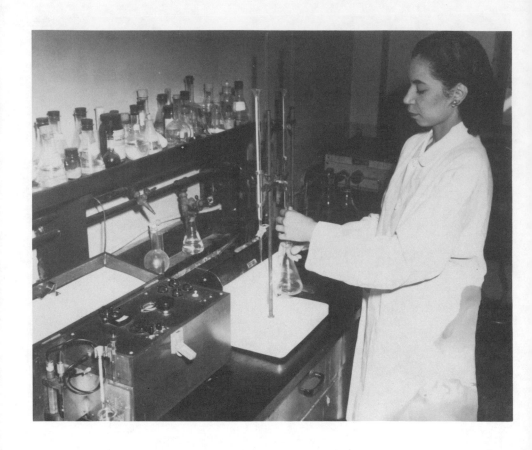

Tuskegee Institute Chemistry Laboratory

(GEB records.1045.Alabama 12.
Courtesy Rockefeller Archive Center)

**1964 Spelman College Students Elected to *Who's Who*.
Author Alice Walker is at far right.**

(Courtesy Spelman College Archives)

The Beginning: Late Nineteenth Century

Lists of Antebellum Black Women Students at Oberlin

Ellen NicKenzie Lawson with Marlene D. Merrill, excerpt from
The Three Sarahs
(New York: Edwin Mellen Press, 1984, 309–312, reprinted by
permission)

10 LIST OF ANTEBELLUM BLACK WOMEN COLLEGE STUDENTS AT OBERLIN

B.A. Recipients

Mary Jane Patterson	1862	North Carolina
Frances Marion Jackson (Coppin)	1865	Washington, D.C.
Frances Josephine Norris	1865	Rome, Georgia

B.A. Candidates

Elizabeth Evans	1862-64	North Carolina
Georgiana Mitchem (Adams)	1855-57	Peoria, Illinois

Literary Degree Recipients

Lucy Ann Stanton (Day/Sessions)	1850	Cleveland, Ohio
Frances A. Williams (Clark)	1853	Cincinnati, Ohio
Ann Maria Hazle	1855	New Bern, North Carolina
Louisa Lydia Alexander	1856	Mayslick, Kentucky
Emma J. Gloucester (White)	1856	Brooklyn, New York
Sarah Kelly Wall (Fidler)	1856	N.C. & Harveysburg, Ohio
Sarah Jane Woodson (Early)	1856	Berlin Crossroads, Ohio
Blanche V. Harris (Brooks/Jones)	1860	Monroe, Michigan
Susan E. Reid (Foster/Oliver)	1860	Port Gibson, Mississippi
Maria Waring (Baker/Williamson)	1861	Pennsylvania
Mary M. McFarland (Hayes)	1864	Natchez, Mississippi
Marion Isabell Lewis (Cook/Howard)	1865	Chattanooga, Tennessee

Literary Candidates

Alexander, Maria Ann (Gibbs)	Mayslick, Kentucky
Alexander, Rachel	Mayslick, Kentucky
Allen, Sarah J.	Chillicothe, Ohio
Alston, Elizabeth (Sampson)	Raleigh, North Carolina
Atkinson, Mary	Columbus, Ohio
Banks, Sarah Ellen	Detroit, Michigan
Boyd, Maria	Cincinnati, Ohio
*Brown, Emma V. (Montgomery)	Washington, D.C.
Chancellor, Ann	Chillicothe, Ohio
Coburn, Jennie	Mississippi (?)
Copeland, Laura (Avit)	Oberlin, Ohio
Darnes, Mary Ann	Cincinnati, Ohio
Darnes, Josephine	Cincinnati, Ohio
Davidson, Chorilla (Alston)	Oberlin, Ohio
Elliot, Rebecca	Cincinnati, Ohio
Ferguson, Maria L.	Richmond, Virginia
Ferguson, Parthena	Cincinnati, Ohio
Freeman, Amelia F. (Shadd)	Pittsburgh, Pennsylvania
Freeman, Ada E.	Brooklyn, New York
Gilliam, Georgina	Sharpsburg, Pennsylvania

Gloucester, Eloise H.	Brooklyn, New York
Hazel, Elizabeth N.	New Bern, North Carolina
Harris, Frankie E.	Monroe, Michigan
Henderson, Eleanor	Zanesville, Ohio
Holman, Louisa	Oberlin, Ohio
Huffman, Lucinda	Louisville, Kentucky
Hunter, Harriet E.	Indianapolis, Indiana
Iredell, Sarah	Philadelphia, Pennsylvania
*Jones, Matilda	Washington, D.C.
Kinson, Sarah (Margru) (Greene)	Sierre Leone, West Africa
Lewis, Mary Edmonia (Indian)	New York, New York
McGuire, Mahala (Gray)	Eaton, Ohio
Morgan, Rebecca (Cady)	Quincy, Illinois
Nesbit, Ophelia (Bell)	Cincinnati, Ohio
Peck, Louisa E.	Pittsburgh, Pennsylvania
Randolph, Americus	Morrow, Ohio (?)
Sedden, Mary C.	Cincinnati, Ohio
Stanley, Sara	New Bern, North Carolina
Taylor, Mary E.	Philadelphia, Pennsylvania
Thomas, Amanda (Well)	Oberlin, Ohio
Tilley, Virginia C.	Louisville, Kentucky
Tinsley, Ann (Baltimore)	Cincinnati, Ohio
Tucker, Georgina	Brooklyn, New York
Wall, Carolina (Langston)	Harveysburg, Ohio

* Prepared at Miner's School in D.C.

11. LIST OF ANTEBELLUM BLACK WOMEN PREPARATORY STUDENTS ONLY AT OBERLIN**

Preparatory School

Allen, Mary	New Orleans, Louisiana
Alston, Mary (50-52)	Raleigh, North Carolina
Bonnar, Virginia	Chicago, Illinois
Bowman, Angelina	Pittsburgh, Pennsylvania
Brugman, Mary E.	[Winston ?], North Carolina
Buckner, Georgie	St. Louis, Missouri
Burnett, Mary J. (Chambers)	South Carolina
Byrd, Priscilla	Oberlin, Ohio
Cage, Frances	New Orleans, Louisiana
Cage, Lizzie	New Orleans, Louisiana
Cage, Amelia	New Orleans, Louisiana
Campton, Jennie	Oberlin, Ohio
Campton, Fannie (Thomas)	Oberlin, Ohio
Campton, Mary (Tate)	Oberlin, Ohio
Carter, Letitia A.	Cincinnati, Ohio
Carter, Cora B.	Cincinnati, Ohio

6

Carter, Susan E.	New Albany, Ohio
Casey, Emily	Cincinnati, Ohio
Casey, Louisa	Cincinnati, Ohio
Chancellor, Elizabeth	Chillicothe, Ohio
Clark, Laura	Cincinnati, Ohio
Cooper, Mary	Columbus, Ohio
Cunningham, Rebecca	Chillicothe, Ohio
Dale, Mary L.	Detroit, Michigan
Degrove, Evelyn	New York, New York
D'Anglas, Addeline	Oberlin & Louisiana
D'Anglas, Etienne Honorine	Oberlin & Louisiana
D'Anglass, Belinda (Watson)	Oberlin & Louisiana
D'Anglass, Leontine P.	Oberlin & Louisiana
Douglass, Mary E.	Louisville, Kentucky
Douglass, Rosetta (Sprague)	Rochester, New York
Duncan, Clara	Pittsfield, Massachusetts
Edmondson, Mary	Washington, D.C.
Edmondson, Emily	Washington, D.C.
Everett, Ellen	Louisville, Kentucky
Ferris, Elizabeth	Oberlin, Ohio
Ford, Mary Ann	Cincinnati, Ohio
Francis, Julia Ann	Rochester, New York
Freeman, Clara	Pittsfield, Massachusetts
Gee, Frances	Gallipolis, Ohio
Gilliam, Josephine	Sharpsburg, Pennsylvania
Gilliam, Henrietta	Sharpsburg, Pennslyvania
Goins, Isabella	Louisville, Kentucky
Green, Louisa B.	Chillicothe, Ohio
Hackley, Fannie	St. Louis, Missouri
Harlan, Mary	Cincinnati, Ohio
Henson, Charlotte	Dawn, Ontario, Canada
Holman, Julia	Lynchburg, Virginia
Jarvis, Elizabeth	Oberlin, Ohio & Virginia
Jarvis, Lucy	Oberlin, Ohio & Virginia
Jarvis, Martha (Huckleberry)	Oberlin, Ohio & Virginia
Jarvis, Susan	Oberlin, Ohio & Virginia
Jarvis, Mary	Oberlin, Ohio & Virginia
Jones, Adora	Cincinnati, Ohio
Jones, Rebecca	Cincinnati, Ohio
Latta, Elizabeth	Cincinnati, Ohio
Lee, Georgianna	Detroit, Michigan
Lewis, Laura	Xenia, Ohio
Lewis, Mary Edmonia	New York, New York
Lloyd, Penelope	Louisville, Kentucky
Ledzan, Hannah	Oberlin, Ohio
Livingston, Mary E.	Jamaica, W.I.
Lyon, Abigail A. (Johnson)	Fitchville, Ohio
Massey, Margaret A.	Columbus, Ohio
Miner, Delia M.	New Orleans, Louisiana
Miner, Josephine H.	New Orleans, Louisiana

itchem, Emeline	Peoria, Illinois
)rris, Maria	Cincinnati, Ohio
itterson, Mary S. (Leary/Langston)	Oberlin, Ohio
ity, Harriet	Cincinnati, Ohio
: Pompella, Elizabeth	Cincinnati, Ohio
:ed, Frances E.	New York, New York
)binson, Victoria R.	Lebanon, New York
:ott, Sarah (Tillinghast)	Oberlin, Ohio
:ttle, Cornelia (Townsend)	Corinth, Mississippi
impson, Clarissa A.	New Orleans, Louisiana
nith, Agnes	Cincinnati, Ohio
nith, Carrie	Litchfield, Ohio
iylor, Ann (McKinney)	Cincinnati, Ohio
iylor, Elizabeth P.	Oberlin, Ohio
iompson, Mary L.	PauPau, Michigan
:abue, Helen	Louisville, Kentucky
iughn, Sarah	Gallipolis, Ohio
iring, Sarah	Beaver, Pennsylvania
iring, Emily P.	Oberlin, Ohio
itson, Sarah J. (Barnett)	Cincinnati, Ohio
:ldon, Eliza	New York, New York
:stfall, Frances	Quincy, Illinois
)odson, Hannah	Berlin Crossroads, Ohio
)od, Josephine	Lexington, Kentucky
iunger, Catherine (Warren)	Osceola, Missouri

This list does not include those black women college students who prepared the Oberlin Preparatory School as most college students, white and black, died in the preparatory school. There were at least 152 identifiable black .en at Oberlin (college and preparatory school) in the antebellum years.

CAROLINE WALL (LANGSTON)

This photograph is from J.M. Langston's <u>From The</u> <u>Virginia Plantation to The National Capitol</u> (1894). Wall studied in the Ladies' Literary course at Oberlin in the 1850s before her marriage to John Langston, lawyer, congressman and diplomat.

9

MARY JANE PATTERSON

This photograph is reprinted by courtesy of the Oberlin College Archives. Patterson received the B.A. degree in 1862, the first black American woman to be awarded this degree. (No personal documents for Patterson surfaced in the course of this research.)

A college official once described Mary Jane Patterson as a "superior scholar, a good singer, a faithful Christian, and a genteel lady." Her graduation address concerned the "Hero of Italy," the republican Garibaldi. She taught at the Institute for Colored Youth in Philadelphia and was principal of the Preparatory High School for Colored Youth in Washington, D.C., predecessor of the famed Dunbar High School.

A Black Oberlin Woman in the 1860s

Fanny Jackson Coppin, excerpt from *Reminiscences of School Life, and Hints on Teaching*
(New York: Garland Publishing, 1987, 11–18)

Finally, I found a chance to go to Newport with Mrs. Elizabeth Orr, an aunt by marriage, who offered me a home with her and a better chance at school. I went with her, but I was not satisfied to be a burden on her small resources. I was now fourteen years old, and felt that I ought to take care of myself. So I found a permanent place in the family of Mr. George H. Calvert, a great grandson of Lord Baltimore, who settled Maryland. His wife was Elizabeth Stuart, a descendant of Mary, Queen of Scots. Here I had one hour every other afternoon in the week to take some private lessons, which I did of Mrs. Little. After that, I attended for a few months the public colored school which was taught by Mrs. Gavitt. I thus prepared myself to enter the examination for the Rhode Island State Normal School, under Dana P. Colburn; the school was then located at Bristol, R. I. Here, my eyes were first opened on the subject of teaching. I said to myself, is it possible that teaching can be made so interesting as this! But, having finished the course of study there, I felt that I had just begun to learn; and, hearing of Oberlin College, I made up my mind to try and get there. I had learned a little music while at Newport, and had mastered the elementary studies of the piano and guitar. My aunt in Washington still helped me, and I was able to pay my way to Oberlin, the course of study there being the same as that at Harvard College. Oberlin was then the only College in the United States where colored students were permitted to study.

The faculty did not forbid a woman to take the gentleman's course, but they did not advise it. There was plenty of Latin and Greek in it, and as much mathematics as one could shoulder. Now, I took a long breath and prepared for a delightful contest. All went smoothly until I was in the junior year in College. Then, one day, the Faculty sent for me—ominous request—and I was not slow in obeying it. It was a custom in Oberlin that forty students from the junior and senior classes were employed to teach the preparatory classes. As it was now time for the juniors to begin their work, the Faculty informed me that it was their purpose to give me a class, but I was to distinctly understand that if the pupils rebelled against my teaching, they did not intend to force it. Fortunately for my training at the normal school, and my own dear love of teaching, tho there was a little surprise on the faces of some when they came into the class, and saw the teacher, there were no signs of rebellion. The class went on increasing in numbers until it had to be divided, and I was given both divisions. One of the divisions ran up again, but the Faculty decided that I had as much as I could do, and it would not allow me to take any more work.

When I was within a year of graduation, an application came from a Friends' school in Philadelphia for a colored woman who could teach Greek, Latin, and higher mathematics. The answer returned was: "We have the woman, but you must wait a year for her."

Then began a correspondence with Alfred Cope, a saintly character, who, having found out what my work in college was, teaching my classes in college, besides sixteen private music scholars, and keeping up my work in the senior class, immediately sent me a check for eighty dollars, which wonderfully lightened my burden as a poor student.

I shall never forget my obligation to Bishop Daniel A. Payne, of the African Methodist Episcopal Church, who gave me a scholarship of nine dollars a year upon entering Oberlin.

My obligation to the dear people of Oberlin can never be measured in words. When President Finney met a new student, his first words were: "Are you a Christian? and if not, why not?" He would follow you up with an intelligent persistence that could not be resisted, until the question was settled.

When I first went to Oberlin I boarded in what was known as the Ladies' Hall, and altho the food was good, yet, I think, that for lack of variety I began to run down in health. About this time I was invited to spend a few weeks in the family of Professor H. E. Peck, which ended in my staying a few years, until the independence of the Republic of Hayti was recognized, under President Lincoln, and Professor Peck was sent as the first U. S. Minister to that interesting country; then the family was broken up, and I was invited by Professor and Mrs. Charles H. Churchill to spend the remainder of my time, about six months, in their family. The influence upon my life in these two Christian homes, where I was regarded as an honored member of the family circle, was a potent factor in forming the character which was to stand the test of the new and strange conditions of my life in Philadelphia. I had been so long in Oberlin that I had forgotten about my color, but I was sharply reminded of it when, in a storm of rain, a Philadelphia street car conductor forbid my entering a car that did not have on it "for colored people," so I had to wait in the storm until one came in which colored people could ride. This was my first unpleasant experience in Philadelphia. Visiting Oberlin not long after my work began in Philadelphia, President Finney asked me how I was growing in grace; I told him that I was growing as fast as the American people would let me. When told of some of the conditions which were meeting me, he seemed to think it unspeakable.

At one time, at Mrs. Peck's, when we girls were sitting on the floor getting out our Greek, Miss Sutherland, from Maine, suddenly stopped, and, looking at me, said: "Fanny Jackson, were you ever a slave?" I said yes; and she burst into tears. Not another word was spoken by us. But those tears seemed to wipe out a little of what was wrong.

I never rose to recite in my classes at Oberlin but I felt that I had the honor of the whole African race upon my shoulders. I felt that, should I fail, it would be ascribed to the fact that I was colored. At one time, when I had quite a signal triumph in Greek, the Professor of Greek concluded to visit the class in mathematics and see how we were getting along. I was particularly anxious to show him that I was as safe in mathematics as in Greek.

I, indeed, was more anxious, for I had always heard that my race was good in the languages, but stumbled when they came to mathematics. Now, I was always fond of a demonstration, and happened to get in the examination the very proposition that I was well acquainted with; and so went that day out of the class with flying colors.

I was elected class poet for the Class Day exercises, and have the kindest remembrance of the dear ones who were my classmates. I never can forget the courtesies of the three Wright brothers; of Professor Pond, of Dr. Lucien C. Warner, of Doctor Kincaid, the Chamberland girls, and others, who seemed determined that I should carry away from Oberlin nothing but most pleasant memories of my life there.

Recurring to my tendency to have shaking agues every fall and spring in Washington, I often used to tell my aunt that if she bought me according to my weight, she certainly had made a very poor bargain. For I was not only as slim as a match, but, as the Irishman said, I was as slim as two matches.

While I was living with Mrs. Calvert at Newport, R. I., I went with her regularly to bathe in the ocean, and after this I never had any more shakes or chills. It was contrary to law for colored persons to bathe at the regular bathing hour, which was the only safe hour to go into the ocean, but, being in the employ of Mrs. Calvert, and going as her servant, I was not prohibited from taking the baths which proved so beneficial to me. She went and returned in her carriage.

After this I began to grow stronger, and take on flesh. Mrs. Calvert sometimes took me out to drive with her; this also helped me to get stronger.

Being very fond of music, my aunt gave me permission to hire a piano and have it at her house, and I used to go there and take lessons. But, in the course of time, it became noticeable to Mrs. Calvert that I was absent on Wednesdays at a certain hour, and that without permission. So, on one occasion, when I was absent, Mrs. Calvert inquired of the cook as to my whereabouts, and directed her to send me to her upon my return that I might give an explanation. When the cook informed me of what had transpired, I was very much afraid that something quite unpleasant awaited me. Upon being questioned, I told her the whole truth about the matter. I told Mrs. Calvert that I had been taking lessons for some time, and that I had already advanced far enough to play the little organ in the Union Church. Instead of being terribly scolded, as I had feared, Mrs. Calvert said: "Well, Fanny, when people will go ahead, they cannot be kept back; but, if you had asked me, you might have had the piano here." Mrs. Calvert taught me to sew beautifully and to darn, and to take care of laces. My life there was most happy, and I never would have left her, but it was in me to get an education and to teach my people. This idea was deep in my soul. Where it came from I cannot tell, for I had never had any exhortations, nor any lectures which influenced me to take this course. It must have been born in me. At Mrs. Calvert's, I was in contact with people of refinement and education. Mr. Calvert was a perfect gentleman, and a writer of no mean ability. They had no children, and this gave me an opportunity to come very near to Mrs. Calvert, doing for her many things which otherwise a daughter would have done. I loved her and she loved me. When I was about to leave her to go to the Normal School, she said to me: "Fanny, will money keep you?" But that deep-seated purpose to get an education and become a teacher to my people, yielded to no inducement of comfort or temporary gain. During the time that I attended the Normal School in Rhode Island, I got a chance to take some private lessons in French, and eagerly availed myself of the opportunity. French was not in the Oberlin curriculum, but there was a professor there who taught it privately, and I continued my studies under him, and so was able to complete the course and graduate with a French essay. Freedmen now began to pour into Ohio from the South, and some of them settled in the township of Oberlin. During my last year at the college, I formed an evening class for them, where they might be taught to read and write. It was deeply touching to me to see old men painfully following the simple words of spelling; so intensely eager to learn. I felt that for such people to have been kept in the darkness of ignorance was an unpardonable sin, and I rejoiced that even then I could enter measurably upon the course in life which I had long ago chosen. Mr. John M. Langston, who afterwards became Minister to Hayti, was then practicing law at Oberlin. His comfortable home was always open with a warm welcome to colored students, or to any who cared to share his hospitality.

I went to Oberlin in 1860, and was graduated in August, 1865, after having spent five and a half years.

A Black Oberlin Woman in the 1880s

Mary Church Terrell, excerpts from *A Colored Woman in a White World*
(New York: Arno Press, 1980 (rpt.), 1940)

While I was in the high school I had to decide what course I would take when I entered college. I chose the Classical Course, which necessitated the study of Greek and which was often called the "gentlemen's course," because it was the one generally pursued by men who wanted the degree of Bachelor of Arts.

Few women in Oberlin College took the Classical Course at that time. They took what was called the Literary Course, which could be completed two years sooner than the Classical Course but which did not entitle them to a degree. They simply received a certificate.

Some of my friends and schoolmates urged me not to select the "gentlemen's course," because it would take much longer to complete than the "ladies' course." They pointed out that Greek was hard; that it was unnecessary, if not positively unwomanly, for girls to study that "old, dead language" anyhow; that during the two extra years required to complete it I would miss a lot of fun which I could enjoy outside of college walls. And, worst of all, it might ruin my chances of getting a husband, since men were notoriously shy of women who knew too much. "Where," inquired some of my friends sarcastically, "will you find a colored man who has studied Greek?" They argued I wouldn't be happy if I knew more than my husband, and they warned that trying to find a man in our group who knew Greek would be like hunting for a needle in a haystack.

But I loved school and liked to study too well to be allured from it by any of the arguments my friends advanced. I was very much impressed and worried by the one which warned that I couldn't get a husband. But I decided to take a long chance. I wrote to my father and laid the matter clearly before him, explaining that it would cost more to take the course that I preferred and that few women of any race selected it. My dear father replied immediately that I might remain in college as long as I wished and he would foot the bill.

CHAPTER 5

I ENTER OBERLIN COLLEGE

IN THE FOLLOWING FALL I entered the senior class of the preparatory department of Oberlin College, which has since been abolished. I boarded in the old "Ladies Hall," which was destroyed by fire and has been replaced by Talcott Cottage. The tables in the dining hall seated eight, and it was customary for students to choose those whom they wanted to sit at their respective tables for the term of three months. In the middle of the term some friend would invite me to sit at a table which she was arranging for the one to follow, and I would accept. Somebody else would extend me the same invitation and I would also accept that, forgetting that I had already promised to sit with another group. Each of these girls would send in my name as one of the eight who had accepted her invitation for the following term. Then, when I was seated at one table and failed to appear at another at which I was expected, naturally there would be more or less confusion, and explanations had to be made. The lady whose duty it was to attend to the dining room declared that I gave her a great deal of trouble, because too many people wanted me to sit at their table.

If I were white, it might be conceited for me to relate this. But I mention these facts to show that, as a colored girl, I was accorded the same treatment at Oberlin College at that time as a white girl under similar circumstances. Outward manifestations of prejudice against colored students would not have been tolerated for one minute by those in authority at that time. Occasionally, a colored girl would complain about something which she considered a "slight," but, as a rule, it was either because she was looking for trouble or because she imagined something

[39]

disagreeable which was not intended. Later on, however, conditions affecting colored students changed considerably.

My associates in college were, naturally, members of my own class. Until I reached the junior year I had only one colored classmate, and she lived at home. I boarded in Ladies Hall three years all together: during my senior preparatory year, when I roomed with a girl of my own race; during my freshman year, when I roomed alone; and during my senior year, when I roomed with my colored classmate. Throughout the whole period in Ladies Hall, never once did I feel that I was being discriminated against on account of my color.

In my senior preparatory year I had one of the best teachers in the entire course—"Prin White," as he was familiarly called, who was principal of the department. Prin White taught us Greek and he was as vivacious, interesting, and inspiring as a teacher could well be. He had very high standards for his pupils. Some thought they were too high, but he succeeded in making most of us live up to them. When a student was called upon to explain the case of a noun or the mood of a verb, Prin White required him not only to give the rule for the construction, but, along with the rule, to give a sentence in Greek illustrating the point.

For a time I was the only girl in this Greek class with 40 boys. It was a joy to read the *Iliad* with Prin White. He entered so enthusiastically into the spirit of that matchless poem that his students caught the inspiration. I still have my recitation card. He marked on a scale of 6. When he handed me my card showing 5.9, he said in his quick, nervous way, fixing me with his keen, blue eyes, "Miss Church, you should be proud of that record." Praise from Prin White was then and still is praise indeed. And I can thrill even now, 58 years after the incident occurred, when I think of it.

I also remember another incident in my college days with pleasure and pride. It was when my Latin teacher complimented me, because I scanned a certain passage in Virgil well. I can recall those Latin lines today, and the genuine feeling with which I read them.

The Greek professor in college was also one of my favorites. He looked like an ascetic, tall and straight and thin. I usually sat on the front seat in his class and drank in every word he said. I took much more Greek than the curriculum required, both be-

[40]

cause I enjoyed the Grecian authors and because I was fond of my teacher.

One day Matthew Arnold, the English writer, visited our class and Professor Frost asked me both to read the Greek and then to translate. After leaving the class Mr. Arnold referred to the young lady who had read the passage of Greek so well. Thinking it would interest the Englishman, Professor Frost told him I was of African descent. Thereupon Mr. Arnold expressed the greatest surprise imaginable, because, he said, he thought the tongue of the African was so thick he could not be taught to pronounce the Greek correctly.

Later on Professor Frost became president of Berea College. For years before his administration this institution had admitted colored and white students on terms of equality. But shortly after Professor Frost became president the Kentucky Legislature passed a law, with Berea specially in mind, forbidding any school or institution to receive both white and colored students unless the one race or color should be established in a separate department not less than 25 miles from the other: and this on penalty of a fine of $1,000 for the institution, $1,000 for each of its teachers and $50 for each of its pupils. In his autobiography President Frost expressed keen regret that Berea was forced to debar colored students on account of this law.

In my freshman year I attended the Bible class regularly and believe it benefited me greatly. I really looked forward to it with enthusiasm and pleasure, because I was allowed to ask questions about the passages in the Scriptures which troubled me. And no verse came nearer shaking my faith in the justice of God than that one which states, "I the Lord thy God am a jealous God, visiting the iniquity of the fathers upon the children unto the third and fourth generation of them that hate me, and showing mercy unto thousands of them that love me and keep my commandments."

I could not understand why a just and loving father should make children suffer for the sins committed by their forefathers. The injustice of the law of heredity stunned me. It seemed terrible to me that the children of drunkards should inherit a tendency to drink immoderately and the children of thieves might have a hard time to be honest, and so on through the category of vices. The teacher was patient with me and did his best to show me why such a dispensation was just, but I was never able

[41]

26

to see it in that light. However, I decided not to try to understand it any longer. I finally brought a semblance of peace to my mind by saying, "I am finite, and if I understood all the plans of the Infinite I should be equal to Him in wisdom, which would be unthinkable and absurd, of course." Even so, my poor brain often whirled and my heart was often sad, as I wrestled with the problem of heredity.

When I tackled geometry in the preparatory department of the college I met my Waterloo sure enough! I struggled hard to do the work, but I did not understand how to go at it properly and I barely pulled through the course. How I loathed plane geometry! It wounded my pride and "hurt my feelings," because it was so hard for me to understand.

I did a little better in solid geometry, but I did not set the world afire even in that. Finally, I grew desperate and decided it was a waste of time and energy for me to try to understand propositions, and I calmly made up my mind to commit to memory the letters on a figure and say "big TAB is to little tab as big AB is to little ab," without having the slightest idea what it was all about. No teacher who wished to show off his class in mathematics would ever have called on Mollie Church to recite in college, any more than a teacher in the public schools would have exhibited my drawing book to display the skill to which her pupils had attained. When visitors came to our class in the public schools and asked to see our books in which we had done free-hand drawing or had copied objects, no teacher ever showed mine. She usually managed to put it at the bottom of the pile.

Try as hard as I might, I could never learn to draw. If I set out to draw a straight line it would turn out to be crooked. And if I wanted to draw a crooked line it was more than likely to be straight. My brother inherited some of my mother's talent for painting and drawing, while I inherited none. My brother, Thomas Ayres Church, wrote a book on *The Roller*, a canary which is taught to sing tunes, and he drew all the illustrations himself. They were exceedingly well done. He was the first person in this country to write a book on this subject. The best publishing houses sold it and it had a ready sale.

In my freshman year I was elected class poet unanimously, and read a poem at the Class Day exercises, which were held a short while before Commencement. I chose as my subject "The Fallen Star," and imitated the hexameter used by Longfellow in

[42]

Hiawatha. In the same year I wrote another poem which a classmate liked so much she quoted one of the stanzas in an essay she read at an exhibition given by her literary society when we were juniors.

Because I had written several effusions of which my teacher approved, I had been rather generally regarded as the class poet. When the time came to elect speakers for the Junior Exhibition, it was the consensus of opinion among the majority of my classmates that I would be elected class poet. After a classmate had nominated me, another presented the name of a young man who had never written a poem in his life, so far as the class had heard, and had never exhibited any talent in that direction, so far as the class knew. After a great many ballots had been cast, I wanted to withdraw my name, but some of my classmates who sat near me held me down in my seat. Finally the young man was elected. I believe I am justified in thinking that if a white girl had won the same reputation for writing poetry that I had, and had been recognized by the class as I had been in my freshman year, she would probably have been elected class poet for the Junior Exhibition instead of a young man who had previously exhibited no talent or skill in that direction at all. Some of my classmates criticized the successful candidate severely, because he did not withdraw in my favor after five or six ballots had been cast, as he probably would have done if his rival had been a white girl.

But I did not allow this episode to embitter me at all. On the contrary, it encouraged and comforted me greatly to see how many of my classmates stood by me so long. I knew also that they finally voted for the young man, so as to break the deadlock, after they saw that a few of his friends were determined to elect him. There is no doubt whatever that on this one occasion, at least, the fact that I am colored prevented me from receiving the honor which many members of my class thought my record proved I deserved.

Right after the Junior Exhibition I attended a party which was always given by one of the professors and enjoyed myself immensely. My mother had sent me a beautiful silk dress from New York, which I wore. I am sure that nobody who saw me that day thought I was suffering because I felt I had been a victim of race prejudice in failing to be elected to write a poem

[43]

for "Junior Ex." I know now better than I did then that "blood is thicker than water" when several racial groups come together to elect a representative for the whole.

But I received almost every other honor that my classmates or the members of my literary society could give me. While I was still in the senior preparatory class, a young woman in the senior college class rushed after me one day and insisted upon having me join Aelioian, the literary society to which she herself belonged. She was one of the most brilliant and popular members of her class, and I felt honored to have such a student solicit my membership in her society. She did not have to persuade me long to gain my consent to join Aelioian. I am glad I began work in this society so early in my course. I was eligible for admission, even though I was only a senior in the preparatory department, because a girl in that class was as far advanced in her studies as one taking the literary course would be in college.

In addition to the literary work required, the drill in parliamentary law was invaluable. All I ever knew about it I learned in Aelioian. After I went out into the "cold world," when I was called upon to preside over meetings of various kinds, I would have been greatly embarrassed if I had not been prepared for this service by the drills given me in Aelioian. The ability to speak effectively on one's feet was also acquired in this society.

I was elected twice to represent Aelioian when it had a public debate with L. L. S., the other women's literary society. The first time I was a sophomore, and the last time I was a junior. I considered the latter selection a special honor because as a rule the society elected a senior to represent it in the public debate held with L. L. S. before Commencement. This was the most important exercise given by the society, so that no greater honor could be conferred upon a member than to be elected disputant to represent it in a debate with its rival on that occasion.

For a while I was one of the editors of the *Oberlin Review*, the college paper, and I was quite excited when I saw the first article I had ever written for publication appear in print.

I enjoyed attending the Thursday lectures, at which either one of the professors or some distinguished man from out of town appeared. The literary societies brought the best orators, the most famous singers, and the finest orchestras to Oberlin, so that when one had finished her college course, if she had availed

[44]

29

herself of the opportunities offered her, she would have seen and heard the most distinguished speakers and the greatest musicians in the United States.

A building was presented by a generous woman to the women's two literary societies, and after it was completed a committee was appointed from each society to decide how the rooms should be furnished. Aelioian placed me on a committee of three to represent it. And so, I could cite numerous instances to show that the members of my society did not discriminate against me on account of my race.

Since my college society conferred upon me every honor in its gift, and my classmates failed only once to recognize me as I believe they would have done under similar circumstances if I had been white, I feel I have little reason to complain about discrimination on account of race while I was a student in Oberlin College. It would be difficult for a colored girl to go through a white school with fewer unpleasant experiences occasioned by race prejudice than I had.

I attended all the class receptions and every social function which the college gave and was sure of a cordial reception wherever I went. The sister-in-law of the acting president of the college decided to have a lawn tennis club, when that game was just beginning to be popular, and I was one of twelve girls she invited from the whole institution to become a member of it. If I attended Oberlin College today, I am told, I would not be so free from the annoyances and discriminations caused by race prejudice as I was fifty-six years ago.

Although for many years there was as much "social equality" to the square inch in Oberlin College as could be practiced anywhere in the United States, I have heard the authorities state that there had never been a case of intermarriage between the races in the whole history of the school. The prediction of the prophets and the near prophets in this particular was never fulfilled. All sorts of dire calamities were threatened by those who strongly opposed the admission of colored students. It was predicted that if white and colored students were allowed to associate with each other on terms of "social equality," the most disgraceful things would be happening all the time. There would be intermarriages galore, of course, and the whole tone of the school would be low. The opponents of equal opportunities for

[45]

30

colored people have proved over and over again that they have not the gift of prophecy.

For a long time I led the singing in a Sunday evening prayer meeting in Ladies Hall. At one of these meetings an incident occurred which made an indelible impression upon my mind. It was customary for those who attended these meetings to bear testimony concerning their experiences as Christians or to offer prayer. On one such occasion I stated that, although I tried to be a Christian, I sometimes did things which I knew a good Christian should not do.

"For instance," I said, "I sometimes whisper in a class, when I don't intend to violate the rule or disturb the order, because I am thoughtless but not deliberately obstreperous. I fear also that I giggle and laugh too much and am not serious enough." And then I expressed the hope that the Christians present would pray for me that I might change my giddy ways and become more quiet and sedate.

As soon as I had finished, a tall, pale, very thin woman, heavily swathed in black, leaned forward from the back seat, fastened her sad eyes upon me, pointed her bony finger at me, and said most impressively, "Young woman, laugh and be merry while you can, and as much as you can. Don't try to suppress laughter and be serious in youth. Some day when you grow older, when the cares and sorrows of life press hard upon you, you'll want to laugh and can't."

About a week after that this woman committed suicide in Cleveland, Ohio, by jumping into Lake Erie. Both her husband and her young daughter had died within a short time of each other and she could not become reconciled to their loss. She had come to study in the college, hoping to divert her mind from grief, but she did not succeed. Many a time since that Sunday evening prayer meeting I have tried to laugh when the sorrows and cares of life have pressed hard upon me, and couldn't.

While I was still in college I had the first bitter experience of inability to secure employment on account of my race, during a summer vacation which I was spending with my mother in New York City. I thought it would be a fine thing then to earn money with a lot of leisure on my hands. I had heard my college friends talk about desirable positions which students were able to secure during summer vacations. One of them had been em-

[46]

31

ployed by a wealthy woman who wanted a young, intelligent girl to read aloud to her, write letters for her, and act in the capacity of secretary. I thought I would try to get such a job. Accordingly, I fared forth several times to answer advertisements calling for such service. At least three of the women whom I went to see told me that I possessed just the qualities they desired and were very complimentary indeed. I thought I had secured employment three times, but three times I was doomed to disappointment.

Just as I was leaving her room one of the women who had practically engaged me said: "I observe you are quite swarthy. You speak English too well to be a foreigner, unless you were born in the United States, or came here when you were a baby. What is your nationality?" "I am a colored girl," I replied. If I had told her I was a gorilla in human form, she could not have been more greatly shocked. Never before in all her life had she come in contact with an educated colored girl, she said. She really didn't know there were any in the world. While she had no prejudice against colored people herself, she said, her servants were white and she was certain they would leave if she employed a colored girl.

On a certain Friday afternoon one of the women whom I went to see engaged me positively and directed me to begin work with her Monday morning. But on Sunday afternoon a messenger brought me a letter saying that her daughter had seen me, as I was leaving the house, and had asked about my nationality. Her coachman would come at seven o'clock that evening for a reply, she wrote. When he came I gave him a note in which I frankly admitted my racial identity. At ten o'clock that night the coachman returned with an answer to my confession of race in which my employer told me she was very sorry to cancel her agreement with me, but under no circumstances could she employ a colored girl.

Months before I graduated from Oberlin I realized that the carefree days of my youth would soon be a thing of the past. I dreaded leaving my friends behind and "going out into the cold world." But the desire to get my diploma and receive my degree was an obsession with me. When I said my prayers at night I used to emphasize the fact, as much as I dared while talking to the Lord, that He could send any affliction whatsoever upon me

[47]

32

He saw fit, if He would only let me live to graduate. I begged Him earnestly not to let me die before Commencement Day.

I do not see how any student could have enjoyed the activities of college life more than I did. Learning my lessons as well as I could was a sort of indoor sport with me. I had my troubles and trials, of course, because occasionally I broke the rules by going skating without permission, for instance, or breaking the study-hour rule, or sitting up after ten o'clock, but that was all included in the course, I thought. I learned one thing outside of the curriculum. Breakfast began at quarter past six in the morning. That did very well in the fall and spring, but in the cold, bitter winter it was terrible to have to arise while it was dark as midnight in a room with a temperature miles below zero, make a fire to keep from freezing to death, and dress in time to be at the breakfast table at fifteen minutes past six.

I did not eat very much at that period. But students were obliged to be in the dining room for morning prayers. So I calculated to a nicety the exact time when the bell would ring for the students to turn from the table to hear the Bible read. I would hop out of bed just five minutes before that happened, and I learned to dress myself so quickly that I was never late for morning prayer during the whole time I boarded in Ladies Hall.

Neither one of my parents came to see me graduate from college. My mother sent me a wonderful black jet dress, for the young women who graduated from the "gentlemen's course" always dressed in sombre black then. She also sent me a pair of opera glasses as a graduation present. While the gift was greatly appreciated, it did not compensate me for her absence on an occasion to which I had looked forward with such anticipation of pleasure for so many years.

[48]

33

CHAPTER 6

ACTIVITIES DURING COLLEGE COURSE

DURING MY FRESHMAN YEAR I had a thrill which comes once in a lifetime. Sticking out from under my door when I came to the Ladies Hall at noon one day was a letter postmarked Washington, D. C., addressed to me in a handwriting I had never seen before. During my college course it was most unusual for me to receive a letter from a stranger, so I tore it open eagerly to see from whom it came. And then I was dumb with surprise. It was an invitation from the wife of a United States Senator to visit her during the Inauguration in Washington. It would require a word artist of the first magnitude to describe my rapture at such a prospect, so that my readers would feel the same exuberance of spirit which I experienced when I received this letter from Mrs. B. K. Bruce, wife of Senator Bruce.

I was certain my father would let me accept the invitation. He and Senator Bruce had been friends for many years. The Senator had a large plantation in Mississippi not far from Memphis, and Father used to purchase mules and supplies for him, since the planter knew very little about doing such things himself. For many years it was Senator Bruce's custom to stop with Father as he passed through Memphis on his way to and from his plantation.

After receiving the permission to accept the invitation I began immediately to study ahead. I knew I could not enjoy myself in Washington if I did not make up my college work before I went. So I read all the Latin and Greek assigned for that term before I started my great adventure, leaving the dreaded mathematics till I returned.

[49]

Moral Training for Black Women: Selections

Black Women's Higher Education: A Man's Perspective from
the 1880s
William T. Alexander, Excerpt from *History of the Colored Race
in America*
(New York: Negro Universities Press, 1968 (rpt.), 1887)

APPENDIX.

HIGHER EDUCATION OF WOMEN.

" In stately halls of learning,
  'Mid philosophic minds,
Unraveling knotty problems,
  His native forte man finds;
But all his 'ists and 'isms
  To Heaven's four winds are hurled;
For the hand that rocks the cradle
  Is the hand that rules the word.

"Great Statesmen govern Nations,
  Kings mould a people's fate;
But the unseen hand of velvet
  These giants regulate.
The ponderous wheel of fortune
  In woman's charm is pearled;
For the hand that rocks the cradle
  Is the hand that rules the world."

" If I were asked to what the singular prosperity and growing strength of the Americans ought mainly to be attributed, I should reply, to the superiority of their women — *Democracy in America.*

Woman's Higher Education may be defined as that education which follows that of school, consisting of moral precepts to govern the conduct of life, and to regulate it in our relations to society, and lay broad foundations for the character of those whom it is our duty to instruct and train for lives of future usefulness.

Said Amie Martin: "Young girls, young wives, young. mothers, *you* hold the sceptre; in your souls, much more than in the laws of Legislators, now repose the futurity of the world and the destinies of the human race."

The women of the Colored Race need to well understand their duty to one another, and to the world at large, their rela- .tion to society, and the good that may be accomplished by rightly understanding what is expected of them, and what may be accomplished by them, in elevating their people.

Society, as we now find it, reveals the fact that many are

awake to the necessity of engrafting into their people the higher culture of their powers, and their labors have resulted in accomplishing much good. As a race, they are truly susceptible of this higher culture, but much work is yet required to obliterate the moral evils contracted through long years of bondage, and we trust that this essay may serve as an inspiration to many to lend their influence in gaining this desired end.

More than two thousand years ago, Isocrates, a distinguished writer of Athens, gave utterance to his views concerning the chief requisite toward contributing to the happiness of a people or a State. He laid great stress upon the importance of bestowing the strictest attention upon the education and early training of the youth, in order to gain this end. Word for word, what he then uttered is applicable to the present condition of our society. The history of social life is always repeating itself, as is the history of Nations, and those people are the wisest who take the lessons to heart. To a second Isocrates, a disciple of the Athenian orator, is attributed another discourse, which consists of moral precepts for the conduct of life and the regulation of the deportment of the young, illustrating the fact that, link by link, through long centuries, has the culture of one generation been carried down and connected with the next. for the ultimate advancement of mankind. The individual may perish, the race become extinct, but the effect of culture throws reflected light down the channel of time.

All systems may be said to have descended from previous ones. The ideas of one generation are the mysterious progenitors of those of the next. Each age is the dawn of its successor, and in the eternal advance of truth,

> " There always is a rising sun,
> The day is ever but begun."

It is thus true that there is nothing new under the sun, since the new grows from the old as boughs grow from the tree; and though errors and exaggerations are, from time to time shaken off, yet, " the things which cannot be shaken" will certainly abide.

Carlyle says: " Literature is but a branch of religion,

and always participates in its character." It is still more true that education is a branch of mental philosophy, and takes its mould and fashion from it. For it is evident that as philosophy, in successive ages, gives varying answers as to man's chief end and *summum bonum*, so education, which is simply an attempt to prepare him therefor, must vary accordingly. Humboldt hints that the vegetation of whole regions bespeaks and depends upon the strata beneath; and it is certainly true that we cannot delve long in the teacher's plot without coming upon those moral questions that go down to the centre.

Richter delighted to preach the doctrine of an ideal man, and that education is the harmonious development of the faculties and dispositions of each individual. No one knew better than he that (in Carlyle's words) a loving heart is the beginning of all knowledge. This it is that opens the whole mind, and quickens every faculty of the intellect to do its fit work. This it is which influences and controls the manners, and, with proper training, distinguishes the well-educated from the ill-educated. It is the women of a Nation who make the manners of the men.

It has been said that there is scarcely any soul born into this world in which a self-sacrificing, steady effort on the parents' part may not lay broad and deep the foundations of strength of will, of self-control; and, therefore, of that self-reverence and self-knowledge. which, combined with the possession and love of noble ideas, will enable men and women not only to have good manners, but to be true and useful to God and mankind. The regeneration of their society is in the power of the colored woman, and she must not turn away from it. The manners of men, the hearts of men, the lives of men, are in her hands. How does she use her power? We look with pride upon the thousands of colored women scattered all over our broad land, true and noble representatives of the ideal woman, inspired by a lofty ambition, and a desire to elevate their people to higher walks in social life, but, alas, all are not so. We see living answers to this sad truth in every circle of society around us. There is no sadder sight in this world than to see the women of a land grasping at the ignoble honor and rejecting the noble; leading the men, whom they should guide into high thought and active sacrifice, into petty slander of gossip in conversation, and into discussion of dangerous and unhealthy feeling, becoming in this degradation of their directing power the curse, and not the blessing of social intercourse—becoming what men in frivolous moments wish them to be, instead of making men what men should be; ceasing to protest against impurity and unbelief, and giving them an underhand encouragement, turning away from their mission to bless, to exalt, and to console, that they may struggle through a thousand meannesses into a higher position, and waste their divine energy to win precedence over a rival; expending all the force which their nature gives them in their false and sometimes base excitements, day after day, with an awful blindness and a pitiable degradation; exhausting life in amusements which fritter away, or in amusements which debase their character—not thinking of the thousands of their sisters who are weeping in the night for hunger and for misery of heart. This is not our work, some say, this is the work of the men. Be it so, if you like. Let them be the hands that do it; but who, if not women, are to be the hearts of the redemption of their sex from social wrong?

Still nearer home lies the point which is nearest the heart of those interested in the higher culture of women, namely, the proper education of the colored youth. Our miscalled education looks chiefly as to how a young girl may make a good figure in society, and this destroys in her the beauty of unconsciousness of self. She grows up and enters society, and there is either a violent reaction against conventionality, or there is a paralyzing sensitiveness to opinion, or there is a dull repose of character and manner, which is all but equivalent to stagnation. We see many who are afraid of saying openly what they think or feel, if it be in opposition to the accredited opinion of the world; we see others who rejoice in shocking opinion for the sake of making themselves remarkable—perhaps the basest form of social vanity, for it gives pain and does not spring from conviction. Both forms arise from the education which makes the child self-conscious, leading the mind to ask that degrading question, "What will people say of me?"

Colored women should guard closely against this, for, to make your children live only by the opinions of others, to train them not to influence, but to submit to the world, is to educate them to think only of themselves, is to train them up to inward falseness, is to destroy all eternal distinctions between right and wrong, is to reduce them to that level of uneducated unoriginality which is the most melancholy feature in the young society of the present day. Let them grow naturally, keep them as long as is possible unconscious of themselves; and, for the sake of the world, which, in the midst of all its conventional dullness, longs for something fresh and true, if not for their own sakes, do not press upon them the belief that the voice of society is the measure of what is right or wrong, beautiful or unbeautiful, fitting or unfitting for them to do. This want of individuality is one of the most painful deficiencies in our present society. The ratification of this evil lies at the root of Christianity, for all Christ's teachings tend to produce individuality, to rescue men from being mingled up, indistinguishable atoms, with the mass of men; to teach them that they possess a distinct character which it is God's will to educate; distinct gifts which God will inspire and develop.

We want men and women who will think for themselves, and study deeply the great lessons that may be learned by the development of their own individual character. And now we see a desire manifested among the colored people, a longing for some fresh ideas to come and stir the stagnant pools of life.

This may be best accomplished by the angels of our households wherever there is one who, in the face of manifold discouragements of daily life, "borne down by the little carking cares that sap out love so slowly but so surely," still bears up, and by example and conversation—

43

—Teaches love to suffer and be pure,
That virtue conquers if it but endure,
That noblest gifts should serve the noblest ends,
That he's the richest who the most befriends;
That through life's journey, dark or bright the day,
Fate's not unkind, whatever men may say,
If goodness walks companion of their way.

It is the preacher's province to inspire women with a desire to do their share of the great work, which should be and which is their mission, namely, the purification, improvement and re-generation of mankind by living up to doctrines which, though everywhere professed, are seldom followed. These verses from the grand poem of Whittier to "Our Master," reveal wherein we fail:

* * * " O Love ineffable!
Thy saving name is given;
To turn aside from thee is hell,
To walk with thee is heaven!

"Not thine the bigots' partial plea,
Nor thine the zealots' ban;
Thou well canst spare a love for thee
Which ends in hate of man.

"We bring no ghastly holocaust,
We pile no graven stone;
He serves the best who loveth most
His brothers and thy own."

Judged by such a test, who can say, "I am a Christian?" Rather will not some of the teachings of barbarian philoso-phers put us to shame! Only by instilling into the minds of children, from their earliest years, a love of justice and truth, sympathy with all their kind, reverence for all goodness, and a a conscientious desire to know and to do the right, can we hope to have a generation of Christian men and women worthy of the republic which confers upon them its unsurpassed rights and privileges. Then will our colored communities be influ-enced by other principles than those by which so many of them are now governed.

As we study closely into the lives and principles of the colored people, we find there, as among the other races, not only those who have worked earnestly and untiringly for the ad-vancement of their race, in a literary and commercial sense, but in that higher education and culture which lends a charm to life, and infuses others with a desire to engraft into their own lives this same principle. It is this same cause that engaged the labors and made the pens of Amie Martin, Harriet Martineau, Lucretia Mott, Lucy Colman and a host of others, eloquent in the advocation of the truest and highest principles of life. This higher culture is now occupying the minds and hearts of numbers of our colored women, who realize that under *the domestic roof* are formed those opinions and those moral feelings which inspire the masses to lead better lives and guard closely their moral character. This principle is that which sustains institutions and governments, or the lack of which will cause them to fall.

Women are formed to become instructors, for while they hold immediately in their hands the morality of their children, those future sovereigns of the earth, the example they may give and the charm they may diffuse over other periods of life, furnish to them means for the amelioration of every evil. Whatever in political organization is not founded on the true interests of families, soon disappears or produces only evil; and these interests are chiefly confided to women, particularly as the attention of men is otherwise directed. As also in the material arrangements, it is principally to women that the care of health, and the care of property has devolved; so in the spiritual department, it is they who communicate or awaken sentiments which are the life of the soul—the eternal impetus of actions. Their influence is immense in the vicissitudes of life. There is then constant action and reaction between public and private life, and thence may result a double advancement in civilization; for, if domestic administration were generally better understood, a purer element would be poured into society by a thousand channels.

That which it seems most necessary to form in our colored women, is a prompt ability to decide correctly of what every moment requires. Principles elevated, firm, and founded on reflection, joined to her natural gifts can alone render her capable of fulfilling that mission of instruction for which she is designed.

45

It is through her children that a woman rules posterity; that she leaves, for good or for evil, indelible marks on the universe; that the tendencies inherited from the past are transmitted to the future—acquired qualities as well as natural qualities—and so we come back to the assertion of the Athenian philosopher, as to the importance of educating our youth aright. Just in proportion as Colored Mothers train aright their children, so we will see the race advance, and not until then. The Spartan Mothers taught their children war and love of country, and we see in that people bravery, such as the world had never before witnessed, and so may we inspire within our children a lofty ambition, and noble sentiments.

Children should be taught the laws of health, and that for every violation of these laws, they will suffer the penalty. Well has Dr. Clark said, "Let Eve take a wise care of the temple God made for her, and Adam of the one made for him, and both will enter upon a career whose glory and beauty no seer has foretold, or poet sung."

Not the happiness of life, perhaps, but its blessedness is learned in living for others; and, as Dr. Kingsley says, it is the glory of a woman, that for this end she was sent into the world, to live for others rather than for herself; to live, yes, and often to die for them. Let her never be persuaded to forget that she is sent into the world to teach man that there is something more necessary than the claiming of rights, and that is the performing of duties; to teach him also that her rights should be respected, and her wrongs redressed; that her education should be such as to draw out her powers of mind to the best advantage and their fullest extent; that there is something more than intellect, and that is purity and virtue. Surely this is woman's calling—to teach man; to teach him, after all, that his calling is the same as hers, if he will but see the things that belong to his peace; to temper his fiercer, coarser, more self-assertive nature, by the contact of her gentleness, purity, self-sacrifice; to make him see that not by blare of trumpets, not by noise, wrath, greed, hatred, ambition, intrigue, puffery, prejudice, bigotry, is good and lasting work to be done on earth; but by helpful hands, by sympathizing hearts, by wise self-distrust, by silent labor, by lofty self-control, by that greatest of all virtues, that charity which hopeth all things, believeth all things, endureth all things, by such an example in short, as women *now*, in tens of thousands of homes, set to those around them; and such as they will show more and more, in proportion as their whole womanhood is educated to employ its powers without waste and without haste in harmonious unity

Let her begin girlhood, if such be her happy lot, to quote from Wordsworth:

> " With all things round about her drawn
> From May-time and the cheerful dawn;
> A dancing shape, an image gay,
> To haunt, to startle, and waylay."

Let her develop onward:

> " A spirit, yet a woman, too,
> With household motions light and free,
> And steps of Virgin liberty.
> A countenance in which shall meet
> Sweet records, promises as sweet;
> A creature not too bright and good
> For human nature's daily food;
> For transient sorrows, simple wiles,
> Praise, blame, love, kisses, tears, and smiles "

But let her highest and final development be that which not nature but self-education alone can bring.

Let the higher education of women be undertaken and carried out with such ends in view, and in another generation some of the most perplexing problems of social science will be solved. "Good teachers make good scholars, but it is only mothers that form men," cannot be too often repeated, for in this truth we have the key to the reformation of mankind.

47

A.

Mrs. E.C. Hobson and Mrs. C.E. Hopkins, excerpt from "A Report Concerning the Colored Women of the South"
(Occasional Paper No. 9. Baltimore: Trustees of the John F. Slater Fund, 1896)

B.

Letter from S[ophia] Packard to J.D. Rockefeller, December 29, 1883
(Rockefeller Family Archives. RG1, box 20, folder 233)

C.

Raymond Wolters, excerpt from *The New Negro on Campus: Black College Rebellions of the 1920s*
(Princeton: Princeton University Press, 1975, p. 13, reprinted by permission)

D.

Jeanne L. Noble, excerpt from *The Negro Woman's College Education*
(New York: Teachers College Press, 1956, p. 24, reprinted by permission)

A. It is perhaps unwise at this time to give full expression to our views regarding the moral condition of the negro women. It is sufficient to say that the reports that had been made to us by others, before we undertook our investigations, were fully confirmed, and we hope that in the near future the women of the South will become so interested and roused to the importance of the subject that they may be inclined to cooperate with the women of the North in some plan for the elevation of these descendants of their former servants.

"Thus many blacks suspected that the extraordinarily strict regulations still in force in their schools during the 1920's were prompted by a racist belief that Negroes were particularly sensuous beings who could not discipline themselves and were not prepared to exercise free will."

" But it appears that many possibly have been predicated on reasons relating to her foremother's sex role as a slave. . . . Her education in many instances appears to have been based on a philosophy which implied that she was weak and immoral and that at best she should be made fit to rear her children and to keep house for her husband."

B. "We [Sophia Packard and Harriet Giles, founders of Spelman] who are here and see their [ex-slaves'] needs know full well that the elevation of this race depends emphatically upon the education of these women. For 'tis woman that gives tone and character to any people."

C. "Thus many blacks suspected that the extraordinarily strict regulations still in force in their schools during the 1920s were prompted by a racist belief that Negroes were particulary sensuous beings who could not discipline themselves and were not prepared to exercise free will."

D. "But it appears that many of the Negro woman's [college] rules and regulations may possibly have been predicated on reasons relating to her foremother's sex role as a slave....Her education in many instances appears to have been based on a philosophy which implied that she was weak and immoral and that at best she should be made fit to rear her children and to keep house for her husband."

Virginia State University: A Woman's Recollection of 1887–1889

Ruth Brown Hucles, excerpt from "Virginia State College as I Knew It as a Student and Worker"

(Records of the Vice-President of Virginia State College [James Hugo Johnson, Jr. Papers. Correspondence, 1957.] Special Collections, Johnson Memorial Library. Reprinted by permission of Virginia State College, Petersburg, Va.)

State College as I knew it as a student in 1887-89 was very different from State College as I see it today. In the fall of 1887 when I arrived at the foot of Fleets Hill, as this location was then called there was no winding driveway nor graded walkway leading to the building. The only way to reach the building was by climbing from the foot of the hill to the summit on rocks hewn by the hand of nature into stairways. The grounds were ungraded and no beautiful trees and grass-covered lawns greeted you when you at last reached the summit of the hill.

The building now known as Virginia Hall, the oldest and most antiquated on the campus was then in the process of erection only one story having been completed on the front.

The building now known as Colson Hall was the old family residence of Mr. Fleet after whom the hill was named and was used for the boys dormitory. As there were more boys than girls two other frame buildings called the House of Representatives and the Senate, were also used as dormitories for the boys. Virginia Hall was supposed to have been built in the shape of the letter T but since only the long end of the T was completed, the girls, about 45 in number including day students, occupied the second floor of that end of the building now used for a .

There were 13 rooms on this floor, number 13 being the bath room. But since there were no water connections this room was occupied by two girls, one of whom was a classmate of mine, the late Mrs. Josie Matthews Norcom. The bath tub filled with quilts and blankets was converted into a studio couch and many a problem in higher mathematics was solved on that studio couch, the bath tub. Number 12 next door was familiarly known as monkey town, for in assigning the rooms it just happened that all the worst looking and noisiest girls were assigned to #12. You know we had a wonderful time in that room.

Our rooms were furnished with iron cots and with mattresses, a bare table and wash stand. All other equipment including window shades, bed linen, blankets, table covers, pitcher and bowl, lamps and oil, was furnished by the students. Water was brought from a spring located to the rear of President Gardy's house, in earthen pitchers and nothing was sadder than to forget the hour allotted for going to the spring for this pitcher of water. Every evening from 4 to 5:30 was the hour, and oh what joy for this was an opportunity to meet the boys. They were allowed to fill the pitchers and escort the girls to the brow of the hill but now further for Miss Lucy Morse, our matron, was always standing there smiling and saying, "This was, girls."

Our rooms were lighted with kerosene oil lamps since electric lights were unknown as well as electric cars. The only car we remember was the Dummy, a funny looking vehicle drawn by two white mules. This was an interurban car and oh how happy we were when on a holiday we were allowed to visit the Central State Hospital and ride part of the way on the Dummy.

The building was heated by one large stove in the hall and what a scramble there was on cold mornings to be the first to dress by this stove. The first floor of this end of the building was used for laundry, dining room, pantry and classrooms while the kitchen was in the basement. I can't speak of the kitchen without referring to dear old Mr. Riddick, the chef. He was a typical Chesterfeildian and just as proud of his "boys" as he called the college boys as if he had been the Vice President. In fact, had his mind been on his culinary art instead of trying to run the college, there would have been better bread and fewer roaches.

On Sundays we went to church in a body, the boys forming a line and marching double file in front and the girls following, chaperoned by a teacher. As we passed through the streets of Petersburg, we heard both favorable and unfavorable comments.

Very little recreation was provided as we were supposed to go to school to study and not to play. Cards and dancing were prohibited and athletic sports were not popular. The only form of recreation we indulged in was a grand march on special occasions when the boys and girls marched together around the chapel and turned square corners.

The personnel of our faculty consisted of a president, secretary-treasurer, 5 professors, 3 female teachers and a matron. Nevertheless, we had an intensive and extensive curriculum and V.N.C.I. stood second to none in the state of Virginia at that time.

The personnel of the student body consisted of the F.F.V.'s and a few from Washington, D.C. for only wealthy families could afford to pay $60 board and tuition for a 9 month's term at an exclusive college.

The late congressman, John Mercer Langston, was our president and as I look back upon those by-gone days, I see Mr. Langston standing in the hall with his long snow white whiskers and hair gazing proudly as we marched in chapel singing "John Brown's body lies a-moulding in the grave." This was State College as I knew it as a student in 87-88.

After working as teacher 2 1/2 years State College adopted me into its official family as the wife of the Treasurer and Business manager. Our wedding reception was held in this chapel with the entire student body present. My work continued here for 19 years after, for although not on the pay roll, the welfare of State College was always uppermost in the minds and hearts of its former graduates. State College stands for loyalty, for courage, for the subordination of individual ease and individual gain to public ends of lasting importance. These are the traditions of service we are called upon to maintain. All the traditions of this place call us to the service of God and our fellow men. May it be our lot to face the problems of today in a spirit of self-consecration bound to our duty not by laws alone, nor by creeds alone, but by the honor of the service.

Higher Education for African-American Women: A Justification

Anna Julia Cooper, excerpt from "The Higher Education of Women"
(*The Southland,* April, 1891, 199–202)

Now I would that my task ended here. Having shown that
a great want of the world in the past has been a feminine
force; that that force can have its full effect only through the
untrammelled development of woman; that such development,
while it gives her to the world and to civilization, does not
necessarily remove her from the home and fireside; finally,
that while past centuries have witnessed sporadic instances of
this higher growth, still it was reserved for the latter half of
the nineteenth century to render it common and general
enough to be effective. I might close with a glowing prediction
of what the twentieth century may expect from this
heritage of twin forces—the masculine battered and toil-worn
as a grim veteran after centuries of warfare. but still strong
active and vigorous, ready to help with his hard-won experience the young recruit rejoicing in her newly found freedom,
who so confidently places her hand in his with mutual pledges
to redeem the ages.

> "And so the twain upon the skirts of Time,
> Sit side by side, full-summed in all their powers,
> Dispensing harvest, sowing the To-be,
> Self-reverent each and reverencing each."

With a view of enlightenment on the point, as the achievement of the century for the higher education of the colored women, I wrote a few days ago to the Colleges which admit women
and asked how many Colored women had completed the B. A.
course in each during its entire history.   These are the figures returned: Fisk leads the way with twelve; Oberlin next with five;
Ann Arbor, Wellesley and Wilberforce three each, Living-
stone two, Atlanta one, Howard, as yet, none.

I then asked the principal of the Washington High School
how many out of the large number of female graduates from

his school had chosen to go forward and take a collegiate course. He replied that but one had ever done so, and she is now in Cornell.[*]

Others ask questions too, sometimes, and I was asked a few years ago by a white friend, "How is it that the men of your race seem to outstrip the women in mental attainment?" "Oh," I said, "so far as it is true, the men, I suppose, from the life they lead, gain more by contact, and so far as it is only apparent, I think the women are more quiet. They don't feel called to mount a barrel and harangue by the hour every time they imagine they have produced an idea."

But I am sure there is another reason which I did not at that time see fit to give. The atmosphere, the standards, the requirements of our little world do not afford any special stimulus to female development.

It seems hardly a gracious thing to say, but it strikes me as true, that while our men seem thoroughly abreast of the times on almost every other subject, when they strike the woman question they drop back into sixteenth century logic. They leave nothing to be desired generally in regard to gallantry and chivalry, but they actually do not seem sometimes to have outgrown that old contemporary of chivalry—the idea that women may stand on pedestals or live in doll-houses, (if they happen to have them) but they must not furrow their brows with thought or attempt to help men tug at the great questions of the world. I fear the majority of colored men do not yet think it worth while that women aspire to higher education. Not many will subscribe to the "advanced" ideas of Grant Allen already quoted. The three R's, a little music and a good deal of dancing, a first rate dress-maker and a bottle of magnolia balm, are quite enough generally to render charming any woman possessed of tact and the capacity of worshipping masculinity.

My readers will pardon my illustrating my point and also giving a reason for the fear that is in me, by a little bit of personal experience. When a child I was put into a school near home

*Graduated from Scientific course, June, 1890, the first colored woman to graduate from Cornell.

that professed to be normal and collegiate, i. e. to prepare teachers for colored youth, furnish candidates for the ministry, and offer collegiate training for those who should be ready for it. Well, I found after a while that I had a good deal of time on my hands. I had devoured what was put before me, and, like Oliver Twist, was looking around to ask for more. I constantly felt (as I suppose many an ambitious girl has felt) a thumping from within unanswered by any beckoning from without. Class after class was organized for these ministerial candidates (many of them men who had been preaching before I was born). Into every one of these classes I was expected to go, with the sole intent, I thought at the time, of enabling the dear old principal, as he looked from the vacant countenances of his sleepy old class over to where I sat, to get off his solitary pun—his never-failing pleasantry, especially in hot weather—which was, as he called out "Any one!" to the effect that "*any* one" then meant "*Annie* one."

Finally a Greek class was to be formed. My inspiring preceptor informed me that Greek had never been taught in the school, but that he was going to form a class *for the candidates for the ministry*; and if I liked I might join it. I replied—humbly I hope, as became the female of the human species—that I would like very much to study Greek, and that I was thankful for the opportunity, and so it went on. A boy, however meager his equipment and shallow his pretensions, had only to declare a floating intention to study theology and he could get all the support, encouragement and stimulus he needed, be absolved from work and invested beforehand with all the dignity of his far away office. While a self-supporting girl had to struggle on by teaching in the summer and working after school hours to keep up with her board bills, and actually to fight her way against positive discouragements to the higher education, till one such girl one day flared out and told the principal "the only mission opening before a girl in his school was to marry one of those candidates." He said he didn't know but it was. And when at last that same girl announced her desire and intention to go to college it was received with about the same incredulity and dismay as if a brass button on one of those candidate's coats had propounded a new method for squaring the circle or trisecting the arc.

Now this is not fancy. It is a simple unvarnished photograph, and what I believe was not in those days exceptional in colored schools, and I ask the men and women who are teachers and co-workers for the highest interests of the race, that they give the girls a chance! We might as well expect to grow trees from leaves as hope to build up a civilization or a manhood without taking into consideration our women and the home life made by them, which must be the root and ground of the whole matter. Let us insist then on special encouragement for the education of our women and special care in their training. - Let our girls feel that we expect something more of them than that they merely look pretty and appear well in society. Teach them that there is a race with special needs which they and only they can help; that the world needs and is already asking for their trained, efficient forces. Finally, if there is an ambitious girl with pluck and brain to take a higher education, encourage her to make the most of it. Let there be the same flourish of trumpets and clapping of hands as when a boy announces his determination to enter the lists, and then as you know that she is physically the weaker of the two, don't stand from under and leave her to buffet the waves alone. Let her know that your heart is following her, that your hand, though she sees it not, is ready to support her. To be plain, I mean let money be raised and scholarships be founded in our colleges and universities for self-supporting, worthy young women, to offset and balance the aid that can always be found for boys who will take theology.

The earnest well trained Christian young woman, as a teacher, as a home-maker, as wife, mother, or silent influence even, is as potent a missionary agency among our people as is the theologian; and I claim that at the present stage of our development in the South she is even more important and necessary.

Let us then, here and now, recognize this force and resolve to make the most of it—not the boys less, but the girls more.

Women Students at Atlanta University, 1894: Rules, Report and Photo

Atlanta University Dress Regulations,
What the Normal Graduates of Atlanta University are Doing
(Atlanta University Archives)

ATLANTA UNIVERSITY

DRESS REGULATIONS

These govern not only the boarding girls, but also day students when on the campus.

In order to promote the interests of true democracy, to discourage extravagance and cultivate habits of reasonable economy, the following regulations have been adopted:

I. Material. In general, good taste suggests that it should be inexpensive, inconspicuous, and appropriate. For example, dresses, blouses or middies may be made of cotton, linen, rayon, natural color pongee, or wool for cooler weather.

In addition to the above, a silk dress or blouse of soft shade and tone may be worn to church, street, or social function.

A simple white dress of cotton, linen or wool (preferably cotton) is required of those who take part in public exercises.

II. Trimming. This may be of braid, same or contrasting material, embroidery of small design and size. Be careful not to overtrim.

III. Shoes should have the low heel and not be too fancy.

IV. Jewelry. Only a wrist watch or simple pin or ring can be worn.

V. Girls should bring to school work aprons, and rubbers, umbrella and coat for stormy weather.

VI. The interpretation of these regulations, and their alteration, if necessary, is in the hands of the preceptress in charge, with the members of the dress committee as advisers.

We earnestly ask all parents not to seek admission for their daughters unless they are in sympathy with the spirit of these regulations.

63

WHAT THE NORMAL GRADUATES OF ATLANTA UNIVERSITY ARE DOING.

————— ⁂ —————

The thirteen young women shown in the picture on the other side of this sheet were graduated from the normal course in 1894. Since then they have been employed as follows :

They have been teaching in the public schools of the cities and larger towns of Georgia — four of them in Atlanta, one in Augusta, one in Savannah, one in Athens, one in Rome, one in Cuthbert, one in Marietta, one in Jenkinsburg, one in Lovejoy, one in Lithonia.

In the schools where they have taught they have had at least 600 pupils under their direct instruction. Some of these pupils they will eventually send to become students in Atlanta University, as they themselves were, many of them, sent by the earlier graduates who trained them.

Most of them have also been engaged in Sunday-school or Temperance work, and have accomplished something in the moral uplifting of those around them.

With their knowledge of cooking, sewing, and other domestic arts, they have been able to do something in improving the home life of the people among whom they have taught.

Trained, all of them, in the arts of nursing the sick and in the treatment of "emergency cases," they have been able, as occasion offered, to relieve suffering and hasten the restoration of the sick.

Some of them will eventually be married, and the homes which they establish will be centres from which strong influences for good will flow forth to bless the communities where they live. Nearly half of the married female graduates of Atlanta University are teaching school besides caring for their homes.

Atlanta University is training many other young women (and men) for equally useful lives. To do this an annual tuition scholarship of $40 is needed to supplement the payments of each student. These scholarships are furnished by many Christian Endeavor Societies, Sunday schools, churches, and individuals. Students' letters are sent to those who contribute these scholarships.

For further information address

PRESIDENT HORACE BUMSTEAD,

ATLANTA UNIVERSITY, ATLANTA, GA

July, 1895.

64

A New Century Opens: Rules and Policies

Atlanta University Student Life c. 1900

Excerpt from an interview with Bazoline E. Usher by Gay
Francine Banks, March 22, 1977

(Black Women's Oral History Project, Schlesinger Library, Radcliffe
College, Cambridge, Mass., reprinted by permission)

BEU: Some of them did their own [laundry]. Those who were on part-time basis and paid just a part of their regular fee, did their own laundry. There was a place for them to do it and tubs and ironing spaces. But those who paid full board, there were a few who paid full board, had theirs done. There were women there who were laundresses and who did the work for the teachers. See, teachers had their laundry done too. And the laundry wasn't very much. But they were limited, quite limited, as to how much they could put into the laundry. So they didn't have very much. The girls and a very few boys paid full fare, so most of the boys had theirs done there. And I can recall how the boys used to come over with their bags. They had little laundry bags and they'd come over and get their laundry from North Hall, but whatever they had was very simple.

Just a few of the girls, as I can recall; I recall girls who were sent there by their white fathers, most of them were able to pay full board, as I can recall. And some others paid full board too. Full board wasn't very much. You did one hour's work a day. Everybody had a job, had something to do, everybody, regardless of what they paid. And those who were on full board had one hour and those who paid part time, did two hours. I was a part-time student, so I had two hours of work. But some of my work was like this. One, I sat at the table of the dean and it was the dean's business to collect absentees. And so during the meal, I went around all the tables; I think there were twelve tables in the dining hall. I went around all the tables and collected the names of those who were absent. Some of them having excuses would be absent. Very often, you know the boys would stay out and things of that sort, so they took the attendance at every meal, and that was one of my jobs, and they gave me credit for about an hour a day on working on that. I did that three times, we had three meals a day.

GFB: So what about other students? What other types of jobs did they do?

BEU: Some of them took care of the teachers' rooms. They spent some times in there, straightening up the room. Some of them did hall duty, swept in the halls. Some of them waited tables. And most of them worked inside at various types of things. Some of them really worked in the laundry, and some of them worked in the kitchen preparing food, you see. There were certain chores that they had to perform. Some of them took a little time and some took more time. But it was expected that you did two hours of work. Most of the time it didn't take two hours, but it was a job and you did it and you got credit for that two hours of work.

GFB: Right. So how were the classes set up during that time? Did you have all the classes, say, like in the morning or were you spread out all over the day?

BEU: Classes were just about all day. Because we had so many students who came from the city. They walked all the way from across town, over to Atlanta University, and see, they had to have classes for those. You just got your job in before school hours, see. I think the school ran from eight until twelve and then from one till four. That's about how it was. And there were no night classes. They didn't have night classes because everybody retired early. I can recall there was no one who stayed up late. And in fact, the preceptresses, we called them, saw to it that everybody went to bed on time.

GFB: What time was that?

BEU: At ten o'clock. Of course, we had lamps, oil lamps. That's another thing, that's another job somebody did, filling the lamps. You take your lamp, every lamp had a name on it, you take your lamp down to the oil room and there was somebody who did that every day. There weren't too many jobs, but they were all figured out and assigned.

GFB: So did you have to eat breakfast, like at a certain time every morning, a set time?

BEU: Yes, we used to have breakfast at a set time. There is a clock over there that rings off, it strikes and rings too. But now sometimes the time was on the clock and other times there was an electric bell that rang through the building. But we had breakfast at a certain time and then lunch at a certain time and then dinner. Except on Saturdays. We didn't have three meals on Saturday or Sunday. We had breakfast and dinner and didn't have lunch. They took a lunch with them from the dinner table.

GFB: Oh, something like a little doggy bag?

BEU: That's right, a bag, that's right.

GFB: So, I wonder if it was similar to the one we get today.

BEU: Well, I guess maybe. They didn't have the third meal. And we had something, they gave you something, I don't know what it was. I don't recall, just a little something, most of them didn't have... and what they would do, they would pass it on to somebody else or something of that sort. And they'd always be going down to the corner to buy something from the store. See, the students who boarded on campus couldn't leave the campus, but they could meet other students, you see. Other students would come to visit them and they would go the store for them. I remember two or three stores right close by. They were always going to those stores, getting something, especially on a Saturday.

GFB: Why didn't they let boarding students, why didn't they let them go off campus?

BEU: Well, they went off campus only by permission and with a matron, with somebody who took them. The girls would go to town on Saturday afternoon. Other afternoons, I guess some other afternoons, but there was a woman who came and chaperoned the girls. Boys were allowed to go off campus certain hours after school, but the girls were not. The girls stayed on the campus unless they had special permission and were accompanied by somebody who was in charge.

GFB: Right. Because I know that happened at Spelman, the young ladies used to have to wear their dresses and gloves when they went downtown. Was that required of A.U. girls?

BEU: No.

GFB: No?

BEU: No, they didn't have to do that. They expected them to look presentable, of course. All I know is I just wore whatever I had. It was very presentable because I came from the country, and my mother made all of my clothes; they were very simple dresses and I was small. I didn't pay full board, but it happened that my laundry was done for a long period of time before they found out I wasn't paying full board. Then I began to do it myself. Sometimes there was a young man there who would take my things home. Sometimes my things were sent home and my mother did it for me.

The 1901 Decision to Bar Women from North Carolina A & T

Quoted by Carrye Hill Kelley in "Profiles of Five Administrators"
(*The Agricultural and Technical College History-Digest*, 55 (5):21)

. . . We gave co-education a patient trial for several years, but at a meeting of the Board held in May 1901, we decided to abolish the girl department, and make the institution strictly a college of agriculture and mechanics. The step was taken with due deliberation. There were several reasons for this change. In the first place, the girls are by nature not well fitted for agricultural and mechanical pursuits, and their presence in the college hampered the work, and there was an evident disinclination on the part of both sexes to engage in the harder kinds of manual labor in the presence of the other, both feeling called upon to wear their best clothes in order to impress the other. It was human nature, and nothing could prevent it. The dormitories were absolutely inadequate, the girls being crowded seven or eight in a room, and consequently there was much sickness. There was no separate building where the girls could be properly isolated, and the arrangements for them were bad.

. . . In addition to these reasons, the opportunity for some designing Negro to hatch out a scandal was unsurpassed, and good use was made of it, but investigation would usually reveal that one individual wanted another man's job. We have found that this desire to pull down another in order to get the position is a weakness of many of the race, and a scandal is the favorite way of getting rid of the incumbent.

. . . We have been delighted with the change, and consider it one of the greatest of the improvements that have been made at the college. . . .

Defense of Black Women's College Education

Untitled article by Mary Church Terrell
(*New York City Independent*, March 14, 1901)

The newspapers representing the negroes of the United States have got hold of Mr. W. H. Thomas's "The American Negro," reviewed by us a few weeks ago, and are treating it with the utmost severity. We also are receiving numbers of articles in reply to it which we cannot print. From one of these, written by Mrs. Mary C. Terrell, of Washington, D.C., president of the National Association of Colored Women, we give the following extract representing her own personal knowledge:

In order to prove the utter worthlessness and total depravity of colored girls, it is boldly asserted by the author of "The American Negro" that under the best educational influences they are not susceptible to improvement. Educate a colored girl and a white girl together, he says, and when they are twenty years old the colored girl will be either a physical wreck or a giggling idiot, while her white companion will have become an intelligent, cultured, chaste young woman. It would be interesting to know where the author of this book made his observations, or from what source he obtained his information.

I was sent to Oberlin, Ohio, when a child, and graduated both from the high school and the classical course of the college. During the nine years I remained in Oberlin I became acquainted with many colored girls who were attending school and with whom I have since kept in more or less constant touch. As far as I am able to learn all of these women are useful members of society, either pursuing their chosen vocations or presiding over their own homes.

About twelve years ago I taught at Wilberforce University, near Xenia, Ohio, for two years, and after that I was instructor in the Washington High School for the same length of time. I therefore came in contact with hundreds of colored girls, not one of whom, to my knowledge, is leading a life of shame. I am also personally acquainted with colored women who have graduated from Ann Arbor University, Cornell and the Chicago University, from Oberlin, Radcliffe, Smith, Wellesley, Vassar and other institutions throughout the North, South, East and West, and not one of them is either a giggling idiot or a physical wreck. On the contrary, they are a company of useful, cultured women who would be a blessing and a credit to any race. Many of them obtained high rank in the institutions from which they received their degrees. The white instructors of colored girls cheerfully testify to their intelligence, their diligence and their success.

Since I have had a far better opportunity to observe colored girls at closer range during their high school or college course than the author of "The American Negro," I feel that I am better qualified to judge the effect which an education has upon their minds, their manners and their morals. Finally, I repudiate as false the charge that colored children are more shameless and bolder in their wrongdoing than the children of other races. I was trustee of the public schools of the District of Columbia for five years, and I came in close touch with both the white and the colored teachers. I observed that their complaints and criticisms concerning the mental density and the moral obliquity of their pupils were about the same without regard to race or color. Children are very much the same the world over, as every one who has traveled much and observed closely will testify.

Women's Life at Tuskegee, 1911–1915

Excerpt from an interview with Hattie Simmons Kelly by A. Lillian Thompson, September 5, 6, 8, and 9, 1976
(Black Women's Oral History Project, Schlesinger Library, Radcliffe College, Cambridge, Mass., reprinted by permission)

ALT: Did your mother make your clothes for you to come to Tuskegee?

HSK: Mother made most of them and then she had a lady make some and then, you see I knew I was going to have to wear a uniform.

ALT: Oh. Did you wear uniforms?

HSK: Oh yes.

ALT: What was that like?

HSK: We wore uniforms every day. The blouse was blue wash material, the skirt was blue.

ALT: Every day?

HSK: Yes. But on Sunday, the blouse was white. In the afternoons and on Sunday afternoons as soon as you came in from chapel, you see, you could change your uniform and wear your own clothes. My sister Alberta had just gotten married. I don't know what year she married, but she had just gotten married as I can recall and if she hadn't just gotten married, she had had all of her clothes made to get married. But she didn't like some of the things my mother had made, so she gave me many of the things, because she had been working for a good while. She gave me many of the things that she had made for herself. So I came here well-dressed.

ALT: Did you find it difficult to adjust, coming from a household where there was strictness and discipline to a campus where you were absolutely free to do what you wanted to do?

HSK: Do you think we were free on this campus then to do what we wanted to do? Then you're wrong. I could take the strictness on the campus because I came from a home that was strict, but many girls could not.

ALT: What was it like? What was the nature of it?

HSK: We could not go off the campus without an admit. It was very difficult to get an admit to leave the campus. Everything we wanted was right on the campus. You couldn't go to town without a chaperone. You had to get a ... sometimes the older girls, I told you about Mary Ross. My roommate was much older than the rest of us and she was one of the chaperones. There were many older girls who were chaperones, but they were very, very strict. We couldn't go to chapel up on the street. The girls had to go down through the bottom to chapel and no boys spent any time over on the girls' lawn at all. When there were calling hours, they could come to the buildings to call. But ...

ALT: And that was a formal arrangement where they would be announced at the door? Coming to call, describe what would happen.

HSK: Well, there were girls on duty, who sat right near the door and they'd call for the girls and somebody would get the girls and they would go to the living room and they would sit and call.

ALT: They wouldn't go out and stroll about the campus?

85

HSK: No.

ALT: They had to sit right there in the dormitory?

HSK: That's right.

ALT: Were there chaperones there?

HSK: Oh yes. The lady in charge of every building and then there were girls called duty girls. Girls on duty on every floor. You see ... they were very strict ... your room was inspected, your trunks were inspected, your closets, your clothes, everything was inspected and you were given demerits if everything wasn't just right. And when you went to chapel, you marched out of chapel and the physical education teachers stood there as you marched out, if there was a button off your blouse, or if it was soiled - the white blouses on Sunday - you were pulled out of line and that was on Sunday.

ALT: Oh, really?

HSK: They would pull you out of line. The man from the military department inspected the boys and I can see Booker T. Washington standing at that podium in chapel, he'd stand there and look. I, however, was in the choir and did not march out. We were in the choir and we'd have rehearsal right after almost every service. We'd have a little rehearsal - especially the night services.

But they were very strict. We were really confined to the campus. There were a number of girls whom I know who lived in the community, but we didn't visit them and we didn't know where they lived.

ALT: Did you have dances or sororities or anything of that kind?

HSK: We didn't have sororities and fraternities. Sororities and fraternities did not come to the Tuskegee campus until the '40s, but we did have all sorts of social organizations. The Christian Endeavor and Little Men and Little Women. I can't remember all the names. But the most important dance was military, although this military was not connected with the government.

ALT: Describe what you mean by being military.

HSK: Well, we had captains and lieutenants, but they were not captains in the United States service, but in school.

ALT: You mean the school just decided that you would be a captain and you'd be a lieutenant and whatever?

HSK: Yes. That's right. There were men in charge whom I guess had been in some service. The men wore uniforms too, but their uniforms were made in the tailor shop and the ... social affair that was most prominent was what we called an officers' hop. Those of us who went, went with officers, but every girl had to come to White Hall, made no difference what building or dormitory you lived in, you came to White Hall and you were inspected to see if you were dressed properly and everything.

86

ALT: What would be proper dress for something like that?

HSK: Well, we were wearing long dresses then anyway, I think. I can remember one
long dress I had was kind of split skirt, the blouse had ruffles all down
and ruffles around here. And the men came into White Hall for you and then
you'd walk over to the dining room; the dances were always in the dining
room. And we did dances like the Skating Schottische, it sounds like this ...
the Waltz Oxford. Those kinds of dances were the kind of dances where you
take hands and dance. I don't think ...

ALT: A young man didn't put his arms around you?

HSK: I don't think we had any dances other than when you whirled around, you
see, you'd have to put your arms around the girl.

ALT: What kind of music did you have for that? Did you have orchestras?

HSK: Orchestras. We always had good music. We always had good music because the
orchestra played every Sunday. I think they played Sunday morning and
Sunday nights, it's vague to me now, but I know the orchestra ...

ALT: Did you enjoy the dances?

HSK: Oh yes. I could not dance when I came to Tuskegee. You see, good girls
didn't dance.

ALT: Did you feel guilty when you learned how?

HSK: No. I don't know why I didn't, but I didn't. I didn't feel guilty at all.
But then, you didn't dance, we didn't go to dances in small towns. Maybe
city girls did, but you see, I was from a small town and we didn't go to
dances. We had church parties and things. But I remember my boyfriend
taught me to dance. He was very popular and somehow, I don't remember, but I
remember the matron allowed him to teach me to dance because we knew I was
to go to the next hop.

Mary McLeod Bethune in 1915: A Student's Perspective

Excerpt from an interview with Lucy Miller Mitchell by Cheryl
Gilkes, August 22, 1977
(Black Women's Oral History Project, Schlesinger Library, Radcliffe
College, Cambridge, Mass., reprinted by permission)

LMM: With Mrs. Bethune, there were just no short cuts, and another
part of the character training, shall I call it, would be through
these phrases that she would use, like "Whatever you do, do it to
the best of your ability." Over and over, you would find,
"Whatever you do, do it to the best of your ability." And so this
feeling about the thoroughness to this day, any kind of sloppiness
disturbs me greatly. I think another contribution that I would
say she made to my life, Cheryl, was her attitude toward work.
For instance, she would say, "Any work is honest however humble,"
and "In whatever you do, strive to be an artist." Wasn't that a
concept? To have it drilled into you, that whatever you do,
strive to be an artist.

Orderliness was another concept that became a part of my life, an
even as I grow to be almost eighty years old, I cannot bear to be
disorderly. It may be just a tiny thing, but it does become a
part of the expression of your living. I can remember many times
as adolescents will, we'd be tired at night and we'd sort of just
drop our clothes anywhere. This is when I became a boarding
student at the school, and she would come around and look in our
rooms at night, and we had these clothes just strewn all over the
place. Gently we were awakened, we had to get up and put those
clothes in a neat way on our chairs. I give those little
incidents because it does show a facet of this woman and the
influence that she had on these students. . . .

This was a woman of strong religious beliefs. We all had to
gather once a day--and this was a small group of 150 girls--for
her chapel talks. And I say here that she wove into the warp and
woof of our personality and character her philosophy of life, her
inspiration, her deep religious fervor; it was all there. And sh
gave to us a feeling that through God's power all things are
possible. But it was also a time, and you'll see the relevance o
this a little later, Cheryl, but it was also a time when she
drilled into her students our obligation to help the less
fortunate of our people. Again one of her constant expressions
was, "You are being trained to serve, go out into the community
and be an example of what education and training can mean to an
individual." . . .

A Home for Black Women at the University of Iowa, 1908–1929

"The Iowa Federation Home" from *Lifting as They Climb: Historical Record of the National Association of Colored Women and Other Items of Interest*
(1933; fac. Ann Arbor, Mich.: Xerox University Microfilms, 1976)

from Lifting as They Climb: the National Association of
Colored Women, pp. 151-54

THE IOWA FEDERATION HOME

IOWA CITY, IOWA

PURPOSE

Since the fall of 1908, there has been an increasing number of
Negro young women enrolled at the State University.

For several years, these young women, being few in number,
easily found homes with the various faculty members, where they
served as domestics, earning their board and room and sometimes a
little spending change; but by the year 1915, the number had
increased to about seven, some of whom could not find suitable
housing in which to live, the Negro population of Iowa City, being
quite small, so a delegation of these young women visited the State
Federation of Colored Women's Clubs, in session at Cedar Rapids,
and pleaded with these women to give to give them some assistance
in the procuring of a dormitory, where they might have comfortable
quarters at a nominal price as well as more time for study and some
social environment, similar to that in the regular university
dormitories.

LOCATION

In may [sic], 1917, Mrs. S. Joe Bowman, retiring president of
the Federation appointed a committee to devise some means of
assisting the Negro young women at the University. In August,
1919, this committee headed by Mrs. Helena Downey, selected the
present building, a twelve room modern two story residence, at 942
Iowa Ave., a wide boulevard which is exceedingly beautiful as well
as famous in the history of Iowa City and the university. This
committee launched a statewide drive to procure $5,500 with which
to purhcase it; and in the year 1919, the Home was taken possession
of and turned over to the young women each of whom contributed what
she could toward the furnishings and upkeep. They lived together
as a large family, presided over by Mrs. Jas. L. Dameron, the
matron selected by the Trustees of the Federation.

IMPROVEMENTS

The situation continued until the Home was fully paid for,
when with the able assistance of Mr. A.A. Alexander, a general
contractor and a graduate of the University, it was remodeled and
beautified. The running expenses as well as the salary of the

matron were taken over by the Federation and each student was required to pay a nominal fee for her room rent and for the one meal which was served by the Matron, the students being allowed to prepare their own breakfast and lunch.

During the summer of 1929, the Home was again renovated and re-decorated within and without. A house secretary was added to the staff of workers, as well as a custodian for the winter months. Having been approved by the Dean of Women of the University, the home is now operated under practically the same regulations as the regular university dormitories, which provide that except where excused for some special reason, all residents of the Home are required to take all their meals at the common table which is provided by the Matron.

EQUIPMENT

For bed rooms the Federation provides rugs, beds, pillows, dressers, study tables and chairs. Students furnish their own bedding, towels, etc.

Two bath rooms, one on each floor, with an "Autohot" water heater furnishing hot
water at all times, a well equipped dining room and kitchen all lighted by electricity, and a laundry room in the basement. All of these with a telephone in the Home add to the comfort and convenience of the young women.

A spacious parlor equipped with a piano and library is also provided, in order that the residents may have means of recreation and the cultivation of sociability.

EXPENSES

The charge for the use of room and other facilities of the Home is $2.50 per week, with an additional charge for meals of $3.50 per week, all of which is payable monthly in advance, to the House Secretary, selected by the Trustees of the Federation.

NEED FOR HOME

That this Home has justified its existence and filled a long felt need during the past ten years is demonstrated by the increase of from seven young women in our State University ten years ago, to twenty-five at the present time; but because of the congested condition only seventeen are housed in the Home at this date (September, 1929), of whom seven are from Iowa, six from Missouri, and one each from Illinois, Alabama, Mississippi and Oklahoma. This Home is not only benefitting the young women of Iowa, but has during this period, been an incentive for young women of our group from the various sections of the country, being the only Home in American maintained by colored women at a State University, with the aid and assistance of popular subscription. It would appear,

also, that the presence of this aggregation of young women at the
Iowa University has had a tendency to increase the attendance of
our young men; for, during this same period there has been an
increase of from about ten to about one hundred Negro men,
according to the record of Atty. S. Joe Brown, who finished there
about thrity years ago, there were then only two young men and no
young women of our race enrolled and prior to that time no Negro
young women had ever been enrolled. The record shows that at this
time the University has a total enrollment of about nine thousand,
of which about four thousand are young women for the accommodation
of which the State maintains only two dormitories, housing about
three hundred eight-four young women, leaving the vast majority to
seek shelter elsewhere. The Colord [sic] Women of the State
Federation, taking cognizance of this situation and realizing the
improbability of our girls being numbered among these less than
four hundred housed in the regular State dormitories, felt that
they could render no more commendable service than the
establishment of this Home.

The College Alumnae Club: An Early History

"History of the College Alumnae Club"
(Proceedings of the Conference of College Women, April 6–7, 1923)

EIGHT

HISTORY OF THE COLLEGE ALUMNAE CLUB

Bertha C. McNeill

On March 11, 1910, ten women graduates of various colleges met in the home of Mrs. Mary Church Terrell at 326 T Street to discuss the wisdom of forming a college women's club. At that time everyone was in favor of the idea, and that evening a permanent organization was effected.

It was decided that the club be called the College Alumnae Club. There were to be six meetings a year. The first president was Mrs. Mary Church Terrell. Other presidents have been Dr. Sara Brown, Dr. G. R. Simpson, Miss L. D. Slowe, Miss Rosa Lane, Miss Charlotte Atwood, and Mrs. L. M. Holmes.

The purpose of the club was threefold:

To promote a closer social union among our women graduates.

To give incentive and opportunity for individual activity and development, intellectually and socially.

To enhance our influence and usefulness in the various movements for the civic good.

Membership was open to any woman holding a Bachelor's degree in Arts, Science, Philosophy, Literature, or Music from any college or university recognized by the College Alumnae Club. Such was the beginning of the College Alumnae Club.

Since that first meeting there have been enrolled over one hundred women, represnting Albany State, Atlanta, Columbia, Cornell, Chicago, Dickinson, Fisk, Howard, the Universities of Michigan, Pennsylvania, and Vermont, Oberlin, Ohio State, Radcliffe, Smith, and Wellesley. Membership is now limited to graduates of those colleges and universities appearing in the lists of accredited schools, prepared by either the Carnegie Foundation or the bulletin of Dr. Thomas Jesse Jones. Articles of Incorporation were filed in 1920.

The club in order to promote closer social union among its members has served refreshments at its regular meetings and held annually a picnic, dinner, or banquet. Meetings were often held at the homes of members until the growing numbers made the homelike atmosphere of the Phyllis Wheatley Club of the Y. W. C. A., acceptable as a regular meeting place.

There has been little done by the Club to develop members intellectually, nor has there been opportunity to measure such growth except through the papers prepared for the programs. The study of the drama during 1920-1921 gave exceptional chance for scholarly theses. One evening also has been given to the original work of the members. The Club has given further evidence of its appreciation of individual achievement by inviting the community to meet Dr. Eva B. Dykes and Dr. Georgiana R. Simpson, the two members who have won the highest academic distinction—the degree of Doctor of Philosophy.

As for the part played by the College Alumnae Club in the various movements for the civic good, a brief glance at the minutes reveals the help given during the War to the Home Relief Corps by members, who served as friendly visitors; the celebration of the one hundredth anniversary of Harriet Beecher Stowe, an open letter to President Wilson asking clemency for the soldiers who took part in the Houston riot; a resolution to Congress in favor of Woman's Suffrage; the joining of the National Woman's Party by a number of the club; a lecture on the care of the feeble-minded by Dr. Alexander Johnson; sums of over one hundred dollars to the Social Settlement and the Young Women's Christian Asociation; other contributions to the Juvenile Protective League and charitable institutions; and many other expressions showing sympathy and interest in both local and national questions. Besides, civic leaders have been invited to the Club as guests and speakers.

Greatest emphasis, however, has been placed on work with girls of the high and normal schools. During the early days of the Club, Reading, Travel, and Ethics Clubs were formed with high-school girls. A reception for the graduates of the high and normal schools and Howard University was given each year for several years. Attempts to reach the mothers of these girls in order to discuss the problems confronting them were made, and round-table talks with the mothers themselves to lead the discussions were inaugurated. Members were asked to serve as friendly advisors in each of the high schools. That they might become more interested in college and know something of college life, graduates of some of the colleges gave inspirational talks on their college experiences to high-school girls, who had been invited for the occasion.

TEN

Members of the club who were not teaching were asked to give talks to high-school groups. A scholarship of fifty dollars has been instituted in both the Armstrong Technical and the Paul Lawrence Dunbar High Schools for the girl who is recommended by the Principal of each school and the Scholarship committee of the Club. The award is almost entirely determined by scholarship. Four girls have already received fifty dollars from the Club. Efforts are now being made to increase the Scholarship Fund.

Now the College Alumnae is in the midst of one of its biggest attempts—the launching of a federation of colored college women—the dream of one of its members.

Having refused to be discouraged by failures of the past, heartened by the achievements of the present, the College Alumnae Club is looking to a future of greater usefulness.

Opportunities for the Educated Black Woman in the 1920s

Eva D. Bowles, "Opportunities for the Educated Colored
Woman"
(*Opportunity,* 1, (March 1, 1923), 8–10)

Opportunities for the Educated Colored Woman

By Eva D. Bowles

Administrator, Colored Work, Cities, Young Women's Christian Association.

More and more the thoughtful woman is realizing that the business of living is a serious matter. In past generations the thought of a proper career for a woman was a home and the rearing of children. Who would vouchsafe to say that the present day woman should not feel this first and foremost? However, woman has found her place outside the home as well, and may we consider the doors that are open to her should she desire to enter. It is perfectly reasonable to assume that the educated Negro woman seeks a career as naturally as any of her sex. She, perhaps, labors under the handicap of her race and thru the past years prescribed limitations have been placed upon her, especially in pursuits other than teaching. During the past few years because of the changing world, barriers have been breaking away, and by degrees she has achieved success in avenues of life where formerly she dared not approach. She has not been wanted, especially, but she was needed.

The profession of teaching was perhaps the first one open to the Negro woman. The last available census reported 22,528 Negro women teachers. The range in standards is vast—from the untrained country school teacher in a four months' Negro school, to the position in cities like New York and Chicago where they are accepted as teachers rather than Negro teachers. There are schools of high standing such as Baltimore, Washington, St. Louis, Kansas City where Negroes are taught separately. They have reached this present standing thru the great interests and increasing efficiency of the Negro teachers. One of these cities has 396 Negro women teachers in their public schools, less than one-fourth are products of the local school system. The greatest number of teaching positions are open in the elementary grades where too often the poorly equipped woman is placed and where experience and character are needed in moulding the youth of the race. The positions in the Kindergarten are becoming more numerous as the school systems grow better. A number of our Negro schools are taking forward steps and providing for the mentally defective. There is a need for teachers to qualify in a specific way to occupy these positions. In one of our large cities there is a flawlessly equipped high school where the following qualifications are required of all teachers: They must be graduates from Northern colleges of first standing and have at least two years' experience in teaching. In order to maintain the standards set, they continue their studies thru summer courses and weekly extension study courses. The ability to qualify for these positions commands an attractive salary. The minimum salary is $1,600. Grade school principalships have in several instances been filled by women and after apprenticeship there is no

reason why Negro women, as well as Negro men, should not hold the position of a High School principal. As registrar of a school, college or university women have been successful. Standing in the highest ranks of educational leadership is the Dean of Women in our universities. We are glad that Howard University and a few other good schools have created this position and we look forward to other universities for the education of Negro youth as an inspiration in the developing of Negro womanhood.

Turning from the well trodden paths of the pedagogue, let us consider opportunities opening in Social Work. In the year 1900, the City of New York produced the first accredited Negro Social Worker, Miss Jessie Sleet, who was employed by the Charity Organization Society as Case Worker until 1909; and in 1906, Negro nurses were employed in the San Juan Hill District, West 63rd Street. During the past few years the Urban League has been foremost in creating opportunities for social workers. "In its forty local organizations at present about 150 Negro Social Workers are employed, about half of whom are women. There are three executive secretaries, about ten special industrial workers, and other case workers, home economic workers, health nurses, girls' club workers, juvenile court workers, etc. Fellowships are provided by the Urban League to Social Workers. This year four are women. This field is not confined to organizations especially interested in Negroes. It is the function of the Urban League to place Negro workers in all social organization, .. g general work, especially in cities with a considerable Negro population." Since leadership is one of the greatest needs of the Negro race the Young Women's Christian Association has given particular attention to the training of Negro women. No different standards apply to the Negro candidates desirous of making the secretaryship of the Young Women's Christian Association their profession than to candidates of the white race.

On January 1st, 1923, there were 107 Negro women holding secretaryships in the Young Women's Christian Association. The qualifications for such a secretary are that they shall be members of Protestant Evangelical churches, women of good education (graduates of accredited colleges or the equivalent) a real faith in the purpose of the Association, ability to work with all kinds of people, energy, self control, good health, sufficient ability to carry and plan thru a piece of work and a willingness to look forward to a period of service in which the returns in the way of reward for good work are not altogether in the terms of salary. Trained Association workers are much in demand, as the local organizations develop and larger numbers of secretaries are needed to carry the program and administrative work. The range of salaries for local workers is $1,300 to $2,000 per year. The inroads towards educational and better conditions that have been made possible by the Slater and Jeanes Funds for Negroes in rural communities bring the challenge to the Negro woman of the best calibre in equipment to meet these tangible, social and economic problems. The field of Social Work has tremendously expanded. In Boston, New York, Pittsburgh, Philadelphia, Chicago and many other large cities, Negro women are successfully filling positions with the Associated Charities, Juvenile and Women's Courts, Day Nurseries, Community Service, Child Welfare organizations, Travelers' Aid Societies, Playground Associations and as school visitors, visiting nurses, parish visitors, etc. Information has just been received concerning a new opening in a middle west city to the effect that this city is planning to open a psychiatric clinic. The qualifications for the Negro worker are that she be a graduate from a school of Social Work with six months of case work experience. While the social consciousness has developed more rapidly in Northern cities, our Southern communities are fertile fields for well equipped and conscientious women social workers. Perhaps, the outstanding Negro woman social worker in the Southland is Mrs. Janie Barrett, who is superintendent of the Industrial Home for Wayward Girls, Peaks, Virginia.

Altho most of the 30,074 Negro women in the professional world are teachers, there is an ever increasing group entering the world of law, medicine, nursing and business. In 1910 we had two women lawyers. There is an increasing number of practising physicians and pharmacists. There are a few Negro women in our Northern medical colleges and several in our medical institutions in southland. There is a possibility of a career in combining the profession of medicine with the technical aspect of social work, child welfare, community health and positive health measures particularly. Too much encouragement cannot be given to the nursing profession. Not only the combination with social service but as

a profession in itself—also a profession that may expand to the extent that women may carry the administrative and executive positions of the largest sanitariums. There are now approximately 50,000 Negro business establishments with an annual volume of business amounting to $1,500,000,000 operated by Negroes and in which women are beginning to share. Of course these establishments are small and are dealing to a large extent with personal service but they are growing. Of the larger business offering a future for employment, the insurance companies possess perhaps the best opportunities. There are about 60 of these writing over about $75,000,000 in insurance a year. Dr. Sadie Mossell was taken over by the North Carolina Mutual as their statistician as soon as they learned of her preparation. The late Madam C. J. Walker and Mrs. Malone of the Poro Institute have demonstrated the fact that Negro women can not only create business, but manage large establishments. A visit to Poro College, St. Louis, can bring to the most skeptical person the knowledge and confirmation that in spite of traditional and present day handicaps the Negro woman can take her rightful place in business. Mrs. Maggie L. Walker of Richmond, Va., holds the distinction of being the first Negro woman president of a bank.

The World War bridged over many years in woman's economic development and along with all women the Negro woman was given a chance and she made good. This fact has given her courage and strength to take no backward steps, but go on thru the doors already open and with the creative power with which she is so richly endowed, press on into other realms. She will have the wisdom to minimize her handicaps, by thorough preparation, with the cultivation of a pleasing personality, with the developing power to think straight, by an appreciation of true values and with the power of adaptability. Thru rich experience and growing patience will come poise, balance and charm of ideal woman leadership.

Working One's Way Through College: A Kentucky Woman's Experience in the 1920s

Alice Allison Dunnigan, excerpt from *A Black Woman's Experience—From Schoolhouse to White House* (Philadelphia: Dorrance & Company, 1974, 74–87, reprinted by permission)

Chapter 8

WHERE THERE'S A WILL

Monday was a busy day in the Allison household, trying to get a few things ready for school. We had learned from the school catalogue that girls wore uniforms. This was to my advantage, as it was to the average poor girl. That is why the policy was adopted in the first place.

The girls' class uniforms for winter were navy blue serge middy suits, similar to the middies worn by sailors. In the fall and spring when the weather was warm, girls wore white cotton middies and the same blue skirts. The Sunday garb was a navy blue suit (called coat-suit) with a white blouse.

Fortunately I had a blue middy suit. Since they were fashionable in those days almost every girl owned one. I took some of my savings and bought two white cotton middies. Aunt Katie (my father's neighboring sister) gave me her beautiful blue suit with a white lace dickey for dress-up wear. My blue taffeta dress with the gold beaded sunburst, made for my high school class night exercise, was my only party dress. That completed my wardrobe with one change of undies and a change of stockings.

I didn't even have a trunk to pack my things in. Again Aunt Katie came to my rescue. She searched her attic and came up with an old trunk with a broken lock. My father tied it on the back of the buggy and hauled it to the blacksmith shop to have the lock repaired, and had it back home in time to pack.

So with all in order, I was ready to leave on the evening train with Mildred, John and Willie. We left home happy and gay. Because this was the first time away from home for any of us, we were beginning to become a little sad, homesick and edgy with each other by the time we were ready to change trains in Louisville around 2:00 A.M.

When we reached the Frankfort campus early Tuesday morning we were still a little homesick and lonely. The students were unfriendly to newcomers but were welcoming their friends from previous years with open arms, kisses and handshakes. That made us feel more alone and friendless. Mildred and I were assigned to the same room. This was to

111

our liking, since we had been friends all through the earlier school years.

We unpacked our clothes, went over to the administration building, registered and signed up for classes. I carried along my own money, whatever was left of my forty dollars, after buying two middies and paying my own trainfare of $7.50. I paid my own registration fee (I don't remember how much it was), and a month's board of fifteen dollars. Then I returned to the reception room in the girls' dormitory and sat alone gazing out of the window, watching the students running down the walk to meet and greet old friends as they arrived on campus.

I was feeling pretty low in spirits when a lady came to ask if I would help serve supper since I didn't seem very busy. I gladly agreed. After supper I was asked to help wash the dishes, which I did without objection.

When the dishes were finished I asked this lady (whom I later learned was the stewardess, named Mrs. Harrison) if I might have a regular job waiting tables and washing dishes. She answered negatively. "We have already assigned girls to these jobs," she stated coldly. "We're using the same girls we used last year. Some of them are just a little late arriving, that is why we are short-handed tonight. We always use the same girls from year to year until they graduate. Then others are selected from a long waiting list. You're new. You'll have to register for the job. Then your name will go on the bottom of the list and you'll have to wait your turn."

Heavy-hearted I left the dining room thinking there's no reward for favors rendered. Early the next morning, around seven o'clock, I heard my name being paged in the hallway. I stuck my head out of the door and was told that Mrs. Harrison wanted to see me in the dining room immediately. I dressed as quickly as possible and hurried down the stairs to be told that she wanted me to help serve breakfast. She then assured me that this job was mine if I still wanted it. "If those other girls were sincerely interested in their jobs they should have reported for duty on time."

This was another of my most happy moments. Once again my prayers had been answered. I recall again the encouraging motto which my mother whispered to me as I left home. "Always remember that 'where there's a will, there's a way.'"

There was no money attached to this job. I only received "half-

75

112

board." That meant $7.50 was deducted from my board each month. No cash was involved, still I was happy. I wrote my parents immediately, proudly informing them of my job and explaining what the benefits would be. "Remember I had already paid my board for a full month," I wrote. "Now this will amount to two months' board. You will not have to send me any money until November, then it will only be seven-fifty plus whatever you can spare for spending change."

My mother sent me ten dollars in November and the same amount each month thereafter. That meant that I only had $2.50 a month for spending change. I was grateful for that, and dared not make her unhappy by asking for more. Out of this allowance I had to skimp, save and plan to be able to take care of bare necessities. This included secondhand books, which I paid for on installments, and other school supplies, such as pencils, pens and notebooks. Out of this sum also came money for a few cosmetics, chiefly soap, and a pair of stockings now and then. Sometimes I was forced to wear stockings with runs as wide as two fingers before I could save enough to purchase a new pair.

There was no money for cleaning my clothes, so my blue serge skirt was worn until it was stiff and smelly with grease and funk. As long as the weather permitted the wearing of white middies, I could get by very well because I could keep them clean by washing, but when I was forced into the one blue serge middy, the situation changed. Since this uniform was unwashable, I was forced to go to class smelling of body odor and dishwater, and was offensive to be near.

This became very embarrassing and when I could bear it no longer I was forced to write my mother explaining the situation, much as I hated to burden her with my needs. She immediately sent me two homemade, navy blue cotton middies. None of the other girls were wearing cotton middies in the winter, but I welcomed them because I could at least keep them clean and odorless. I actually cried when the box arrived—out of humility, gratification and appreciation for my mother's concern and undoubted sacrifice.

Next, the waitresses were requested to wear white aprons on the job. Once again I had to reluctantly write home for them. My mother cut up an old white dress which I left behind, and made aprons, bleached and laundered them nicely and sent them to me. Although they were plain homemade aprons with no fancy, frilly ruffles like some which my co-workers were wearing, I kept them spic-and-span, neatly starched and ironed, and wore them with great pride. However ragged

76

my one change of underwear and stockings had become, I continued to wash them every night in order to keep them clean. (In the winter I would place them on the radiator overnight to make sure that they were dry enough for wearing the next day.)

The duties and responsibilities of the job were very taxing and very wearing. Breakfast was served from seven to seven-thirty; dinner from twelve to twelve-thirty; and supper from five to five-thirty. Waitresses had to be on the job a half hour before each meal, seven days a week, to see that the tables were set up properly and the food ready for service as soon as the students were seated. Each waitress was responsible for two tables seating twelve and fourteen respectively. She also had to wash the dishes for her own tables after each meal. This required some real rushing, especially if she happened to have an eight o'clock or a one o'clock class.

Compulsory chapel exercises (for all except waitresses) were held daily from eleven-thirty to twelve. Many times visitors were invited to speak during these exercises. Although they were always forewarned to make their remarks brief, many would completely disregard time, prolonging the chapel period, delaying the midday meal, and compelling the dishwashers to work overtime. This would cause them to be late, or absent, from their one o'clock class. An arrangement of this kind placed undue hardship upon the waitresses, since most of the instructors showed no sympathy, or understanding, for the working student—she was required to toe the mark timewise and scholastic-wise, just like the students who had plenty of leisure time. No excuses were accepted or even listened to.

Pantry work was not only a rush job but a heavy one. The kitchen was in the basement of the girls' dormitory, and the dining room was on the first floor. Food was sent up on a dumbwaiter to a serving room, called the pantry, adjoining the dining room. Sometimes food servers were so slow sending up the food that the waitresses would find it quicker to run down the steps, get the food, and rush back up the steps in order to get their people fed within the allotted time.

In their rush to get the dishes cleared away after meals, waitresses often found themselves carrying big trays of dirty dishes into the pantry for washing. Sometimes the trays would be loaded with twenty-six glasses, many half-filled with water, making them entirely too heavy for a girl to carry. (Again it is necessary to remind our young readers that there were no automatic dishwashers in those days. Each

77

dish had to be washed, rinsed and dried by hand then stacked on the table ready for the next meal.)

As the year went on, waitresses found themselves faced with an almost insurmountable problem. Dishes were broken from time to time until the supply got so scarce that there were not enough left to go around. The school had no budget to buy another supply. So each waitress was responsible for seeing that her two tables had sufficient dishes to serve her people. If a waitress came into the dining room early and found she was short of a plate or two, or a few glasses, she would swipe some from another table. She would then have to stand by her table to safeguard them until mealtime. If the losing waitress happened to be a little late coming down and found her table short of dishes, someone at that table would be short of a meal since they had no dish from which to eat. In such case the waitress was always to blame. She had to endure the anger and abuse of the students. The dishless student would lambaste the waitress, humiliate her, call her all kinds of names, protest loudly, beat on the table with the silver, causing an embarrassing situation which usually left the poor waitress in tears.

Note that these deprived students took their hostility out on the helpless, harried waitress and not on the administration as they should have, or as they would do today. There were no pickets, no boycotts, no mass protest on the campus, and no confrontation with school authorities who were really responsible for not demanding necessary supplies from the state Department of Education.

Student protest for better food and better service would have been justified in that situation, especially since their meals consisted almost daily of only beans (of different varieties) and bread for dinner, and canned peaches or stewed prunes and white bread and butter for supper.

The harassment which waitresses had to accept from fellow students was almost more than they could bear. So one by one they gave up their jobs. New girls had to be brought in. They had to be trained. This doubled the hardship of the original waitresses. The confusion became so great that Mrs. Harrison found it necessary to resign, leaving no supervision over the girls. Without proper guidance the situation became still worse.

The oldest girl on the job, from the standpoint of service, was

78

elevated to acting supervisor. The other girls resented taking orders from another student, so they gave her no cooperation or respect. They took out their hostility and frustrations on her, making her so miserable that eventually she had to resign.

With all of the changes, the work got more difficult and more strenuous both physically and mentally. By May, the month before school closed, every girl who started work at the beginning of the term, except me, had quit the job. I tried desperately to hold on because I had hoped and prayed so hard for a job, and because I needed it so badly. Finally it got to be too much for me and I became ill. The doctor ordered me to give it up. He forbade me to do any more heavy lifting, and advised against rushing and worrying.

So on the last month of the term I was forced to call upon my parents to pay the full fifteen dollars for board. They complained violently for having to pay this extra money right at the end of the term when they also had to send my trainfare home.

In addition to the work schedule, we also had to abide by the school's very rigid academic and social rules. The regimentation of the girls was as severe as the rules adopted by the military. The day began at 6:00 A.M. with reveille and ended with taps at 10:00 P.M. From breakfast until suppertime our activities were about as normal as those on any average college campus during that era.

After supper we were allowed to socialize on the campus for one hour. At the sound of the six-thirty bell we were herded inside for a half-hour bed preparation. From seven until nine we were confined to our own rooms for a "quiet hour" study period. From nine until ten we were allowed to visit other girls' rooms. Exactly at ten o'clock the bugle would sound: "G-o to b-e-e-d, g-o to b-e-e-d, go-to-bed, go-to-bed, g-o to b-e-e-d." And the lights would go out.

This routine was not altered in any way to suit the working girl. While the other girls were sitting on the campus in the early evening chatting with their dates, the waitresses were still washing dishes. When they finally finished and went to their rooms, the study period was about over and the visiting hour had begun. The dormitory corridors would be ringing with lively conversation, loud laughter, ukulele sounds, singing voices and echoes of dancing feet projected by those jolly girls who had finished their homework and were now visiting friends, playing cards, or engaging in some type of games and

79

fun. While the working girl would just be settling down to begin her study in the midst of all the noise and confusion.

Being tired, sleepy and fatigued, I would become so very annoyed with the loud-mouthed, good-time, carefree, card-playing girls that I developed a violent dislike for cards, a hate which lingers with me until this day. Since that time I have had very little patience with, or respect for, carefree people who seem never to accept responsibilities or to have anything serious or worthwhile on their minds.

At ten o'clock when the lights went out the working girl would be just beginning to study. Kerosene lamps were prohibited in the dormitory due to fire regulations. So I found it necessary to lie flat on the floor and study by candlelight. The candle had to be placed on the floor below the level of the windowsill so that the reflection could not be detected by the night watchman who constantly patrolled the campus. If the candle should be placed on a table or desk its flickering light could be seen by the guard, who would report it to the matron. She, in turn, would investigate, giving demerits to the girl caught using it.

Giving demerits, was the school's method of punishment. A student who broke any of the rules would be given a number of demerits depending on the nature of the crime. When a student received a certain number of demerits, she (or he) would be suspended. Or if a greater amount were received the student might even be expelled. I received about five demerits during the entire school year.

It was customary in schools of this type for students to adopt a "play" family. Practically every student had play sisters, play brothers and even a play mother and a play dad. I was no exception. My play son was Henry Ford, one of the kitchen helpers. It so happened that one day while all of the waitresses were standing around the pantry table waiting for the dumbwaiter to bring up the food for service, Henry came up the basement steps, casually placed his arm around my waist and affectionately greeted me with "Hi, Mom!" At that moment one of the teachers passed through. He chided us for such unbecoming behavior and reported the incident—exaggerated all out of proportion—to the matron.

We were called on the carpet and chastised for such unbecoming conduct. We both explained the harmless incident but were not sure whether our explanation was accepted. I was frantic for fear of being

80

117

expelled. I thought of all the trouble I had gone through just trying to get into school, and all of the worries trying to get an in-school job. I could visualize my mother's disappointment in me. I feared that I had betrayed Dr. Russell's trust. I could just hear the gossiping hometown folks whispering about the "innocent" country virgin who had to be sent home from school about a boy. They would never tell it like it was, but would make it sound like a notorious scandal.

All of my mother's early training came into focus at this point. Her warning about overfriendliness with the opposite sex was recalled. Her concern about what people thought and said regarding character, frightened me almost beyond endurance. I thought I would die with fear and humiliation.

The matron sounded so villainous, making us feel like scum of the earth guilty of some heinous crime. She called all of the pantry girls in and questioned each separately about the incident. They all told the same story.

I was questioned at length on whether Henry was my boyfriend. Disinterested parties were called in to attest to the fact that Henry was only a play son, and that I had been regularly dating another fellow. Several anxious, frightening days passed before the final verdict was rendered. I gave thanks to God that both Henry and I were finally cleared of any suspicious misconduct. So each of us got off with only five demerits. (I don't recall how many demerits rated explusion, but I think around twenty.)

Recreation for working girls was very limited. I had an interest in athletics, and was very good at basketball and volleyball. But I couldn't play on the girls' basketball team because I had no time to practice or travel. So my athletic desire had to be satisfied in the gymnasium during the regular physical education class.

All students, including working girls, could take part in the campuswide social activities. But even then they had to adhere to strict rules. Regardless of how informal an affair was, whether a movie, a lecture, a concert, or a social, a girl could not be escorted by a boy unless she received from him a formal invitation written in the third person on appropriate stationery, and properly answered, also in the third person, by the girl. This was true even if the affair was given in Hume Hall, just across the lawn from the girls' dormitory. The invitation, properly spaced, had to read like this:

81

Mr. So and So
Requests the pleasure of
Miss Alice Allison's company
to the
Halloween Social
at
Hume Hall
Thursday Evening, October thirty-first
Nineteen hundred twenty-four
Eight o'clock

Invitations had to be delivered to the girls' dormitory sometime during the morning of the affair. They were stuck under the individual's door before the noonday meal. Answers written in the same format were required from the invitee, either accepting, or expressing regrets. These replies were expected in the matron's office that afternoon in time for distribution to the young men at supper-time.

Around forty-five minutes before the designated time for an affair to begin, fellows would come to the girls' dormitory and find seats in the reception room to wait for their dates.

As the girl came downstairs she would be greeted at the foot of the steps by her escort, and the two would be reseated in the huge reception room. At a given time a gong would sound and the couples would line up and stroll across the campus to their designation. Two faculty members would lead the line, two would bring up the rear, and several others would walk along on either side of the line at a certain distance apart. The same procedure was followed on the return to the dormitory. Two faculty members would stand on either side of the dormitory door to see that there were no goodnight kisses. The boy would depart with only a friendly handshake from his girl—but never a kiss.[1]

Students of my day enjoyed most of all the small private parties sponsored by some organization, such as a social club, sorority or fraternity. But I never had an opportunity to attend any of these affairs. These privileged guests were admitted by invitation only.

1. This is a far cry from dormitory rules a few decades later when college students today are not only demanding that male and female students share the same building, but are asking for practically unlimited inter-room visitation rights.

82

Since the poor working student had neither money nor time   devote to social clubs or Greek-letter organizations, they missed out on most of the fun. Furthermore, working students were usually snubbed by the so-called high society. They were seldom, if ever, dated by the campus hierarchy so they had no chance of receiving invitations to the more swank affairs.

Working people were considered the *hoi polloi* of the campus, therefore, they found it expedient to seek companionship among those in their own social stratum. The girls who worked in the dining room were slurringly referred to as "pantry rats." My boyfriend, who worked in the kitchen, was commonly known as a "kitchen kat." He was a nice-looking young man, quiet, refined, kind-hearted and very attentive to me. But like the rest of us who had to rush around, working in a hot kitchen, sweating, and lacking sufficient time to properly bathe, or failing to have adequate clothes for frequent changes, he, too, went around sometimes smelling like a greaseball with halitosis feet. Because of this he was often slurred by fellow students.

One of the most popular groups on the campus was the athletic club. It would throw big parties for football or basketball teams on their return from an out-of-town game. And they would really beef it up if our team won. Likewise they would give big after-game parties for every visiting team. These parties were usually held in the reception room of the girls' dormitory. Girls who had no fellows on the team felt terribly discriminated against as they sat in their rooms, often trying to study, only to be disturbed by the swinging music and gay hilarity below.

Although the music sounded good, it might be mentioned that dancing was prohibited on campus during that particular year (1923-'24) when Dr. F. M. Wood, a Baptist minister, was serving as president. Young people had to content themselves with "grand marching" as a means of entertainment at social functions. This policy was abolished the following year and dancing was resumed after Dr. G. P. Russell returned to his former position as president of the college.[2]

2. Dr. G. P. Russell served as president of KNII from 1912 until his ouster in 1923 due to a change in political administration. As result of public pressure, he was returned to his former post in 1924 after only one year of absence, serving in that capacity until his resignation in 1929.

83

One night when the athletes' party was in full swing, even after the ten o'clock curfew, the lights upstairs were out and the girls, who were supposed to be tucked snugly in bed, got a bright idea. A group decided to sneak down the back stairs and take a peek at the socialites. Dressed in our outing-flannel granny-gowns (as all girls wore in those days before fancy, frilly nightgowns and lacy, silk pajamas came into vogue) and old stocking legs (called susies) on our heads instead of the big, colorful rollers, or fluffy slumber bonnets that are worn today, we lined up on the stairway. Each of us took turns standing on the bannister and peeking through the transom over the side door, which was never used and presumedly always locked. All of a sudden, someone at the top of the stairs gave a push and the girls came tumbling down the steps, falling against the door with such impact that it swung open and the nightgowned girls piled up in the middle of the party parlor floor.

All of the commotion brought the matron and her student assistant scampering down the front steps with flashlights, while the girls hustled up the back stairs making it to their own rooms or somebody else's room and into bed and under cover with eyes closed pretending to be asleep when the matron inspected each room.

This broke up the party time in the girls' dormitory. Perhaps the athletic parties were held thereafter in the gym, or some other building on the campus.

All of this campus life was great fun for me. It was an exciting, interesting, wonderful experience. There were continuous activities, never a dull moment. The year was chugged full of all kinds of adventures, many pleasant and some heartrending. The latter was due chiefly to the poverty which I was forced to endure, going week after week without a single penny and many times hungry.

Some of the girls sneaked tiny kerosene stoves into the dormitory for the purpose of heating straightening combs and curling irons. There were no electric curlers or combs in those times as far as we knew. My roommate had such a stove, so we bought a little frying pan. I could sometimes slip a potato or two from the pantry and we would have French fries in our room.

Sometimes I could persuade the school butcher to slice for me a small steak from a hunk of beef. Our beef was raised and butchered on the school farm. Whole cows were hung in the cold storage room in the basement of the girls' dormitory in the area of the kitchen, and

84

roasts and steaks were cut from the carcass as needed.

Sometimes I could sneak out a loaf of bread, taking it upstairs in my bosom. My friends and I were usually so hungry that we could consume the whole loaf of dry bread at one sitting. I had to make out with what I had because many times I didn't have three cents (the price of a postage stamp) to write a letter home to ask for additional spending change, even if I had a mind to.

Schoolgirls without sufficient clothes to keep clean and neat, were faced with all sorts of humiliations, and got little attention or respect either from the teachers or the more fortunate students. If they were burdened with too heavy a workload they often found themselves tired and listless, sleepy and dull, thus, they became objects of ridicule. In spite of all of this I tried hard to stick it out to the end.

When I became ill and was ordered by the doctor to give up my pantry job, I was very upset. I had one month to go before the end of the term. I didn't want to lose what I had gained. I was afraid to write home to my parents right away for fear that they might tell me to come home.

When I did inform them near the end of the term they did send me money to square off my bills. But I knew I would not be able to return to school the following year. I would not be physically able to fill the same job, and there were no others available. I knew that without work I would not be able to enroll at all. Considering these facts I began to think how I could best profit from the year's work which I had completed. Then I came up with an idea which I discussed with the dean.

In order to understand my proposal, one would have to know the structure of the institution. Normal schools were composed of a regular four-year high school with two years of normal (or teachers' training) equivalent to freshman and sophomore college classes.

Graduates from eight-grade elementary schools, with sufficient financial backing, could enroll at KNII for the entire six-year course, which would give them a full high school education and two years of college. Upon graduation they would receive a certificate entitling them to teach for three consecutive years, after which their certificate would automatically be renewed for life.

Eighth graders who were unable to stay through the full course, could enroll in a special elementary teachers' training course, which would award them a two-year teacher's certificate for work in

85

elementary schools following two years of study.

Two-year high school graduates, like myself, who were unable to take the entire normal course, could enroll in an intermediate teachers' training course. After two years of study they would be qualified for a four-year teacher's certificate.

Regular spring sessions were conducted in these institutions for teachers who wished to continue their studies after the close of their schools. Since rural school terms were only seven months in Kentucky, teachers could return to KNII in early April for a three-month spring term plus an additional six-week summer session. This would amount to one semester's work. Teachers could continue their studies, springs and summers, until they completed the entire normal course.

I enrolled in the intermediate teachers' training course. Had I remained in this course for two years I would have qualified to teach in junior high schools for a period of four years. When I discovered that I would be unable to return for my second year's study, I asked the dean if it would be possible to be awarded a two-year elementary teacher's certificate since I had already done a year's work beyond the requirement for this type certificate. I realized that this would down-grade my qualifications but I was willing to make this sacrifice rather than lose what I had already accomplished. The dean took my request under consideration and discussed it with a faculty committee.

Later he called me in for further information. They had checked my work record and found that I was dependable, conscientious and sincere. They had looked into my discipline record and found that I had received only five demerits, which were reportedly imposed unjustly. I had a good class attendance record. But they had no exact knowledge of my academic attainment. Since the final grade for the year had not been released, the dean wrote a request for my record and had me hand-carry it to each of my instructors and return the replies to him.

I was a bit apprehensive because I did not know how well I had done scholastically. But I made the rounds and returned the sealed envelopes to the dean. He opened them in my presence and to my surprise my lowest grade was about eighty-six and my highest around ninety-three.

Impressed with my grades, the dean smiled and assured me that anyone who could earn grades like this in spite of all the obstacles I had to face, certainly deserved some reward. Before school closed for

86

the year I had in my hand a certificate authorizing me to teach in any elementary school in the state for a period of two years. This was another of those never-to-be-forgotten moments in my life. So I marked June 1924 as another progressive milestone in my life's career.

When I returned home and proudly presented to my parents a certificate qualifying me to teach school, they were most happy. They circulated the good news to all of their acquaintances. The pastor of our church added to their joy by publicly announcing from the pulpit that I was the first student ever to leave our city and return after only one year's study as a licensed schoolteacher. Dr. Russell practically jumped with joy as he proudly faced my parents with that old cliche, "I told you so!"

The following summer was devoted entirely to job seeking. My first chapter describes the torture I went through trying to find employment, and the final results. Again my mother's favorite phrase echoed in my mind: "Where there's a will, there's a way!"

87

A Black Woman at the University of Cincinnati, 1918

Lena Beatrice Morton, excerpt from *My First Sixty Years:
Passion for Wisdom*
(New York: Philosophical Library, 1965, 30–36, reprinted by permission)

I had long dreamed of college; therefore, clutching my high school diploma in one hand, I launched out into the world of dreams and visualized ascending the stately steps of the University of Cincinnati. I was jubilant beyond bounds, and I talked of nothing but going to College. In this state of ecstasy, I chanced upon my friend, Pearl. You may be assured I flooded her with my rapturous anticipation of college life. When I had run the gamut of my word power, Pearl gasped, "Bea, do you mean you are going to the University of Cincinnati?"

"Yes," I responded, "aren't you?"

"Why, I wouldn't dare try to dress like those girls at the University," she replied. "What are you going to wear out there?"

In truth, I was so transported with thoughts of being a college girl, that the problem of dress had escaped my thinking. In answer to her query, I explained, "I'll wear the same things I wore in high school."

Pearl insisted that the white girls really dressed at the University; nevertheless, I stoutly defended my dominant interest. I was going to the University of Cincinnati in quest of learning regardless of the dress of the black girls or the white girls.

I had planned to be the first one to register on the morning of registration. Accordingly, I was up early and arrived on the campus approximately an hour before registration was scheduled to begin. To my surprise, I discovered nigh fifty freshmen waiting in line. The sight of these predecessors was a startling reminder that other freshmen were aflame with the desire for knowledge. Be that as it may, my white heat to register at the University of Cincinnati continued to glow. I registered for seventeen hours of

30

127

work, the maximum load for freshmen. After enrollment, I read
and reread my academic challenge:

Freshman English	3 hrs
Appreciation of Poetry	2 hrs
French	3 hrs
Economics	3 hrs
Geology	5 hrs
Health	1 hr
Phys. Ed.	
Total credit hours	17 hrs

I was aware of the academic challenges that necessarily
accompany college life. On the other hand, here at the University
of Cincinnati I was summoned to act on problematic situations
in unexpected areas. Although there were rumors of prejudice at
Woodward High School, in my opinion, Woodward was 99.44%
free of racial discrimination. I had expected the same proportion
of fairness at the University.

Unfortunately, in the initial days of U. C.'s academic year,
1918-1919, the seating of students in the classrooms in alphabetical order made the problem of racial discrimination eminent. A
goodly number of the professors followed the alphabetical arrangement in seating the white students but relegated the Negro
students to the last row regardless of literal sequence.

Some of the Negro students made heated and antagonistic
protests. For the first few days I was not personally affected by
the discriminatory policy. Then, I reported to my class in the
Appreciation of Poetry. The professor requested the students to
stand around the walls until he could seat them in alphabetical
order. I listened for my name until I heard Miss Newman's name
called, and observed she was already seated. Miss Newman had
sat directly behind me at Woodward High School because my
name began with M, and her name began with N. I knew an
error had been made, and my naivete caused me to deem it a
purely human error without premeditation. Therefore, with in-
nocence and sincerity, I called out "————, you skipped me."

The professor's face flushed with blood, but he continued to
seat the students without recognizing my address to him. In spite
of his flushed face, my freshman soul still said, "The professor
did not hear you." Heeding this voice, I waved my hand with
vigor, increased the volume and urbanity of my voice, and repeated my statement of fact. The situation was becoming embarrassing, for now all eyes glared at the professor. He turned to
me and asked, "Now, what is your name?"

31

I replied, "I am Miss Morton. You have already seated Miss Newman and M comes before N."

With this information exposed to the class, the professor requested Miss Newman to move down one seat, and grant me alphabetical priority. When the seating of students was completed, I glanced around to survey the large class, and discovered the other five Negroes in the class were compactly seated together on the last row in the room; notwithstanding the initial letters of their surnames ranged intermittently across the alphabet. A strange, uneasy feeling came over me. I had been naive to deem the professor's omission of my name an unplanned human error. I began to suspicion an element of truth in the rumor concerning the prejudice of some professors.

If there were any doubt of deliberate discrimination in the above class, the incertitude was completely removed in my next Freshman English course. I was the only Negro member of the section. Without including me in the M's, the professor seated the white students alphabetically until she came to the last row. Here she placed me in the seat against the wall; then she left one seat vacant, and seated the remaining whites whose names were at the end of the alphabet.

As I write this episode forty-six years later, I am able to record the incident with composure and good will. In 1918, as I sat there in the last row against the wall with an empty seat between my classmates and me, my freshman soul was unutterably hurt. I stared at the cultured professor and pondered man's inhumanity to man. Later, I reflected upon a proper reaction, for I had always tried hard to do what is right. In this important decision, I did not wish to stray from my self imposed rule of noble action.

In the afternoon, I related the occurrence to my mother. I told her I did not approve of an undignified scene; rather, I preferred to prove from that isolated seat against the wall that I was as intelligent, well bred, and affable as any member of the class. Although I had been warned that this particular professor was prejudiced, it was my opinion that her experience with Negroes was limited. I counted it a privilege to have the opportunity to round out and set aright this professor's concept of the Negro student. I wanted her to know the truth about the Negro; then she would be free of prejudice. I did my best in every lesson.

One day, after I had made an oral report on Edgar Allan Poe's "Ligeia," the professor requested me to remain after class. I shall never forget the beautiful words she spoke to me on the excel-

32

lence of my report. The next semester, I was assigned to the same professor's section of English. Again she seated the class in alphabetical order. This time I was placed with the M's, exactly where I belonged; furthermore, there were no empty seats between the white students and me. It had taken a whole semester, but I had won my case and a friend for the Negro. Never again did I hear a rumor that this professor discriminated against Negroes; rather, Negro students who came after me acclaimed her virtues, and expressed a genuine admiration for her professorship.

Before I graduated from the University of Cincinnati, I had one more formidable battle to fight on the line of racial discrimination. Every student was required to take swimming before he received his degree. I had not taken it during my freshman year, because I resented the University's forcing its Negro female students to take swimming only on Friday afternoons after the white females had had their swimming lessons for the week. When the Negro swimmers were out, the water was changed and the pool was made fresh and ready for the Caucasian swimmers on Monday morning. This principle of clear-cut discrimination was contemptible to me, and I could not reconcile my acceptance of it. I had hoped the University would adopt a more liberal policy before my senior year. Therefore, each year I deferred registering for swimming. At the end of my junior year, I received an official notice from the University warning me that I had not fulfilled my swimming requirement, and that I could not graduate without credit in swimming.

My dilemma was unbearable. Should I refuse to attend the segregated swimming classes and forfeit my degree, or should I endure the humiliating Friday afternoon classes and attain my degree? I put both issues on the scales of my life's goal and weighed them with meticulous care. I wanted to help humanity —particularly the element known as the Negro race. I realized that the more knowledge I acquired, the more potent could be my service to my fellowman. If I relinquished my degree to fight for the Negro's right to take swimming in the regular swimming classes, I would limit my educational status, and scarcely augment the black man's collegiate opportunities. One withdrawal would mean little or nothing to the University's practice in the use of the swimming pool. My parents had moved from Kentucky to Ohio that I might achieve a college degree. I felt the evidence was on the side of attaining my academic degree, and with a

33

wounded heart I enrolled in the swimming class which met every Friday afternoon, and completed my requirements for the degree of Bachelor of Arts in three and one half years. I have never regretted my undergraduate decision, because I believe Time has proven I chose the better part. The degree opened doors which otherwise would have been closed to me. Once within those doors, I was free to perform as a self-appointed ambassador of good will and better human relationships.

I was not the only unhappy member of the Friday afternoon swimming class. All of us were dissatisfied with the discriminatory arrangement. My friend, Ida May Rhodes, probably expressed our thinking when she explained that we were getting our knowledge and skills the hard way, hoping that our efforts would facilitate the educative process of younger Negro students who would come after us. To this end, we diligently toiled, and sacrificed many a social pleasure.

In some areas we pioneered. Occasionally when we requested registration in certain courses, the professor would warn, "Your people don't do well in this course." We knew the sweeping generalization was erroneous; therefore, we immediately enrolled in the prohibitive courses and passed them with respectable grades.

Once when I was taking logic, the Alpha Phi Alpha Fraternity asked to have a party at my home on Barr Street. The party was scheduled on the night preceding my logic test. I expressed my regrets to the Fraternity, but explained it would be necessary for me to use the time preparing for my test. Their insistence was so intense that I gave them permission to have the jollity, but made it clear that I would not come in. Mother would be the gracious hostess, but perforce I would go into seclusion and study for my logic. The gala affair continued until midnight. Mother tendered the merrymakers every possible courtesy, but in compliance with my promise, I remained in my room impervious to the music and the frolic. Not once did I peep through the keyhole. The next day I made my A, proving "my people could do well in logic."

Other Negro students proved their caliber in different areas. My friend, Ida May, successfully majored in Greek, some mastered the physical sciences, others the romance languages, etc.

The preceding paragraphs calling attention to racial discrimination at the University of Cincinnati are not included to create a negative attitude toward my Alma Mater, for to me U. C. will

34

131

always be "the magic name I proudly to the world proclaim," and I shall always be a loyal child of old U. C. In later years, I was pleased and honored to become a member of its staff in the capacity of cooperating teacher of the University of Cincinnati; and I rejoiced when one of my former student teachers, Mrs. Roberta Wooten became a member of the faculty of the University of Cincinnati.

In the first quarter of the twentieth century, America was still predominantly fettered in racial discrimination. The University of Cincinnati was a victim of the social environment, and of its fundamental tradition echoed in the words of its founder, Charles McMicken. The cherished desire of this philanthropist was "to found an institution where white boys and girls might be taught." To this end Mr. McMicken gave the city of Cincinnati, by will, most of his estate valued at one million dollars.

It is gratifying to discover the growth the University of Cincinnati has achieved in interracial understanding since the first quarter of the present century.

In truth, Ida May's hope for "the Negro students who come after us" has become a reality—even the Friday afternoon swimming class for Negro females has been buried in the pages of history. The battles of racial discrimination that accosted me in my undergraduate days were grievous and should not have happened; but notwithstanding those ills, I owe a profound gratitude to the University of Cincinnati. It gave me knowledge and skills fundamental to a life of service; it taught me the Negro, or any other ethnic group, is respected and honored if he possesses and evinces brains and character; and it exposed me to great intellectuals whose lives were towers of inspiration. I shall always remember the moral elevation I received from my major advisor in the College of Liberal Arts, Dr. Guy Allan Tawney, Head of the Department of Philosophy. Dr. Tawney used to tell us that a lie destroys the use of language. Dr. Hartman, Associate Professor of Philosophy, was equally as memorable with his assertion: "When the commoner becomes heated, the aristocrat grows cooler and cooler." In the College of Education, there were the two noble gentlemen: Dean Louis A. Pechstein, and Dr. William H. Burton. These giant pedagogues have continued to befriend me down through the years. Dean Pechstein wrote the Introduction to my book, *Farewell to the Public Schools—I'm Glad We Met*, and Dr. Burton wrote a criticism of the same publication. I could continue the list of U. C. faculty members who made significant

35

contributions to my mental, emotional, and spiritual life; but the many names would be tedious reading for those who have not been touched with the magic of their lives. I cannot close the list without affixing the names of Dr. Paul V. Kreider and Miss Helen A. Stanley. To these and others, I say, "Thank you for what you have done for me."

Finally, in answer to the question, "What has the University of Cincinnati been to me?" I choose a line from its Varsity Song:

A fountain of eternal youth,
A tower of strength, a rock of truth.

Dear Alma Mater, I salute you, and I honor you.

36

The University of California at Berkeley in the 1920s

Ida L. Jackson, excerpt from *There Was Light: Autobiography of a University: Berkeley, 1868–1968*
(Garden City, N.Y.: Doubleday, Irving Stone, ed., 249–256, reprinted by permission)

"At the time, 1920, there were eight Negro women and nine Negro men enrolled on the Berkeley campus. Few of us knew each other before arriving there. Our isolation drew us together. The need for social life caused us to combine and organize the Braithwaite Club. All did not participate, as some did not wish to be identified as Negroes on campus . . . The YMCA under the leadership of Harry Kingman and Ralph Scott welcomed the Negro men earlier than any other group. Stiles Hall was always open to them; their participation in sports gave the men at least a speaking acquaintance with some of their non-Negro fellow students."

IDA L. JACKSON

✳

FEW NEGROES, before and during my generation, can trace their ancestry to or beyond their grandparents. It is distressing to most of us to hear the stories of our grandparents concerning the slave era, as well as those stories of our parents' endurance in the South, whether they were born before or after freedom was declared. We Negroes seemed to feel, I suppose, in the days of our youth, that we could obliterate the existence of the sufferings and privations of the past if we did not hear them.

My parents, who had but little formal education, believed religiously that education was the most desirable possession. "Until the Negro gets an education, he can't compete with the white men" and "Get an education, for knowledge is the one thing the white man can't take from you" are expressions which my father constantly drilled into my brothers and me. Five of my brothers had little more than the minimum essentials of an education because of lack of opportunity. Many of my early teachers, both

Negro and white, preached the same doctrine: "Get the type of education the white man gets, behave as the more refined white man behaves and the Negro will be accepted as an American citizen; then the opportunities for advancement will appear for the Negro, according to his skills, education and talents." In my experience and that of many other Negroes, this has proved to be a mirage—to date.

I know little about my grandparents. My father's parents were born in Nigeria, West Coast Africa; he and several of his brothers and sisters were born in Anniston, Alabama. My maternal grandmother was born on the Eastern Shore of Maryland, and my maternal grandfather, a dentist, was born in Marseilles, France. I once visited my mother's birthplace on Canal Street in New Orleans with her and her only sister years later. We were, like most Negroes of our day, of many racial strains: African, American Indian, French and Irish.

My father was born in 1855, and later settled in Monroe, Louisiana, which was then little more than a wilderness. In the latter part of the 1880s he fled from Monroe to save his life, crossing the river on a barge with what few possessions he and my mother could throw hastily into a wagon, and three boys, all under four years of age. They landed on the banks of the Mississippi at Vicksburg, where they started life again from scratch.

My father had escaped from the posse which had set out to lynch him because he had won a case in the courts against a white man involving land owned by my father. This land had been leased to the white, but when the lease expired, he produced a document which stated that my father had sold him the property. The fact that the neighbor farmer's wife, who was white, rushed through the cornfields and warned my parents saved my father's life.

This incident, told to us when we were young, along with many other evidences of friendship of whites at various times in my life, has kept me from hatred of all whites. It is the fairness of the few which plays such a great part in restraining the bitterness and hatred which many Negroes have had to fight.

Father built a one-room house on the outskirts of Vicksburg

shortly after their arrival. He later built another house, in which the other six of us were born. The house grew along with the family and at the time of my birth there were three bedrooms, a parlor, a dining room and kitchen. We had not then worked up to indoor plumbing.

The line dividing the city from the county was just across the street to the north of our property. Our side was in the county and we had to attend the county schools. Many people have heard of the rural schools in Mississippi, that is, what they are like today. At that time, in the early 1900s, the schools were much worse. The county school which my brothers were supposed to attend was miles away from our home and located in a small Baptist church, which was equipped with crude wooden benches, a wood-burning stove, a poorly prepared and poorly paid teacher and no books.

We, like most Negroes in Mississippi, were a poor family, but not the poorest, for our condition then was far better than the mass of Negroes and many poor whites. There were always some extra people at our house who were destitute, needing help. None was turned away. Each year the younger ones of us looked forward to the people who came to live in the little house, and pitched tents in our yard in which they lived during the period when the Mississippi River overflowed its banks.

We had no toys or games with which to amuse ourselves. I had dolls of course, but my brothers created their own games. Card playing was forbidden as a sin. Guessing games of many kinds were favorites as we sat around the table in the evenings. These games had much to do with my being as well informed as I was, for I had to do something to be able to participate. Also, a part of my early learning experience was due to the practice of each brother taking his turn caring for me, and I usually chose some one of his books to satisfy my curiosity. We had very few books: our textbooks, Ridpath's *History*, a volume of Longfellow's poems, a few others whose titles I do not now recall and several Bibles. When there was any argument loud enough to waken my father where he sat nodding in a chair, he would say, "Get your books."

Everybody would scatter and, for a while at least, appear to be studying.

My father was a carpenter, farmer and preacher. My mother discouraged his taking over as preacher, as she said there were too many to be fed already. As a result he preached for the people on the plantation where he had a farm. The church where we were members was located in the far north end of the town. My brothers hated to go to Sunday School, because there they met boys who attended the city public schools and there were fights over being called "country hicks," which caused more trouble at home.

There were two schools for Negroes. One had classes from first through tenth grades, the other, about seven miles from home, had grades eleven and twelve. Our generation was most fortunate, for there were four teachers in the high school who had college training. They gave us their best and an incentive to try. They taught us subjects not in the curriculum of the Negro schools. We read *As You Like It* in the eleventh grade and performed *Othello* as our class play in the twelfth grade. I graduated in May 1914, one of the youngest in my class. I was twelve years old the following October.

Eventually I enrolled in Rust College, one of the several schools supported by the Methodist Episcopal Church and the Stewart Missionary Foundation. There were eleven of these schools in the South and one in the West, the University of Southern California in Los Angeles, a non-segregated school. The two years I spent at Rust stimulated a desire to find something better. I owe much to one of the white women on the staff. She was there as matron, but was transferring to Peck School of Domestic Science and Art as superintendent the next term. My mother permitted me to transfer to New Orleans University, of which Peck was a part, that year at the matron's suggestion. I took examinations and was admitted to the senior class in the Normal School, for by this time everyone thought I should choose teaching as my profession. I graduated at the end of the year, with a diploma from the Normal School and a certificate in domestic science. I was also presented with an

award that I had won n an essay contest conducted by the Stewart
Missionary Foundation thoughout their system of schools. I was
quite pleased when my English teacher, Mr. Morrison, informed
me that I had won the Grand Prize over an entrant from USC.
I was asked to return the next year and assist in the supervision
of the girls in Peck Home, and teach two classes of beginners in
sewing. In exchange for these services I was able to take some
courses in the college department.

During January of this year Mama told me to prepare to move
with her to California. We arrived in Oakland in February 1918.
My brothers had preceded us and had urged her to leave the
South, saying that here in California I could get a better education
free than she could pay for in any of the southern schools, and that
there was no prejudice against Negroes here in California!

After being in Oakland three weeks I sought directions to the
county superintendent's office and applied there for a teaching position. I believe every employee in the office filed past and looked
me over before Mr. David Martin, the superintendent, came from
his office and interviewed me. He was a kind man and seemed
deeply interested in me. He gave me an application form to fill
out and return, but told me that while I no doubt met the requirements for an elementary teaching position, I needed to know California history; there were times, he said, when they hired teachers
and had them take the course while they were teaching. Meantime,
since I was young, why not attend the University of California
and get my degree?

A few weeks later I visited the University of California campus
to see if I could register; my transcript from New Orleans University had been sent. The semester had begun a few weeks earlier,
and the registrar advised against my attempting to enter so late.
Finally I saw the dean of the College of Letters and Science and
was told that if I could enroll in ten units of work, I would be permitted to register.

One of the most difficult problems I faced was entering classes
day after day, sitting beside students who acted as if my seat
were unoccupied, showing no sign of recognition, never giving a

smile or a nod. This I thought of as the "cold spot" on the Cal campus. In contrast, one day I had the privilege and great honor of being spoken to by and chatting with President Benjamin Ide Wheeler. I left inspired and figuratively walking on air.

At the time, 1920, there were eight Negro women and nine Negro men enrolled on the Berkeley campus. Few of us knew each other before arriving there. Our isolation drew us together. The need for social life caused us to combine and organize the Braithwaite Club. All did not participate, as some did not wish to be identified as Negroes on campus, or for other reasons did not join. The YMCA under the leadership of Harry Kingman and Ralph Scott welcomed the Negro men earlier than any other group. Stiles Hall was always open to them; their participation in sports gave the men at least a speaking acquaintance with some of their non-Negro fellow students.

It was during my second semester that the women's gymnasium was burned down. Another Negro student and I had signed up for swimming. The pool at the YMCA on Alice Street in Oakland was made available to the University women students who were enrolled in swimming, but when we two Negro students arrived, we were told that there was some mistake, that we could not use the pool. The San Francisco YMCA did invite us to use their facilities but we could not travel such a distance and still make our classes, to say nothing of the cost of transportation.

Five of the eight women organized the Alpha Phi Club, preparatory to forming a sorority. High moral standards and better than a C plus average, among other things, were required to form a chapter of Alpha Kappa Alpha sorority, the one to which we applied for membership. Few of us qualified scholastically. The approval of the dean of women was necessary. We were put on probation for a semester, with the understanding that if grade points and all else met required standards, she would give her approval. We made the necessary grades, a bit higher than required, and organized the Rho chapter of Alpha Kappa Alpha sorority in 1921. My home on Fifty-eighth Street became our sorority house and AKA was given representation on the Women's

Council. I was elected president of the chapter and became its representative on the council. At last we began to learn something of the functioning of student government on campus, and we began to feel we were a part of things.

Organizing the sorority enabled me, as spokesman for the group, to meet the dean of women, Lucy Stebbins, and her assistant, Mary Davidson. The contact with these two charming women developed into a friendship that proved very valuable to me later and was a source of great joy and inspiration.

As time went on, Rho chapter decided to take a page in the *Blue and Gold*, at forty-five dollars per page. We paid the required fee, went on the date assigned to us to the photographer and posed as directed for our picture. The eagerly awaited date when the *B&G* was off the press arrived; we could hardly wait to see a copy. *But our picture was not included!* Our disappointment knew no bounds. We were never able to see the editor or anyone else in charge. We went to the dean of women's office. She tried to explain in words that would comfort us, but she was unable to offer any acceptable answer. This was a bruise that did not quickly heal.

In 1922 I received my A.B. degree. I had in these two years become acquainted with several of the professors in the School of Education. I participated in a few of the Senior Week activities, and although I walked alone, unnoticed by my fellow classmates, took part in the Senior Pilgrimage. There was another Negro woman graduating, a friend, but she felt we would be snubbed and decided not to participate.

Encouraged by one of my professors, my mother and brother, I decided to try for a master's degree. I had been interested in the reports of the Alpha Army Tests and the then widely accepted notion that the Negro's highest mental age was fifteen. Rare cases indicated that there was development beyond that. Intelligence tests were the criteria and the Alpha Army Test results became the criteria for judging the educability of the Negro.

Dr. J. V. Breitweiser was chairman of my committee for the master's thesis. He offered me great encouragement and help. The subject of my thesis, "The Development of Negro Children in Relation to Education," was chosen primarily because I felt that factors other than mentality (as inherited) affected the IQ of an individual. Sociological and environmental conditions have in recent years been accepted as conditioning factors. Whatever my thesis attempted to prove, the two psychologists who were appointed to the committee failed to approve of my findings and conclusions and refused to give their approval. As a result it was placed in the hands of the Graduate Council, and they approved it. A group of Negro people with whom I had worked, quite unknown to me, asked the University if they could purchase my cap, gown and hood for me, as a gesture of their appreciation.

A Black Woman's Experience at Wellesley

Jane Bolin Offutt, "Wellesley in My Life," in *Wellesley After-Images: Reflections on Their College Years by Forty-Five Alumnae with an Introduction by Barbara Warne Newell* (Wellesley College Club of Los Angeles, 1974)

Wellesley in My Life

SIXTEEN YEARS OLD, sensitive and idealistic, first time away from the family, one of two Black freshmen who were the first Black students for some years—this was I in 1924.

The two of us, though strangers, were assigned the same room in a family's apartment in the village—the only students there. We ate in the college dining room shared by other freshmen. Students were assigned to tables at dinner but at all other meals sat anywhere, provided a table was filled before another table could be started. If my roommate or I were sitting at an unfilled table, the Southern students would come in the dining room, see this and ostentatiously walk out and stand outside the door peeking in until our table was filled. No one in authority, though observing this, interceded in any way.

Also during my freshman year, my roommate told me she had been asked by her French teacher to play the role of an Aunt Jemima type figure (bandanna too!) in a charity fundraising skit outside the Chapel one morning. Though the teacher was not mine, I went to her and remonstrated vociferously. The request to my roommate was withdrawn. Yet I was still deeply hurt by the insensitive protestations and wondrous lack of understanding by a teacher of young people.

In my junior year, though an honor student, I was rejected for membership in one of the houses or sororities supposedly interested in social problems (its name long forgotten) by an unsigned notice surreptitiously slipped under my door during the night.

Once, and only once, I made a reservation to spend the weekend at the Wellesley Club in Boston. I recall my pain as I was

[91]

shown to an attic room, which was the only room on the top floor. No contamination there!

The sharpest and ugliest memory of my Wellesley days occurred in my senior year during a conference, mandatory for seniors, with a guidance counsellor. She exhibited obvious physical shock when told of my plan to study law. She threw up her hands in disbelief and told me there was little opportunity for women in law and absolutely none for a "colored" one. Surely I should consider teaching. In tears, I rushed to telephone my father, a prominent lawyer in New York State. I told him of this insult. He replied that lawyers have to hear such "dirty" things, that he was not happy about my decision but, that as long as he was paying for my education it was solely our business what education he provided for me. So I applied to Yale Law School and was accepted.

When I was appointed a judge at thirty-one by Mayor Fiorello LaGuardia of New York City, it was given wide publicity, since I was the first Black woman judge in the United States. Letters and telegrams came by the hundreds from people, mostly strangers, from all over the world. Included were my law school, high school and even grade school teachers, but not a single note from teacher, president, dean, house mother or anyone (except a few classmates) who was at Wellesley during my four years.

There were a few sincere friendships developed in that beautiful, idyllic setting of the college but, on the whole, I was ignored outside the classroom. I am saddened and maddened even nearly half a century later to recall many of my Wellesley experiences but my college days for the most part evoke sad and lonely personal memories. These experiences perhaps were partly responsible for my lifelong interest in the social problems, poverty and racial discrimination rampant in our country.

I thank you very much for inviting me to submit a memoir for Wellesley's Centennial. You will understand that I report my memories honestly because this racism too is part of Wellesley's history and should be recorded fully, if only as a benighted pattern to which determinedly it will never return and, also, as a measure of its progress.

[92]

148

A Call for Interracial Cooperation from the 1928 National Association of College Women

(Minutes of 1928 Convention of National Association of College Women, April 13, 1928, p. 14)

In the absence of Bertha C. McNeill, chairman of the Inter-racial Policies Committee, the corresponding secretary gave the following report for her. The question of the treatment of our girls in various colleges governed by the other racial group, the committee feels can best be handled by our making contacts with the alumnae of these colleges and interesting them in looking into conditions and bettering them. The committee recommends further that we encourage our girls to take advantage of all the cultural opportunities their communities may afford them and where cultural opportunities are denied that each branch set out intelligently to gain them. The question particularly of opening up the theatre to our group, and further contacts by joining such national and international organizations as the Council on Cause and Cure of War and the Women's International League for Peace and Freedom were urged. The convention felt that the suggestions given by the committee were timely and urged each branch under the guidance of the National Committee to make inter-racial work an integral part of its yearly activities.

Requisites for a Dean of Women: 1927

Tossie P.F. Whiting, "The Dean of Girls."
(*Virginia Normal and Industrial Institute Gazette,* 33 (1), November, 1927, 19–22)

THE DEAN OF GIRLS

Tossie P. F. Whiting
Dean of Women

Since there are many more secondary schools than colleges in our State, I am using the subject "Dean of Girls" in preference to "Dean of Women" for this paper.

With the coming of secondary education for girls, and particularly co-education, came also many perplexing problems, one of the most serious of which was that of the adolescent boy and girl. In the schools for girls only, there were special problems due to the peculiar physical, social, and mental changes through which a girl passes during high school age; but the problem presented a much more complex aspect when the high school became co-educational. The principal, already encumbered with manifold duties, could not assume the responsibility of another problem so complex. The teachers, due to the organization of the high school into departments, did not come into as close contact with the girls as the elementary teachers did. There was thus a lack of that degree of acquaintance and association which would enable the teacher to direct and help the girls. Each teacher in her special sphere felt responsible for her classroom only. She did not assume responsibility for the conduct of her students outside of the classroom. On the other hand, the high school student felt accountable as to deportment to no one except the principal. However, the principal, being engaged with the larger problems of school administration and general supervision, could not give special attention to the supervision of the girls of the school. Thus, the more thoughtful parents and members of the faculty became aware of the fact that the girls needed a more adequate safeguarding, as an indiscreet act of harmless prank often meant a misrepresentation on the part of the community and a serious embarrassment to the girl. It was evident that some one was needed who could have the care and supervision of the girls; some one who could give the major part of her time to their personal interests; some one who loved youth and young people, and who understood the precarious period of adolescence.

As a result, there was created a position in charge of a woman who was responsible for the care and general oversight of the girls. The position has run through a gamut of names: "lady principal," "preceptress," "adviser of girls," and "dean of girls," and for the college, "dean of women." For a while, it was difficult to make a satisfactory adjustment of the new individual on the faculty. Duties of the principal and of the dean of girls overlapped. Teachers, too, sometime felt that their territory was being trespassed upon by the new member of the faculty. After some adjustment and readjustments, however, the dean of girls found her place on the faculty. She asserted her importance and established herself through the work which she did.

Her position, as discovered, is that of dean of the girls and not dean of the school; but if our secondary school is to bring to our youth the refining and ennobling and cultivating influence which its most zealous adherents claim for it, the woman who is to be the leader and adviser of girls should rank with the heads of different departments and with the officers of the school, being only one step below the principal in that she is responsible to him for the proper execution of her duties as dean of girls. Her position is one of leadership; and that being true, certain personal qualifications are prerequisites to her success.

A fundamental qualification is poise of mind and body. Nothing so inspires young people with confidence and trust as to have as their leader some one who has equilibrium of mind as well as of body; someone who is well-balanced, being neither impulsive nor impetuous; someone who thinks quickly and accurately and who decides wisely. The dean need not be very young in years, but she must be young in spirit. When she allows herself to become peevish and nagging, or static and incapable of adjustment to new ideas and new methods, she disqualifies herself for the position, and she must give up her job.

Another requisite is personal magnetism—love for young people and an understanding of and a broad sympathy for girlhood. It is during this period that the dean must cultivate warm friendships among the girls, if she is going to render them the help they need. The thought that "love begets love" is doubly true at this period in a girl's life. This is the time that she does not understand herself. She is feeling her way. She has various whims and fancies. The vicissitudes through which she is passing are inexplicable to her. She feels the need of the sympathy of someone in whom she can confide. The large-hearted dean often gets nearer the girl than her mother, because often the dean is a better student of human nature.

As to literary qualification, the dean of girls should have, at least, a bachelor's degree. The holding of a degree increases her self-respect and demands a larger respect of the students. Furthermore, it secures to her a larger efficiency in her work. College or university training gives her a back-ground which enables her to advise more wisely those under her supervision. It enhances her resourcefulness.

Other qualifications, such as neatness and good taste in dress, a pleasant approach, congenialty, wholesome decorum, an easy but dignified compliance with rules of social etiquette, positiveness, along with a kindly spirit, are essential. Wisdom as to her health, a sense of the proportion of things, and a keen sense of humor will add much to her efficiency. These qualifications will of themselves solve many problems. The dean should set the standard. She is to be the criterion. Young people are very critical, and she who preaches to them must practice what she preaches, or her sermon is of no avail.

We pass now to the function of the dean, which is three-fold. Her work is administrative, academic, and social; in her administrative duties, there are the general problems of the school life, and then there are special problems incidental to the life of the girls. Her function is to be awake to the best interests of the girls, and to convince the faculty and trustees of the necessity of meeting these needs. Too often, men in arranging their school programs do not consider special needs of girls. They can not be supposed to know the needs of girls as a woman knows them; yet, it is sometimes a job to get men to realize this fact.

Aside from handling minor cases of discipline, the dean should be a member of all faculty committees which have to do with the discipline of girls. She should be well acquainted with the school curriculum and with all the school requirements. She should know her girls well enough to suggest, in special cases, the type of schedule a girl might be expected to carry. Her advice should be of value to the committee in its administration of discipline. Her vision should be clear and her judgment keen. She should "see the worst, but deal with the best" in girls. She should have faith in human nature, and have a well of peace in her own heart. The principles of Jesus should serve as her measuring rod.

If the school is a boarding school, additional administrative duties enter. It is the dean's duty to see that her girls live under hygienic and wholesome social conditions both in and out of the dormitory. The dean not only follows up conditions in the dormitory, but keeps in touch with homes in which girls lodge or board, seeing that the girls residing in them are properly cared for.

Where the school is a boarding school, the question of chaperonage, also, gives some concern. The girls need be led to see that the purpose of chaperonage is a greater freedom rather than greater restriction. Dean McLane says that the chaperon should be of some academic rank, and should be an instructor of a few years' experience in the school, so as to have imbibed the spirit of the place, and to have learned the principles for which the school stands.

The academic function of the dean of girls is as important as her administrative function. Her relation to the educational policy of the school can be made concrete by actual membership upon and participation with committees. The dean needs to be well informed on such subjects as ethics, psychology, and sociology. She needs to be able to appreciate individual differences, and to have a knowledge of intelligence tests and their application. She needs to be able to diagnose some physical and mental conditions.

As to her teaching, there is a difference of opinion. Some think that she should not teach; but the opinion of the larger number of thinkers on this subject is that she will lose prestige and give up that which she loves, if she does not. The advice is that she should not have too large a teaching program—one or two subjects being sufficient. In support of this opinion, Dean Lois K. Matthews, of Wisconsin, says: "Since no dean of women can go far without the support, cooperation, and good will of her colleagues, it is vital to her effectiveness that she should teach. Teach to preserve one's soul alive and to keep one's mind upon the distant vision. It is absolutely essential to have a part in the intellectual life of the community."

Now that much is being said about vocations, and that the majority of our young people must prepare for some form of life work, it is highly imperative that the dean be informed on the various professions and vocations, and at the same time be capable of judging the ability and qualifications of the different girls so as to direct them to the profession or vocation for which they are best fitted. There is much material now on Vocational Guidance. Quite a lengthy bibliography could be given any one interested in the subject.

The function to which I now come is social. This is of no less importance than the other two. The social life of the girl is important, and it is going on whether the dean takes a part in the guidance of it or not. Since happy home life is dependent upon the social life of the boy and the girl, the dean who is tactful in directing the young lives, and in leading them to realize the sanctity and beauty of life as it exists all about them, is rendering to society an invaluable service. Dean Talbot, in *The Education of Women*, discusses the changes which have taken place in woman herself and the change of her attitude toward life. She discusses in turn the commercial and industrial change, the educational change, the civic change, the philanthropic change, the domestic change, the social change. A knowledge of these changes and their effect on education is essential to one who today stands as an adviser to girls. The following paragraph, from Dean Talbot, is so meaningful that I quote:

"Happiness, satisfaction, and progress—all demand a new view of the home as a permanent human institution, if the highest welfare of the individual, the family, and the nation is to be secured. Better marriages, higher standards of fatherhood and motherhood, wider scope for the development of individuality, more intelligent appreciation of the role of the family in the state, greater privacy, truer protection, more generous affection—these are the ideals toward which women must work in new and even untried ways in their great, ever old and ever new, sphere."

The dean of girls in the secondary schools must play her part in helping to establish these ideals.

In summarizing, I would say that the office of dean of girls is of inestimable importance; and that with the capable, liberal-minded, well-balanced, sympathetic dean of girls, who executes the administrative, the academic, and the social functions of her office with intelligence and facility, rests largely the salvation of many of our young people.

Standards of Fisk Women

(*Fisk Handbook,* 1928–1929, p. 11)

"The college girl of today starts for a high standard of womanliness which includes scholarship, good health, justice and fair play, self-control, a love of beauty, courtesy toward all and an essential goodness of heart. These standards are foremost in the ideals long held by Fisk women."

Collegiate Womanhood: The Double Bind of Race and Sex

Marjorie L. Baltimore, "Collegiate Womanhood"
(*The Fisk Herald,* 36 (February, 1930), p. 21)

When folk begin to think of college life they usually visualize a "transition period". This period means to a female the change into a glorious womanhood. College presents itself as a means of promoting this change effectively.

Woman the world over is realizing the extreme necessity of a constructive program. Her quiet resourceful ability to solve world problems has at last been recognized.

In her atempt to prove her fitness, woman has encountered many difficulties; tradition of female inferiority, physical weakness, and the double standard of morals. The Negro woman finds herself facing the double handicap of race and sex. These have however served only to strengthen her. She has found college to be the best place to begin the struggle for recognition.

The Fisk woman has by intellectual and social work proved her willingness to fall in line with the great race movement. At present she finds interest in literary and artistic club groups, conversational hours, and athletic programs both for herself and in support of the male teams. She has also cooperated with the religious program of the school.

Civil activities play an important role in the development and advancement of the intellectual sphere. The interest shown by the girls in the meetings, which are definitely not in the school program, is to be commended. The international Fellowship of Reconciliation Movement at the Ryman Auditorium and the Inter-racial Conference at Scarritt College were largely attended by the women.

Classical programs have served to direct their thoughts from the mediocre to the highest type of cultural art. The women went in large numbers to the Ruth St. Dennis and Ted Shawn Classical Dance and to the Roland Hayes concert.

Radicalism is sometimes necessary for emancipation. The overwhelming reaction of women in general after the great war was startling, but has not proved useless. After the thrill had worn off and their purpose accomplished, they became more conservative Some individuals, however, still cling to the idea that woman's prime object is to be shockingly radical. The sooner this false idea is eradicated, the sooner woman's endeavor will be respected and accepted. It is the College Woman's duty to prove her worth; and it is the College Man's duty, as a part of society to believe in her sincerity and fidelity.

—Majorie L. Baltimore

The Women at Tennessee State from a 1927 Male Perspective

Ozaana Vineyard, "Our Girls"
(*Bulletin of Tennessee A&I State College,* 16 (2 & 3),October–November, 1927, 2–3)

OUR GIRLS

Eddie: "Well, this is a little world within itself! It is a perfect paradise."

Billie: "You have certainly spoken a parable, and I shall ditto your statement, for I can surely speak from experience."

Eddie: "This is your first year here, isn't it?"

Billie: "Yes, but not my first in college, for I have been to Howard, Harvard, Morris Brown and many other colleges playing on their teams, and visiting at my leisure hours."

Eddie: "Well after your tour of the fountains of Education, what do you think of old Tennessee State?"

Billie: "Well, I just can't tell you what I think of the place as a whole, but in part I know one thing and that is, State certainly has a bunch of real young women. I have traveled far and wide and I have seen young women of various institutions but none can compare with our girls here. They are perfect in every sense. Modest enough to be real young ladies; now understand me, I don't mean false modesty, but I do mean that portion of modesty which goes to make up the character of real womanhood. Not any of them are far below Venus in physical make-up, and all are certainly well dressed. Why last Sunday while looking from my window I thought that I was in a theatre looking at a Paris shop review, but I awoke to the fact that I was merely looking at our girls out for an evening's stroll on the campus."

Eddie: "You are right old boy, we certainly have some girls; girls from every clime; girls of all the uplifting types; girls that just can't be beaten."

Billie: "Well, if my only opinion of, and reason for coming to Tennessee State was to enjoy the privilege of seeing the largest collection of real honest-to-goodness young, intellectual and women who show their character and what they really are thru their daily and hourly walks and motivations, I believe I would be justified. Do you agree with me?"

Eddie: "Give me your hand, old boy, and let us shake it off. Come on, the Cafeteria is open. Let us get a bit of supper.

Oznana Vineyard

169

Mid-Century: Discrimination by Race and Sex

Mary Elizabeth Branch: Black College President

Tossie P. F. Whiting, "Hail, Our Daughter"
(Manuscript. Mary E. Branch Collection, Manuscript Department,
Moorland-Springarn Research Center, Howard University)

Milton A. Maxwell, "Mary E. Branch"
(*Advance*, (September, 1944), 9–10)

Some years ago, there came to the then "Virginia Normal and Collegiate Institute" a little round-faced, bright-eyed, intelligent-looking girl. John, "Clem," and Hattie had come before her and Helen came later. Brothers and sisters they were. They hailed from Farmville, Virginia, and were representatives of one of the old, well-known families of the State.

Their parents were unusual people. Their father, the late Rev. Tazewell Branch, who lived to the ripe old age of 94 years, was known for his integrity and sagacity and for his wise counselling. He served for two terms during the Reconstruction Period as a member of the Legislature of Virginia. Their mother, a member of one of the first families of Virginia, was cultured in taste, refined in manner, intelligent, and ambitious for her children.

It is not surprising that their children developed into useful men and women. One brother is one of the leading physicians of Camden, New Jersey; another brother is Dean of the Teachers College in St. Louis, Missouri; one sister is principal of the public school in Morristown, N.J.; another sister is a prominent teacher in the public schools of Lawnside, N.J.

But the development and advancement of the "little round-faced, bright-eyed, intelligent-looking girl," known on the campus during her school career here as "Little Bettie Branch" is the reason for this article. While in school she evidenced her intellectual ability by her work in the classroom and by her good judgment on affairs outside of the classroom. She was a favorite among the students of her rank and among those in the college departments. After completing her course of study, she went out to teach.

For a few years she taught in Blackstone, Virginia; but her Alma Mater recognizing her ability offered her a position on its faculty as teacher. She accepted and over a period of years did an exceptionally good piece of work--teaching, serving on committees, and counselling. Counselling should be emphasized, for she was really the students' friend. Both girls and boys sought her for advice and counsel and left her with lighter hearts. In fact, for a few years, along with her teaching program, she lived in the men's dormitory, Johnston Hall, as Matron for the young men of the school. Those were great years for the boys. If you do not believe it, ask some of the fellows who lived in Johnston Hall during those years. The building was neat and attractive, and the young men were genteel and orderly. The girls living in Virginia Hall, as they all were then, had to put forth much effort to make their rooms as attractive as the rooms of the young men were. The young men of the campus were as devoted to Miss Branch as were the girls.

Her poise of body and mind, her characteristic bearing, her personal magnetism, her strong but pleasing personality, her scholarly attitude and her studious inclination won the admiration of all. Everybody on the campus knew and respected "Miss Branch." Among the students she was known as a English teacher. In those days students would be heard to say that you must get "Branch's English" and "Phillip's English" and "Gandy's History."

Miss Branch never stopped growing. She read and studied all the while she was teaching, did regular personal reading, took extension courses, attended summer schools. Then she matriculated at the University of Chicago in regular session and was graduated with Ph.B. Later, from the same university, she won the Master's degree and some credit toward the doctorate.

All the while, Miss Branch has identified herself with the group interests of the race. At present, she is the Mid-Western Regional Director of the Alpha Kappa Alpha Sorority and an active member of the National Association of College Women.

The State College lost a valuable asset to its faculty when Miss Branch transferred to another field, but we were proud of her achievements and of the rapid advancement. She taught acceptably both in Kansas City and in St. Louis since leaving us. In St. Louis she was promoted from the position of teacher to that of Dean of Girls in the Vashon High School in which she was employed. During the early part of this year, Miss Branch was asked to accept the presidency of Tillotson College, a college for women in Austin, Texas. At first, Miss Branch declined the offer because she was satisfactorily located. Repeated requests and the urgency of the call, however, won her. She realized that the position meant increased responsibility, but she was willing to assume it to render a larger service to the young women of our race. Hence on July first 1930 she became the President of Tillotson Teachers College.

We hail and give honor to our Miss Mary E. Branch as President of a college, the second woman of the race to head a standard woman's college.

The Negro American of July, 1930, published in San Antonio, Texas, bears a cut of President Mary E. Branch along with an article headed, "Tillotson under Woman Leadership."

President Branch two months after having taken charge of the work in writing to a friend said,

"The place is beautiful, the prettiest spot in Austin. It stands on a hill like Virginia State. Many, many trees cover the campus; some are quite old and storm ridden. These I hope to replace with young sycamores, elms, and China berries. I shall plant also some fruit trees-- peaches, pears, figs, and pecans. I want a nice pecan grove.

"I've been working hard to increase the student body. I've sent out about 600 letters and 300 catalogues and visited and spoken in eight churches in four cities. I plan to visit four more cities within the next three weeks."

With such a woman as president, Tillotson is compelled to advance. We congratulate the college and the American Missionary Association on securing such an efficient, conscientious person to steer the work of the college at this time.

President Mary E. Branch carries with her to Texas the best wishes and felicitations of her first Alma Mater, the Virginia State College, and of her many friends here.

WE HAIL WITH PRIDE OUR DAUGHTER

Mary E. Branch

MILTON A. MAXWELL

MARY E. BRANCH, LATE PRESIDENT OF TILLOTSON COLLEGE, AUSTIN, TEXAS

WHAT! Put a woman in charge of a run-down college?" Such was the reaction in 1930 when Miss Mary E. Branch was recommended for the presidency of the American Missionary Association's Tillotson College in Austin, Texas.

This response seems strange to us now—particularly to those of us who, before her recent death, had felt the warmth and force of Miss Branch's personality and had known her as a highly respected Negro educator, as the holder of honorary degrees from Virginia State College and Howard University, as the notably successful rebuilder of Tillotson College, as the assistant moderator of our General Council, and as a prophetic champion for her people.

MILTON A. MAXWELL, pastor of University Community Church, Austin, Texas.

In 1930, Tillotson had come upon difficult days. Everything was dilapidated. The five old buildings were in need of repair. The campus was barren and dusty. The student body numbered only 69 girls. Its educational reputation was at a new low. No one was proud of being a Tillotson graduate. The A. M. A. debated closing the school. Obviously more than a man-sized job lay ahead if the college was to be continued and built up again.

But Mary Branch turned out to be just the woman for that size job. She started off by beating the bushes for more students. She pitched in with the girls in planting flowers, shrubbery, and grass. She began making repairs with the limited funds at her disposal. Somehow during the second year she managed to get enough money to offer

Negro high school in Texas. This strategy alone speedily brought Tillotson to the attention of the state and greatly improved the quality of the student body. She kept strengthening the faculty, determined to make the best possible education available to her students. She instituted a four year home economics course which is still unique among Negro colleges of the Southwest. She tackled the library of 2,000 discarded theological books and succeeded in making it a first class library of 21,000 volumes. Each year saw growth in the student body and greater prestige for the school. The graduates began to be sought for teaching positions. In 1935, boys were again admitted. Enrollment continued to grow until it reached almost 500 during the 1943-44 session. Despite heavy loss of boys to the armed services, this was the college's best year, highlighted by the crowning achievement of President Branch's administration—receiving an "A" rating from the Southern Association of Colleges and Secondary Schools.

"Now that makes me feel that I've really done something!" she beamed to her associates. How glad her friends are that she lived to enjoy this tangible reward for her long years of determined effort.

This may sound like just another ordinary success story, until the almost unbelievable limitations under which she worked are taken into account. Then the magnificence of Mary Branch's achievement and the greatness of her stature stand revealed. For Mary Branch was a great person! She was a firm minded, forceful personality, balanced by great charm and kindliness.

She believed in herself. "If I don't believe in myself, how can I ask you or anyone else to believe in me?" Yet she was unostentatious and humble.

Her judgment was excellent. It was her conscious policy to get all the facts she could on any new proposal, to make sure that they were the facts, to talk the matter over leisurely with others, and then to go off by herself and make up her mind. Decisions made that way were usually good and backed up with all she had.

She was a genius at making money

177

go a long way. She had to be. There never was enough. Her reputation as an economizer is almost legendary.

She was determined to have her school measure up to the best standards. She had never wanted anyone to make allowances for her because she was a Negro or because she was a woman. She wanted no one to make allowances for her school. On one occasion she appeared before the General Education Board in New York, seeking a grant. They told her they would like to give her some money and that they knew she needed it, but that Tillotson did not measure up to certain standards. She said she wanted no favors; if they would just tell her what the standards were, she'd be back in a few years and then they could give her the help she needed.

She believed in the average people and the poor. She observed that the world rested on the lowly, and she was their champion. "Equality and justice for all" was her oft-repeated motto. She took pride in helping poor students get a college education. She spent much of her own money on them. She was a courageous spokesman for her race and at the time of her death was president of the Austin chapter of the National Association for the Advancement of Colored People.

Her friends speak of her strong maternal nature. She was forever mothering somebody. Each year she took a girl or two under her wing, often girls no one else would mother. During her twenty years at Virginia State College she not only taught English but was a much-sought counselor of students and the beloved house mother of a men's dormitory. She mothered the girls of Vashon High School in St. Louis for four years, as dean of girls. At Tillotson she took great personal interest in the students and faculty, and they were devoted to her.

And in a sense her fourteen years at Tillotson might be described as they were by one of her closest friends as a mothering of Tillotson College itself, from neglected infancy to self-respecting adulthood.

Her mother heart was a generous channel for the creative power and love of God.

Pay Inequity: One Woman's Experience

Excerpt from interview with Eva B. Dykes by Merze Tate,
November 30–December 1, 1977
(Black Women's Oral History Project, Schlesinger Library, Radcliffe
College, Cambridge, Mass., reprinted by permission)

Pay Inequity: One Woman's Experience

In 1921 the first three black women ever to receive Ph.D. degrees graduated within several weeks of each other. One of them, Eva Beatrice Dykes, taught at Howard University for a number of years before assuming a position at Oakwood College in Alabama where the following incident occurred.

> One of the men teachers here, by the name of Sumpter, said to me, "Oh, Miss Dykes, did you get your promotion?" And I said, "What promotion?" And he said, "Well, you know, all the teachers were promoted." I said, "Well, I didn't get any promotion." So when I saw President Peterson, I said to him, "President Peterson, I understand that some of the teachers got a promotion. And I didn't get one." And I was just like a child, curious, you know, why I didn't. And he said to me in his inimitable way, with his hands stretched out wide—I can see him now, standing on the steps of Moran Hall—"Well, you are a woman. That's why you didn't get it." And he was one of my dear friends. I said, "President Peterson, if I go over here to the store and want to buy a loaf of bread, do I get a reduction because I am a woman? If I want to go downtown and buy clothes do I get a reduction because I am a woman? So that has existed all down through the ages, that discrepancy.

Excerpt from interview of Eva B. Dykes by Merze Tate, November 30-December 1, 1977. Black Women Oral History Project, Schlesinger Library, Radcliffe College, Cambridge Massachusetts. Printed by permission.

Black Women's College Curriculum: Needed Reforms

Lucy D. Slowe, "Higher Education of Negro Women"
(*Journal of Negro Education,* 2 (July, 1933), 352–352, reprinted by
permission)

Higher Education of Negro Women

LUCY D. SLOWE

EARLY HISTORY

It appears that the first Negro woman to complete a college course in America was Mary Jane Patterson, who was graduated in 1862 from Oberlin College with the degree of Bachelor of Arts. This event, happening before the issuing of the Emancipation Proclamation, marks the beginning of higher education for Negro women in the United States.

It is significant, in the light of the subsequent history of college education for Negro women, that the first woman graduate received her training in a co-educational school, and that a vast majority of these women, since this event, have been graduated from the same type of college. There are in the United States today only three colleges maintained exclusively for the education of Negro women—Bennett, Spelman, and Tillotson; consequently the problem of their higher education is essentially the problem of educating "the weaker sex" in colleges with "the stronger sex."

The history of the education of Negro women, therefore, does not parallel exactly the history of education of white women. While Oberlin College opened in 1833 for the admission of all races and both sexes, there was a long period of struggle for the admission of women to college, but, by the time of the founding of Vassar College in 1865, at least three Negro women had been awarded the degree of Bachelor of Arts. By the time any considerable number of Negro women were ready for college, the question of the right of women to a college education had been, to all intents and purposes, settled.

After the close of the Civil War, co-educational colleges for Negroes sprang up in various places in the South and the real education of Negro women began. Howard University, founded in 1867; Fisk University, founded in 1865; Atlanta University, 1867; Shaw University, 1865; Straight College, 1869; Tougaloo, 1869, are among the important institutions which admitted women and men on the same basis.

It is a fact that the segregated college has never played a very important part in the training of Negro college women, hence, even if it were the purpose of this paper to compare the advantages of the co-educational college with those of the segregated college, there would be scarcely enough data to make the comparison worthwhile. There is no counterpart of Vassar, Smith, Wellesley, Mount Holyoke, Wells, Radcliffe, Bryn Mawr, Mills, Barnard, among the Negro institutions. The problem of the higher education of the Negro woman is therefore found in the co-educational institutions. The assumption that women were not endowed with the capacity to pursue standard college courses had been disproved before the influx of Negro women to college. In

352

those who entered co-educational colleges studied the identical subjects studied by men. Indeed, in the early days there was only one course for students to follow—the traditional classical course.

OBJECTIVES OF THE CURRICULA OF THE COLLEGES

In examining the curricula of the various colleges, it is interesting to note that they all are striking in their similarity, and to note further that they are pointed toward the same objective—the training of teachers and preachers. If a history of all the graduates of Negro colleges were available, it would show that the vast majority of these graduates have gone into the teaching profession. This was brought about by the great need for trained teachers for the mass of Negroes and also by the fact that it was the easiest profession for them to enter. It is true that the colleges have trained men for the ministry, for law, and for medicine, but, by far, the largest number of Negro college graduates, men and women, are following the teaching profession. Thus the aims of the founders of these institutions of higher learning to a great extent have been carried out.

CHANGES IN CURRICULA NEEDED FOR MODERN LIFE

Regardless, however, of the purpose of colleges of a past day, if they are to serve the needs of the present time, they must examine and re-examine their curricula in the light of changes in modern life. Since the opening of most of the Negro colleges between 1865 and 1875, momentous changes have taken place in American life af-

fecting every phase of its existence, but no group has been as seriously affected as American women. Any discussion of the education of women must take into consideration the present status of women, their opportunities and their chances for achievement in the new order.

It is the purpose of this paper to discuss the problem of the higher education of Negro women in the light of conditions in the modern world. Since these conditions affect them in the same way that they affect other women, Negro women must be prepared for making their contribution to the problems of the world.

In considering the preparation of women for their places in the modern world, it is well to recall some of the important changes which have come about in our industrial, domestic, political and social life. The vast changes in our mode of living ushered in by the industrial revolution have upset completely the routine of life as it moved as late as 1865. Home occupations have all but disappeared with the possible exception of the preparation of meals, and this occupation is being taken over by numerous restaurants, cafeterias, hotels, etc.

The taking of their traditional work out of the home has sent thousands of women into commercial and industrial pursuits. Women who had always spent their lives in caring for their own homes, in doing the sewing, preserving, and other household tasks for which they usually received no direct pay, found themselves the recipients of weekly wages and their attendant independence. The employment of women in gainful occupations has done more than any other factor to change the home life and the social life of men, women and children. Whether or not the change has been altogether beneficial is beside the point in this discussion; the fact remains that the present industrial system has revolutionized the lives of women and, indirectly, the lives of men. A discussion of the education of women has to take this fact into account.

Scarcely less important than the changes brought about by the industrial revolution have been the changes brought about by the political independence of women. The achieving of the full rights of citizenship by women has had a profound effect upon them as individuals and upon their relationship to their several communities and to their government. Their participation in the civic activities of their communities has extended their interests beyond their homes, their cities, their states and their nation. Negro women, no less than white women, must be prepared for the responsibilities of citizenship if they are to discharge their duties to the government under which they live and if they are to be capable of watching intelligently their own interests, and of using their ballot in preserving and promoting these interests.

The great question before college administrators today is whether or not the curricula of their several schools have been organized to meet the needs of women who must live in and make their contribution to a changed economic, industrial, and political order. In other words, have those who formulate the policies of higher institutions of learning where Negro women study, surveyed our changed modern life and consciously attempted to prepare Negro college women for intelligent participation and leadership in it?

In order to get some idea of what is happening in Negro colleges where women are enrolled the following questionnaire was sent to 76 institutions doing work of college grade:

HOWARD UNIVERSITY
Office of the Dean of Women
(QUESTIONNAIRE ON THE HIGHER EDUCATION OF NEGRO WOMEN)

Name of Institution ....
Location ....
Name of President ....
Name of Dean of Women........................

1. How many women of college grade are enrolled in your school. ....
2. How many are enrolled in the following courses:
    a. Political Science ....
    b. Economics ....
    c. Psychology ....
    d. Sociology ....
3. Have you a woman physician in charge of the health of women students ....
4. How many women teachers on your faculty ....
    a. Full Professor ....
    b. Associate Professor ....
    c. Assistant Professor ....
    d. Instructor ....
5. Do you have a Women's Self-Government Organization................
6. What organizations on your campus give women an opportunity for self-development:
    a. ....
    b. ....
    c. ....
    d. ....

Please send me a list of your rules and regulations governing women students.

Forty-four (44) institutions sent replies that are highly illuminating. Since college education in America has been designed not only to develop scholars but also to furnish intelligent leadership for the masses of the people, it is pertinent to find out what provision Negro colleges have made for preparing Negro college women for intelligent leadership in the sphere of life which they will occupy after graduation.

Enrolled in the forty-four colleges which answered the questionnaire are 14,843 women. Of this total the following figures compiled from the questionnaire are significant in considering the question under discussion.

Subjects which have a direct bearing upon preparation for living in the modern world:

Subject	Number enrolled	Per cent
1. Political Science	615	4
2. Economics	560	4
3. Psychology	1,163	8
4. Sociology	932	7

It is reasonable to suppose that the large number registered in psychology are preparing for the profession of teaching, but the fact that during this year out of over 13,000 women registered in college courses only 615 are pursuing courses in political science and only 560 in economics—subjects basic to understanding modern life— should cause college administrators and faculties to give some thought to what this means for the future adjustment of women to conditions which they must face in the present day world. While it may be inaccurate to generalize from these data, it can be readily seen that if college women are to be intelligent heads of homes, or intelligent members of their communities, more of them must pursue those subjects which have to do with community life in a very fundamental way. The classical courses followed by practically all college students up to very recent times, important though they may be, must be supplemented by those social sciences which enable one to understand the world in which one lives. College administrators and faculties should give serious consideration to this in building their curricula.

TRAINING FOR SELF-DIRECTION

The answers to the questionnaire were suggestive also from the standpoint of the opportunities given to women students for training in the assumption of responsibility and self-direction. Whether or not Negro college women will be able to take their places as leaders in their communities depends, to a large extent, upon the opportunities offered them for exercising initiative, independence, and self-direction while in college. The theory of political science, for instance, studied in the classroom should find concrete expression in self-government associations on the campus.

The returns from the questionnaire seem to indicate that less than 50 per cent of the colleges answering give their students any part in their own government. Of the 44 colleges which replied only 27 per cent have student councils; 6 per cent dormitory self-government; 6 per cent Women's Leagues.

In examining the lists of rules submitted by the various colleges with the questionnaire, it is quite apparent that students in too many schools are governed by administrators and faculties rather than encouraged to govern themselves—the only kind of government worthwhile in an intelligent community. It seems reasonable to say that only in a very small minority of colleges do students participate in the making and executing of the rules under which they live. Such participation is so vital to the development of good citizens that all institutions of higher learning should give serious consideration to this phase of their students' development.

The opportunities which students have in institutions of higher learning for self-development outside the class-room may be judged from the following list of clubs returned by the forty-four schools:

Name	No. of schools where they exist
Y. W. C. A.	30
Departmental	19
Social	16
Sororities	12
Glee Clubs	12
Dramatic	12
Debating	9
Literary	6
Athletic	6
College Forum	5
Home Economics	3
Class Organization	2
Art Club	2
International Club	1
College Prayer	1
Inter Club Council	1
Christian Endeavor	1
Epworth League	1
Self-government:	
Student Council	12
Dormitory Self-government	3
Women's League	3

Of course, it is almost impossible to interpret the results accruing to students by their participation in the activities of these various clubs, but fundamental to all participation in the activities of the world is the ability and training to understand the customs and laws by which people are governed. It does not appear that many colleges where women are being trained are giving them this fundamental opportunity by having them assist in governing themselves.

PECULIAR PROBLEM OF DEVELOPING INITIATIVE IN NEGRO WOMEN

Such opportunity is far more important for Negro women than for white women in this country, although it is important for all women. This point of view seems sound because the social experience of most Negro women is different from the social experience of most white women, and because their own psychology is colored by their peculiar experience. It is true, too, that the philosophy of education in the colleges to which the majority of Negro women go does not seem to be set for the development of the capacities of women for self-directed lives in a modern world.

When Negro women go to college, they go usually from segregated communities where neither they nor their parents have had much experience in the civic life of the community. In many places they have not had the right to vote, nor have they been permitted to participate in the responsibilities of government in their city or state. They have paid taxes, but have had no voice in deciding how taxes shall be spent. They are accustomed to stand by and see policies of government worked out or not worked out, without help from them.

Frequently, Negro college women come from homes where conservatism in reference to women's place in the world of the most extreme sort exists. Regardless of the fact that modern conditions have forced many women to be economically, politically, and socially independent, many parents still believe that the definition of woman found in an eighteenth century dictionary is true today: "Woman, the female of man. See man." Regardless of the wish of many parents that their daughters become adjuncts of "man," modern life forces them to be individuals in much the same sense as men are individuals.

It is to be remembered, too, that much of the religious philosophy upon which Negro women have been nurtured has tended toward suppressing in them their own powers. Many of them have been brought up on the antiquated philosophy of Saint Paul in reference to women's place in the scheme of things, and all too frequently have been influenced by the philosophy of patient waiting, rather than the philosophy of developing their talents to the fullest extent.

Under these conditions, it is inevitable, therefore, that the psychology of most of the women who come to college is the psychology of accepting what is taught without much question; the psychology of inaction rather than that of active curiosity.

With this sort of psychology to begin with, Negro women go in large numbers to co-educational colleges where much of the same sort of conservatism in reference to women prevails. The belief exists that college women must be shielded and protected to such an extent that the most intimate phases of their lives are invaded by rules and regulations. An extreme example of this sort of thing may be seen in the following list of rules in operation in one college:

The President of the College shall have the general command and government of the Institution, watching over its administration, discipline and instruction. He shall have authority to make rules, from time to time, governing the granting of excuses to students, to inspect anything in a student's room or baggage; to suspend or modify regulations, or to publish others when he considers it necessary which shall have the authority of the Board of Trustees until they shall act on the same.

The President's authority over the conduct of students continues until their return to their homes and parents. They remain members of the school until dismissed, honorably discharged or graduated therefrom.

The Deans, under the President, shall have control of all students in all that pertain to discipline and administration. They shall make thorough inspection of rooms, furniture and clothing of students at least once a week. They shall have the right to inspect anything in a student's room or personal baggage.

The government of the College is conceived and executed with a view of making the college a pleasant, busy, and therefore happy, and well-ordered home. Its object is to develop self-control, higher character, and the desire to do the right because it is right. Courtesy and kindness are uniform rules of the Institution. The honor, pride, and interest of students in the success of the College are appealed to, and students who do not study or conform to requirements will be sent home promptly.

* * * * *

No young woman is permitted to leave the grounds of the College unless accompanied by the Dean or her representative.

Communication in any form with the opposite sex is prohibited.

The absence of women or the presence of very few on the policy-making bodies of the colleges is also indicative of the attitude of college administrators toward women as responsible individuals, and toward the special needs of women. An examination of the list of faculties of the colleges in which most women are trained is highly suggestive. It is difficult to interpret that portion of the questionnaire dealing with the rank of women on the faculties of the several institutions, for in some institutions it appears that all members of the faculty have the same rank, and, in several cases this section was not answered.

Reliable sources also point to the fact that few women achieve administrative positions in co-educational colleges, consequently, little stimulus comes to women students from outstanding examples of women who have achieved high rank in their institutions.

These facts point to the necessity of having college administrators and those interested in the higher education of Negro women make special provision for giving Negro college women opportunities for self-expression through self-government and opportunities for becoming acquainted with the problems of the world in which they live.

Emphasis in this discussion has been placed purposely upon the value of social studies and the value of opportunities for self-government and self-development in the education of Negro women, for these seem to be subject to more neglect than any other phase of their college course. However, this emphasis is not given to detract from the importance of the so-called cultural subjects as a part of the college course. Education must fit Negro women, as it must fit all women, for the highest development of their own gifts; but, whatever those gifts, they will not be able to exercise them unless they understand the world they live in and are prepared to make their contribution to it.

HIGHER EDUCATION AND MARRIAGE

Those interested in the higher education of women should bear in mind that women are not only conservators of the race, but they are its real educators. The mother in the home, the first teacher of the young, needs the broadest sort of training if she is to start her children on the road to satisfactory adjustment in life. Not only must she have a liberal education in the traditional subjects of the college course, but she must also understand the economic, political, and social system under which the children of the future must live. She cannot, even if she desires, keep modern conditions out of the home; therefore, colleges which train women must train them to understand the world as it now is, and to aid it in changing for the better.

It should also be borne in mind that the life of married women, including those who become mothers, is quite different from what it was twenty-five years ago; their children as a rule are grown by the time the mothers are forty-five or fifty years of age, and frequently are away from home and no longer in need of the supervision of their mothers. With the span of life lengthened as it has been in recent years, these women have from fifteen to twenty years of comparative leisure which must be provided for in their scheme of education. Many women with college training have achieved distinction in their careers after they have reared their families. From almost any point of view, it seems wise to assume that college women must be trained along the lines of their individual talents, and at the same time must be made conscious of the fact that the world will expect from them practically the same sort of contribution that it expects from men—the contribution of an individual so disciplined that she can direct herself, so informed that she can assist in directing others in this intricate modern world. Institutions of higher learning must furnish the world this type of individual.

Student Life in the 1930s: Tennessee State

Excerpts from an interview with a 1935 Tennessee State
Graduate
(Interview with Lillian Dunn Thomas by Elizabeth L. Ihle, June, 1987)

Tennessee State graduate, 1935

Nashville, TN

Elizabeth Ihle conducted this interview with this graduate of
Tennessee State University in June, 1987. TSG stands for Tennessee
State Graduate.

ELI: What lessons that you learned at Tennessee State were the most
     valuable?

TSG: Well, I'm trying to think. I learned to be a leader
     there. I'd work with people because I was president of a
     club, and I was the treasurer of my sorority. I learned a
     lot from my teachers and other people--I observe well--how
     they do things. You know we had to give speeches when we
     finished in the auditorium in front of the student body.
     I think that helped me a little bit. I'm not a speaker;
     I'm a better workshop person. I think my leadership
     really came from my home and from my teachers and other
     students who were good leaders.

ELI: What were your chief entertainments in college?

TSG: Well, we had pajama parties, and we had dances on the lawn,
     block dances they would call it, and we had beautiful
     dances on the inside. Now, I didn't care for cards, but
     some of them played cards called "Five Ups" or something
     like that. So I never played cards too much.

ELI: But cards were allowed?

TSG: Oh, yes. You could play cards in your room. I'll tell you
     that we were not allowed to cook in our rooms. Now, this
     was fun. One girl--we were in high school then--got a
     bucket, and they went and got a chicken out of a building,
     cooked him in the bucket, boiled him. I remember the
     matron coming, "I smell somebody cooking." Everybody got
     quiet, and she didn't knock on our door. It was us
     cooking that chicken.

ELI: What were some of the fads of the times?

TSG: Some of the fads were...well, you'll be surprised. The skirts were long. I was telling somebody about an evening dress I had. They were long evening dresses, and at times they wore little tea dresses, pretty little organdy dresses, girly looking dresses, with little bows like that and everything, very dainty clothes, I thought. And I used to design my dresses. I would design them, and my mother would have them made.

I enjoyed going to the recitals and things like that that they used to have. Oh, we had--they called it--Sunday evening with speakers to come out from different organizations. Once or twice a month the students would go to the auditorium where they had these speakers. We had another cultural club that I liked. This lady taught girls how to dress, she taught them about using deoderant, she taught them how you should wash yourself: "You've been in school all day, you certainly should come home and when you go to dinner don't put on the dress without your doing that." She had whole different groups of girls. That's some of the things they need now; it was a beautiful thing.

ELI: Is wasn't a course; it was a series of lectures?

TSG: No, a series of lectures that she would give to students in the dormitories. And that was real nice.

ELI: You had to go?

TSG: No, you didn't have to go; you just wanted to go. You see those are some of the things...and now you can give things and some of them don't go. Now they tell you, "I'm not going." But we wanted to go [to] the things that they would do.

ELI: Tennessee State and Fisk appear to be very separate and different schools.

TSG: At that time they were because, well, we thought the Fisk students thought they were better than us, you know. We had friends at Fisk, and they had friends at Tennessee State. There was a kind of rivalry with the games and things like that. I always thought that the Fisk girls really dressed so well. We always thought that they came from very rich homes.

Defense of the Women's College: Spelman's President

Florence M. Read, "The Place of the Women's College In the
Pattern of Negro Education"
(*Opportunity*, 15, (September, 1937), 267–270)

The Place of the Women's College In the Pattern of Negro Education « «

● By FLORENCE M. READ

F UNDAMENTALLY, the aims and aspirations of those charged with the education of women are the same, whether it be in institutions where men and women are educated together, or in separate colleges for women. There is much to be said for each type of school, and each has its distinct value. In any discussion of Negro women's colleges, however, it should be pointed out that the co-education of Negro youth has been fostered primarily because it is the less costly procedure. Southern states have not been willing to set up separate colleges for men and for women, because the overhead costs would be doubled. Church organizations and other educational agencies have followed the same course, not always because they were convinced that co-education was the ter course, but because it was the more expedient.

Whether this course has been the wisest one may be an open question. Yet few would deny that there exists today a definite place in the pattern of Negro education for the college for women, and that the contribution of women to society is bound to be increasingly important as this type of institution develops and reaches its full measure of usefulness.

At the outset, it may appear that the function of the women's college differs little, if at all, from that of the co-educational college. Perhaps the purpose is the same, but to many it seems that the women's college may state its aims more clearly and work less interruptedly to the realization of these objectives.

In the early days of Spelman College (then Spelman Seminary) a proposal was made that Spelman combine with Morehouse, the neighboring college for men, to form a co-educational institution. The reply of Miss Sophia E. Packard, the senior founder and co-principal, was in this wise: "No, I do not favor it. I have never known an institution for both men and women where the interests of women were not subordinated to those of men." So far as I know, the subject was never thereafter seriously discussed.

While Miss Packard's comment may not be quite so true today with reference to the curriculum, it is still true in large measure and in most respects.

The President of Spelman College has for many years been a tremendous influence in the education and training of young Negro women in the South. When Miss Read speaks of the place of the women's college, she speaks from wide knowledge and experience.

Co-educational institutions have some advantages that separate colleges for men and women do not have, but undeniably colleges for women enjoy some noteworthy advantages not possible for co-educational colleges.

In planning the curriculum, it is possible to emphasize features that relate both to general principles and conditions and also specifically to the life of women. To illustrate, in physics by all means teach general theories and principles of matter, heat, light, electricity, et cetera, but in the laboratory problems or experimental work, include a study of mechanical devices found in homes. Frigidaires and Kelvinators, vacuum cleaners, radios, kodaks, sewing machines, heating systems, automobiles, all are part of the experience of most women.

To take another example, women constitute the main purchasing power in this country. Some statisticians say that 65 per cent of the money is spent by women, directly or indirectly. Women need to know about buying. A course in the principles of economics in a women's college may well stress consumer buying in its proper place in the course, giving more attention relatively to that than, say, to monetary theories or credit inflation.

There is a tendency in some quarters to look upon courses planned especially for women as inferior, as requiring less intellectual effort. That need not be, and should not be the case. It is fortunately no longer necessary to prove that women have mental capacity to comprehend the most abstruse subjects.

Women and men are human beings, and personally I do not advocate too great a difference in the curricula of men's colleges and women's colleges. The base should be pretty much the same,—certainly before specialization begins. There is need of subjects that require accuracy and straight thinking for both men and women. The point I am making is that in women's colleges, it is feasible in the organization of the courses to recognize the interests and obligations

267

From the Library, Lincoln University,
Jefferson City, Missouri.

of women as women when that seems advantageous.

Let me say in passing that the teacher, more than the name of the course, is the determining factor of the value of a course. An alert and well-grounded teacher of English literature includes economics and sociology, religion and psychology, in teaching Nineteenth Century Prose. How else really can one teach Emerson and Carlyle, Ruskin and Matthew Arnold? It is a fallacy to suppose that a student is not being prepared for life in the modern world if she does not take a course in criminology. That is why statistics are often misleading as showing the content of a student's course of study. The content depends on the teacher more than on the title of the course.

It is the duty of the college not only to train the mind to the highest point of usefulness but what is even more important, to develop an attitude to life that will mean growth in college and after college, and ability to stand the strain and stress of life. It is in that respect, as much as in the curriculum, that the women's college has a special responsibility. Every person needs an inner source of strength, a power of endurance, the ability to hold one's place against the tide. But women are in a special sense the keep-

ers of social standards, the guardians of spiritual values. Unless the women of any race have high standards of personal and family and community life, those standards will slump and social life will decline. Much attention is given to manners and much attention is given to character in the women's colleges.

In women's colleges, all extra-curricular activities naturally are directed by women. Here women students are not relegated to the offices of vice-president and secretary. It is fine experience for young women to be wholly responsible for YWCA programs and forums and department clubs and class parties. It develops initiative and responsibility and self-reliance. It teaches good sportsmanship. It gives experience with human nature. Mary, as chairman of the committee for the international dinner, learns that Grace may not be talkative in the committee meeting but that she can be depended on to do what she promises, that Vivian has to be watched or she will change the menu or the program from that agreed upon, that Ellen has skill in arranging the decorations but unless prodded constantly will not get them done on time, that Mildred will do nothing but stir up friction, and that Sarah and Jane and Ethel who will see the thing through to the end and help clean up and return borrowed belongings after the dinner is over are jewels in any community. She learns this so much better through her own experiences with people than she can in any other way.

There is another most important lesson she begins to experience that will stand by her throughout her life. Men for generations have known how to work with men. In more recent years, women have learned to work with men, usually in subordinate positions. But women do not so well know how to work with women. It is important for women to learn early in life how to adapt themselves and get results in living and working with women. In college they associate with young women—from country and small town and city, from large families and small, from East and West and North and South. They learn to be more tolerant and understanding. They learn that their own way of doing things is not the only way and perhaps not the best way. Their personalities are broadened and strengthened by these experiences. Then again, young women frequently do not know what a good time they can have by themselves until they try it in college. Community and church work come more easily to them afterward if they have a background of teamwork with other women in college.

As I see it, the three-fold function of a college

(1) to develop to the full the ability of each student to face the practical problems of life and to solve these problems most effectively, (2) to help each student to cultivate her creative and imaginative powers to the full to the end that her life may be rich, happy, and socially useful, and (3) to enable each student to grow spiritually in the same degree that she grows intellectually and culturally. Unless there is this three-fold development, college is a failure. It is not enough that a woman shall be healthy and strong, and trained to earn her living. Nor is it sufficient that she be a cultivated, well-read, alert and socially intelligent individual. The growth must be three-fold, in body, mind and spirit.

The women's college is fitted by tradition and by circumstances to accomplish this highly complicated task of developing the well-rounded person. In the first place, women's colleges are relatively small institutions, and the Negro women's colleges have abided by this tradition. In any form of mass education, such as exists in the great state institutions or in the large private colleges, it is manifestly impossible for either administrators or teachers to know students intimately, or to develop that close association which is inherent in great teaching. No method has ever been perfected that is capable of overcoming this handicap, and it is unlikely that any ever will. In mass education, moreover, it is impossible for the teacher to take the proper interest in the social, cultural and spiritual growth of individual students, and unless this interest is taken, the students' full-rounded development is unlikely. Again, the traditional women's college is a place where culture and all that it implies are an inherent part of the educational process. Teachers here are not expected to be cold-blooded specialists; they are encouraged to relate their teaching to the larger cultural aspects of life. I can illustrate this best, perhaps, by recalling that Mary Lyon, the founder of Mount Holyoke, the pioneer college for women, was herself a chemistry teacher. Yet no one today remembers Mary Lyon as a chemist, but as a great-hearted, far-sighted leader of womankind who perhaps more than any other one person laid the foundation for higher education for women in this country. Finally, the women's college is traditionally a Christian college. And it still remains true that unless there is a firm and well-grounded religious faith having its expression in unselfish living, the whole superstructure of culture and intellectuality will topple.

Let us consider the first of the three major functions of the women's college, the training of the women to meet the material problems of life. Manifestly, a woman must be prepared to face life as it exists today, to be able to earn a living, to be able to handle her resources, and to cope with the manifold difficulties involved in the job of being a bread-winner, a wife and a mother. Even if the economic conditions of life for a Negro woman were ideal, which they are not, she should have this training, for in these uncertain days no one knows what she may be called on to face. A women's college by concentrating on the needs of women can effectively meet this educational challenge. In the larger co-educational institutions, there is grave danger that the obligations to women shall be lost sight of, or at least slighted. This danger that led the founders of Spelman to reject the suggestion that the seminary be united with an institution for men still exists. If Spelman had become a co-educational scheme, it is quite unlikely that the pioneering work in nurse training, in the domestic sciences, in missions education, and in teacher training would have been developed, and that Spelman would have become as she did, the early training school of practical service for Negro women in the far South.

When we enter upon a discussion of the cul-

Instruction in Fine Art, Lincoln University, Jefferson City, Missouri.

tural possibilities of the women's college, the field for great service to the race and to society opens even more widely. Women are, admittedly, the pioneers of our cultural life and the architects of our social structure, the keepers of the standards. As such, Negro women have not as yet asserted their full powers, nor yet begun to exercise their total influence. When Negro women realize that it is "up to them" to bring about better housing, to insure higher standards of health, to raise the taste of social and cultural life, and generally to improve the ways of living, then there will come about a steady revolution towards those goals. This will come when Negro women have mastered the arts of leadership. A young woman who has ably edited a college newspaper, or who has served as a forum leader, or led an interracial conference has earned for herself that measure of self-reliance that will stand her in good stead when she goes back into her community. One learns to lead by leading. In the same way, the young woman who has had full opportunity to develop her dramatic talents, to appreciate and understand good music and literature, and to engage freely in games and sports will carry back with her a full measure of her talents to her people, and if she is worth her salt, will in one way or another share her gifts and enthusiasm with those whom she lives and works. It may seem far-fetched and Utopian, but I cannot but feel that many unlovely sections in the towns and cities of the South may some day be redeemed and made to blossom, largely through the initiative and steady efforts of Negro college women who will bring about a clean-up of unsightly spots, the elimination of billboards, the creation of parks, the beautification of public places, and the general improvement of outward conditions. Along with this would go, of course, the betterment of child life, of schools, of social and recreational facilities, and of social conditions generally. I can think of no greater good that the women's college can do than to train a continuing generation of students who will go out to their myriad home towns, and each in her own way exert a quiet, yet persistent and effective influence in the social settlement of her community.

As to the place in the women's college for the development of Christian character, it must be obvious that here, if anywhere, is favored the quiet, orderly growth of Christian womanhood. The close association of administrators and teachers with individual students, the leisure for quiet thought and meditation, the temptation to be utterly sincere and honest with one-self, the upreaching of ideals, and the opportunity for the functioning of student Christian organizations, all these are possible in the quiet of a women's college campus. In the hurly-burly of the larger colleges, religious activities are likely to be subordinated to second place. Almost inevitably, Christian organizations within these larger colleges languish in their hurried, hectic atmosphere. The ways in which a college-trained woman may advance the cause of the religious life of the community in which she lives are legion. There is no field in which a college woman can work more effectively, exert a wider influence, or better justify her investment of years and money in a college education. As a worker in a church, the Sunday School, the young peoples' society, or the women's mission group, or as a Christian individual, living according to the highest standards of life, the college woman may exert a powerful influence in her community.

Before I leave this discussion and the endless possibilities which the subject opens, I wish to recall a message which was brought to our campus last spring by a great social-educational leader, who is charged with the supervision of the work of the Rockefeller Foundation in China. He told us how because of the limited funds available to educate the people of China's great rural areas, schools were set up where men and women were taught the fundamentals of reading and were enabled to learn sufficient Chinese characters to master simple texts dealing with principles of health, sanitation, and other basic matters. Then these men and women went out and taught what they had learned to others, and so the good was spread in turn to thousands of underprivileged and depressed people. This must be the spirit that motivates Negro education, particularly the education of Negro women, who must go forth from college and share to the full with their fellows what they have gained. It is not enough that a woman shall become a self-contained, economically independent, and completely rounded individual. Neither is it sufficient that she shall have developed her taste for the good things of life and acquired skills in the arts. If the college has succeeded in its purpose, she will be not only willing but eager to share her gifts and use her newly acquired skills to better the lives of all those within the reach of her influence. And by that strange paradox which is the profoundest truth yet discovered or revealed, it is thus that her own life will reach its richest fulfillment.

White Staff Life at Spelman

Dorothy K. Clark, excerpts from her unpublished
autobiography.

(Schlesinger Library, Radcliffe College, Cambridge, Mass., reprinted by
permission)

Dorothy Kneeland Clark served as secretary to Dr. Florence
Matilda Read, president of Spelman College from 1937 to 1940. A
white woman who had a Ph.D. in history from Radcliffe, she provided
a different perspective to Spelman in the late 1930s. Excerpts
from her unpublished autobiography are published by permission from
the Schlesinger Library.

Having discussed her activities within the college, Clark turns to
town-gown relations:

"Outside the enclave [of Spelman] my Atlanta adventure was
quite different. I was well briefed in the beginning by Miss Read
and others. Never invite a racial incident unless the black person
you are with wants it, understands the potentialities, and is
willing to accept the results, and preferably not even then. If
you do get in trouble, there are three men (high in the city
hierarchy) who will help you, but don't expect quick or obvious
aid. If you go anywhere outside the enclave with a black man, you
are breaking the law. (Happily I never had to use my
often-practiced statement, 'I can't help it if my father was a
light-skinned man,' although occasionally a black man was brave
enough to drive with me in the front seat beside him.) If you get
into trouble off campus, head for Spelman. The night watchman was
nicknamed 'Mr. Will-Shoot,' and this was no idle joke. There were
a few rumors about episodes which fortunately did not develop into
anything serious. Irene Diggs had been pursued onto the campus by
two armed men; one of the professors who was a Harvard graduate had
a set-to with a gas station attendant who called him by his first
name. The possibility of an episode hung over us constantly;
however, I must confess that I rather enjoyed that little spice of
danger." (pp. 11-12)

Under Read's leadership, Spelman was transformed from a women's
seminary to a college of first rank. In order to do this, Read had
to walk the tightrope common to presidents of other black colleges:
keeping the students happy with their college life, while
simultaneously pleasing rich white donors, in Spelman's case, the
Rockefellers.

Read was [in 1937] "well aware of the growing impatience among
the students at being regarded as beknighted heathens and at being
subjected to rigid discipline. Her intent was to bring the college
to as close an approximation of the general run of women's colleges
in the United States as possible without alienating any outside
monetary assistance." (p. 69)
Miss Read had a difficult line to tread. The 'old sisters,'
as the students termed most Spelman alumnae, were extremely
critical and straight-laced, at least in regard to their successors
at Spelman." Miss Read's own inclinations and those of most of the
Spelman trustees centered on development of the academic standards
of the college; individual life practices were pertinent only as
such activities detracted from academic achievements. Individual
students had already proved that they could hold their own in
intense competition as they went on to graduate work in well-known
northern institutions. The numbers who could do this, Miss Read
and the trustees believed, must be increased." (pp. 72-73)

Bennett College: Another Black Woman's College

Constance H. Marteena, "A College For Girls"
(*Opportunity*, 16 (October, 1938), 306–307)

A College For Girls

By CONSTANCE H. MARTEENA

A Bennett Art Student

"**W**HEN you educate a man you educate an individual, but when you educate a woman you educate a family."

This ancient adage well expresses the aim and spirit of little Bennett College, in Greensboro, North Carolina. Operated for the past twelve years exclusively for women, its entire curriculum is geared to provide its students the type of education that not only will make them intelligent, alert, and progressive, but that will go a long way towards helping them establish worthwhile homes and happy families as well.

President David D. Jones, who has headed the institution since 1926, firmly believes that there is a very definite place in our educational scheme for a college exclusively for girls. He has envisioned Bennett as a place where young women might have the opportunity to discover themselves, and to learn and grow in the best possible environment.

In its twelve years of existence as a women's college, Bennett has made unusual progress. Beginning with ten students and a few buildings, it has grown until today its student body numbers over 300 and is drawn from twenty-two states. It has acquired an endowment of nearly half a million dollars, and during the past few years it has been able to spend an equal sum on permanent improvements.

The background, attainments, and capacities of each prospective student are studied before she is admitted to the college. A definite program and a course of study is mapped out as soon as she matriculates. Faculty advisors observe her development throughout the four-year period of study and keep a record for her future guidance.

The curriculum is so organized as to surround each student with wholesome and inspiring influences. Formally, it includes four major divisions, Biological and Physical Sciences, Social Sciences, Home Economics, and the Humanities.

A Class in Homemaking

Students are free to major in any of these divisions, but all are required to take a course in "The Art of Living," which aims to give a comprehensive idea and appreciation of life in its everyday setting. The course includes the study of personal hygiene, costume art, personality development, the use of time and money, and family and community life. Informally, Bennett offers a free and happy student life. There are the usual religious, social, and study clubs, but there are also a number of groups devoted to community recreational and civic work.

The latitude of the college extra-curricular program enables every student to find some one thing that she can do well, and enjoy. Students interested in social welfare recently made a study of Negro life in Greensboro, and turned over a summary of their findings to the social service agencies of the city. The student Little Theatre Guild won special recognition last year at the dramatic festival of the University of North Carolina. The college choir has made frequent appearances in churches of all creeds and denominations. A Home-Making Institute, conducted each spring since 1927 by the Department of Home Economics, has proved an excellent means of setting before the student body and the community at large the importance of all phases of home life. A Nursery School and Parent Education Center, recently established, now serves as an observation laboratory for students and parents, further extending the college's influence upon the community.

Thus Bennett has won for itself a definite and important place in the field of Negro education. Staffed by a faculty carefully selected and thoroughly devoted to the educational development of young people, and headed by a man who has given the best of his energy and time to its development, it is generally acknowledged to be a living, a growing, and a thoroughly progressive institution.

Bethune-Cookman College in the 1930s

Notes of Ward N. Madison of the Rockefeller Foundation,
January 2–3, 1938
(Rockefeller Archive Center)

ARM		*ARM*

Dr. Abram L. Simpson
and others
at
Bethune-Cookman College
Daytona Beach, Fla.

January 2-5, 1938

Bethune-Cookman College

I attended the regular Sunday afternoon service held at the College. Some 500-600 persons, practically all white and largely female, filled the auditorium; students of the College sang in chorus, gave dramatic recitations; Mrs. Bethune and Dr. Simpson spoke; a collection was taken (about $80); tea and cakes were served in Faith Hall, and certain articles of food and clothing were on sale. After the meeting I met Mrs. Bethune and Dr. Simpson, and through them several of the faculty.

Returning Monday morning, I went through the buildings with Dr. Simpson, noting especially the small library building where there are seats and tables for about 85 students, inadequate shelf and catalog space, and books in great need of repair. Discussing the library, Dr. Simpson said he sought light on how important the library should be in the Junior College set-up. "We are not getting the best results out of the library at present," he said. "If we get a new library, I want the students to spend the major portion of their time in it; now they have courses from 8 to 4:30 and do not have free time to spend in the library. The Dean wants to keep them in class, releasing them only occasionally."

Continuing his discussion, Dr. Simpson pointed out that at present Bethune-Cookman is a one-sided Junior College, with undue emphasis upon a college-preparatory course and too little emphasis upon "terminal" occupations. There is only one student in home economics, although all have certain training in home economics. "Very few vocations are given here, only stenography and typewriting." "We are all equipped for college-preparatory emphasis; we need an activities building for more emphasis on industrial arts, home economics, etc. I would rather have an activities building than a library, but it is almost as hard now to secure money for vocational activities as for academic pursuits. We need space for painting, woodworking, carpentry, masonry, etc., so that we can put on a program of activities furnishing certain terminal occupations which at present we cannot give because of lack of equipment. And we will have to get rid of some of the older people (teachers) who don't know the new activities. At present many are teaching only 9 to 10 hours, whereas it is legitimate to have them teach 15 to 16."

Enrollment at present is 202, 17 of whom are high school students and 185 in the junior college years. Of last year's graduates, 10 went on to college, and of that number 6 received football scholarships (to Morehouse). The facilities of the College would accommodate 250, according to Dr. Simpson. There are 155 boarding students just now. Some 378 attended the last summer school session. In general, the high school enrollment has been decreasing (it was 48 in February, 1934) and the college enrollment remaining constant or increasing (185 in February, 1934, and 178 for 1936-37).

Dr. Simpson said that he had just gotten out the Bulletin for 1937-38, no issue having been published for a few years past. I marked a few points, especially pages 12, 13, 23, and 85; also pages 14 & 15.

Mrs. Bethune plans to form an executive group within the Board of Trustees. This group, she feels, would be more active and wieldy than the present rather large Board. With reference to the library, Mrs. Bethune said there was on deposit in New York about $13,000 earmarked for the library in memory of Harrison Rhodes, who left his Estate to the College subject to the life interest of his sister. (See letter dated 11/24/37 from Dr. Simpson to GEB.) Mrs. Bethune said there were now about 6500 volumes in the library, many of which are inaccessible due to insufficient space for shelving and cataloging.

In planning for a new library, Dr. Simpson indicated his hope that the new building, if, as, and when erected, might be located at a distance from the street, considerably south of the present site, and thus increase the open area in the center of the campus.

The College has recently received a number of household articles from the home of Mr. Rockefeller, Senior, in Ormond Beach, including blankets, kitchen utensils, and an electric organ. In her address on Sunday afternoon, Mrs. Bethune pleaded for gifts of all kinds, from dish cloths, rakes and brooms to "a ten-dollar bill from each of four persons present." In other years, Mrs. Bethune said, she would have raised a thousand dollars at such a meeting; this time it was eighty.

Mr. Rupert J. Longstreet, Principal of one of the two white high schools in Daytona Beach and a member of the Board of Trustees of Bethune-Cookman College, said he considered the College was doing "a good piece of work and needs more support." He felt it might be "more like Tuskegee and less like Stetson," but that certain things are required by the laws of the state for teachers and that the college curriculum had been adjusted accordingly.

There is a large Advisory Board of the College, made up chiefly of women of means and influence who have contributed of both. The "moving spirit" of this Board, Mrs. C. M. Ranslow, is a nearby Florida resident and one of the most active workers among the white people on behalf of the College. She spoke briefly and emotionally at the Sunday afternoon meeting. The list of members of this Advisory Board is given on pages 61 and 62 of the Bulletin for 1937-38.

Dr. Simpson is Acting President of the College. For the past five years he has been President of Allen University at Columbia, S. C. He stated that his biggest problem was learning how to work with Mrs. Bethune and carry on constructively and with her approval. His budget for the current year is nearly $74,000 as against last year's actual expenses of just over $105,000. The plant is operated in four quarterly periods, the summer session having the largest enrollment.

A Black Student at a White Institution: 1940s Perspective

Edythe Hargrave, "How I Feel as a Negro at a White College" (*Journal of Negro Education,* 11 (October, 1942), 484–486, reprinted by permission)

How I Feel as a Negro at a White College

EDYTHE HARGRAVE

I decided to go to a white college. I lived in the town where it was situated; consequently, I would not have the expense of room and board that would follow if I chose a Negro college; my brother had been graduated from this college; and, also, I had heard it said that a colored student who graduated from that institution was highly respected for his scholastic ability.

I realized, however, that a Negro entering a large institution of thirty-one hundred students of whom twenty were Negroes would lack the social life that goes with a well-rounded education. First of all, being a Negro, I was exempt from all the sororities on the campus. I knew that I would never dress for a sorority "rush" party, or become a pledge. I knew, also, that I would never dance at the Sigma Chi or the Delta Tau houses. Yet, I chose a white college.

I had heard that the professors graded Negro students lower simply because they were Negroes. Yes, I had heard certain incidents about different professors that were surely no encouragement to me. "Don't get him! Why he flunked so and so!"

Some of my Negro friends pointed out that they would never think of going to a white college. "I want the social life," they said. "The social phase of college life is the most important."

Well, I entered a white college with the determination to confront all of the white faces over there, and show them that I could be one of them

scholastically, even if my color were different, even if I were conspicuous. Mine was the determination to be a good student.

Strange it is that regardless of how many Negro faces a white person has seen, another coming before him still causes that extra glance of "look who's here; well!" I found that my biggest task was to accustom the students to my presence in the classroom. I found that upon entering a class for the first time, I met many surprised glances and looks of "Do colored students go here?" or frowns of disgust that said, "Here comes a nigger!" and still little pleasant smiles that said, "I think I would need a smile if I had to enter and try to become one of us!" I found that when I spoke the rooms would be in complete silence to see what the Negro girl was going to say. Well, honestly, my reaction was to show these people that I was a good student. This idea has obsessed me throughout my two years here. Perhaps some may say that I am a "show-off"; but that is not my aim at all. I cannot help feeling, however, that if I am down scholastically, and a Negro also, I might as well leave this place. So in the classroom I talk; I make myself heard; I make my professors realize that I can speak, that I can ably use the English language, that I, too, have prepared my lesson.

Another significant point about being a Negro at a white college is my contact with the professors. Interestingly, I am the only Negro in my classes. Therefore, all of my professors

484

learn my name readily; and I have found that most of them call upon me frequently, some to see what I actually do know, and others to make me feel that I am not being neglected. I find that I have their deepest courtesy and respect; I am always spoken to. I have, however, always had the fear, perhaps unjustly, that a professor might too easily classify me in the C group, and then "feel me out" to see if I might possibly deviate a notch above or below that mark. Maybe such a feeling comes from the Negro hate of slavery, of being classed inferior; but I always make it my aim to show my professors that I am good. I feel that then I gain respect from them because of my scholastic standing, and not respect out of sympathy for my being, I might say, alone here. Now, professors have praised me for my work, told me that I can expect an A if I keep up the good work. I haven't found that keen discrimination that I was told of. I feel that I can get what I deserve. I do not intend to convey the feeling that I am only seeking grades, and if I can obtain the grades, I have conquered the prejudice at this white college. I know that this is not true. I am seeking respect and high rating, not because I am a Negro doing well, but because I am another student at this institution.

In the Physical Education Department I have discovered more prejudice than anywhere else on the campus. I feel (and I quite freely admit) that I will be glad to complete my physical education requirements. I feel more that I am a Negro in those classes; a keen sense of inferiority empowers me there. Maybe it is that the girls are given more freedom with their friends; and that truly a Negro friend is not needed. Maybe it is that embarrassment which follows their revealing that they know a colored girl too well; maybe it is that the girls would never stop laughing at the dorm; maybe it is that dancing with a Negro is disgraceful. I avoided the discomfiture and hurt pride by attending classes with another Negro friend of mine for a while, but since her death, I have been forced to enroll in classes alone. Also, I have been engaging in all the individual sports possible; but there was the time when I was one among three hundred girls at a social dance; and the instructor and one other girl ventured to drag me over the floor, when all of the other girls had run frantically clutching at each other to dance with everyone else but me, simply because I was a Negro, a brown conspicuous person. That was the time I went home and fell across the bed and cried, cried until I was exhausted. That was the time I hated a white college!

It is true that I would enjoy going to the formals in Brant Room at Kumler Dorm and the fraternity dances. It is true that I would enjoy having my brown legs hang over the side of one of those long trucks that take boys and girls on hayrides and to picnics, but I have become adjusted to not attending these affairs. I have never been part of them, so I do not miss them. I take in a Varsity dance now and then, and I know I am free to go to the Senior Ball and Junior Prom, but I am forced to walk around with resentment toward the white students who sing as those trucks roll them toward home, who parade High

Street on Saturday night in their formal attire. I am going to this college to learn. I will let the leadership and activity in various social events await postgraduation. I knew that I could not have these other things upon entering this white college.

Yes, I am a Negro attending a white college. That's all right. I do not go around the campus day after day and hour after hour feeling that I am a Negro, and that I am not treated right. What if I am a Negro here? That attitude would make any dog hang his head. Well, I am keeping my head up. I am going forward. It is true that some of these students might crack a joke about my being a prospective girl friend to one of their fraternity brothers; and then, it is true that I dodge some of my white friends because they treat me too nicely. Somehow they have the feeling that it is their duty to go to the extreme in treating me nicely just because I am a Negro. Maybe they feel sorry for me; I don't know. Their seemingly sincere interest perhaps doesn't affect me as they feel it does. I am not attending this college for sympathy, but for high achievement and respect as another college student.

I dodged the white boy that suddenly became my friend because I had my lesson prepared every day. It was much easier to ask the Negro girl after he once found she was capable; because then his white friends would never know just how inefficient he was. Yes, they ask me the answers and the assignments now, since they have found that I am reliable. I am much too smart to regard this as a distinction, however. I know when I am being used; I have spoken too many times and not been spoken to.

I like this white college. I have become very much broader. I can sit in American Literature now and hear "nigger," "nigger," "nigger" in Twain's *Huckleberry Finn*, hear the Negro dialect in Harris's *Uncle Remus Stories*. History class doesn't bother me with its discussions of slavery, emancipation, and Abraham Lincoln; government class doesn't bother me with discussions of Negro suffrage in the South. I am too broad now. The Red Cap Revue with the little Negro puppet "jitterbugging" under the control of a string moved by a white boy's hand didn't inflame me. Here, I am learning to face life. My aim is to forget the color of my skin, avoid being emotionally aroused because of ill-treatment because of my conspicuousness. I would be a fool to let these immature white students ruin my chance for a college education. I must go on.

It feels all right to be a Negro at a white college if you do not walk around feeling black, feeling conspicuous, if you do not sit in class with your mouth shut because you are a Negro, if you do not feel that every misfortune happened because you were a Negro. Feeling inferior makes one inferior!

219

The Black College Woman of the 1940s

Marion Vera Cuthbert, "Background of the Negro College Woman"
(*A Study of the Negro College Woman,* dissertation, Columbia University, 1942, 11–19)

CHAPTER II

BACKGROUND OF THE NEGRO COLLEGE WOMAN

In 1862, Oberlin College graduated a Negro woman,[1] the first in this country to be graduated with an A.B. degree. The first white woman had been graduated from Oberlin in 1841.[2]

In the middle and late years of the nineteenth century two of the important social questions in the United States centered around the extension of higher education to women and the extension of learning to Negroes.

The first of these struggles was characterized by the same interest which in the Western World has been attached to all other attempts of its women to be accepted as full personalities, which means according them all opportunities open to adult intelligence, as well as allowing them full citizenship responsibilities. Conceding women the right to higher education was fairly general in all parts of the country after the Civil War,[3] and the last decades of the century saw the extension of college education to women both in co-educational institutions and in colleges especially planned for women. With the winning of this right, many women surged into all the avenues of liberalism

[1] Miriam J. Patterson. For the reproduction of the first college diploma and degree received by a Negro woman in the United States (1862) see: *The Aframerican Woman's Journal*, Vol. 1, Nos. 2 and 3, Summer and Fall, 1940, p. 29.

[2] There is some question about the time of granting the first degrees to white women. Mississippi College, founded in 1830, is reported to have granted degrees to two young women in 1832; the Georgia Female College graduated its first class in 1840; but both the nature of these degrees and the type of college represented have been questioned.

"... it was not till 1841 that women graduated in the full and strong course at Oberlin with the A.B. degree." Three women are listed as graduates for that year. (Taylor, James Monroe, *Before Vassar Opened*, pp. 19, 16, 20, 22, 41.)

[3] See Woody, Thomas, *A History of Women's Education in the United States*, Vol. 1, p. 395.

11

then existing in their sphere—the suffrage movement, social work, the fight for the abolition of child labor, and socialism.[4]

The second struggle, giving learning to Negroes, was a most intense matter, for the bitter aftermath of war was involved, and the blocking of the generous impulses of the liberal-minded men and women of the North, who essayed to pierce what was so recently enemy territory, stirred to a crusading zeal the spirits of these carriers of learning to the freed men. The whole story has been told now with comprehension and understanding (43—Parts II, III); only a few parts remain for special illumination by the interpretive scholar.

One such part concerns the role of the white woman teacher of this period. It is a fair assumption both from the numbers of women teachers and from the kinds of tasks inherent in the problem of reshaping the lives of Negro students that white women played a conspicuous part in developing the newly freed people. Their place in the development of education among Negroes is of great importance for two reasons: for the special imprint which the austere concepts of these religious-minded women made on the cultural life of the Negro;[5] for the close parallel between their own struggle for education and that of the Negro group.

"The history of higher education for women generally," according to Johnson, "is recapitulated on a small scale, and with

[4] "Back in that day [last decade of the nineteenth century] those who could leave their own homes were plunging into the woman's suffrage movement, into social settlement life, into assistance in shirt waist and other strikes, into work for family relief, for child welfare, for child labor legislation, for improved recreational opportunities for the masses, for the advancement of the cause of socialism." (Mills, Herbert Elmer, *College Women and the Social Sciences*, p. 4.)

[5] "The teachers had to be persons possessing great faith in the possibilities of humanity and willing to lose themselves in their task and to endure hardships, social isolation, insult, and often personal danger. They lived with their students and taught them lessons in living outside of school hours often more valuable than the lessons learned in the classrooms." (Holmes, *op. cit.*, p. 98.)

"This moral surveillance [of white preceptresses or matrons], as intimate and unescapable as conscience, stalked dormitory halls at all hours of the night, inspected mail, investigated, lectured, warned, punished guilt, and rewarded virtue. No less stern rectitude and concern could have broken the grip of habits adjusted to a now out-moded life of irresponsibility, and re-shaped them to a new and more serious purpose." (Johnson, *op. cit.*, p. 287.)

12

only a slight lag in the case of the Negro college population" (16–56). The entire struggle of white women for status has apparently been closely tied up with the struggle of the Negro for freedom and status. Literature concerning this period shows that women became more conscious of their rights as they worked for the rights of other human beings:

> In 1840 a group of delegates from the United States went to London to attend an international congress for the abolition of slavery. In this delegation were a number of women, and, being women, they were not allowed to take their places in the convention. On returning home, they met together and started a rebellion against the subordinate position imposed upon women by law and custom (87–5).
>
> Lucy Stone or Elizabeth Cady Stanton, lecturing wherever they could get a hearing, might talk nine times on Women's Rights, but the tenth time they would give to Abolition (14–225).

The close connection between race problems and social problems including the further emancipation of women is also pointed out by DuBois (61–69) and others, and striking similarities are to be noted as between the latter-day trends in the development of the status of American women and the development of the status of the American Negro. Groves notes four trends for women from 1900 to 1941: (1) changes in domestic and social habits and reshaping of conventions; (2) greater invasion into industry; (3) progress in women's organizations; (4) the change in feeling, a new outlook upon life (41–325). Precisely the same description could be made of the changes most pronounced in the Negro group, noting particularly in the time span for the Negro group the two decades following the World War.

With regard to higher education, all groups in the country have come a long way since the turn of the century, but for two groups achievement has been beyond that which the most sanguine envisaged—the women of the country and the Negroes of the country.

13

When Thomas Jesse Jones pointed out in 1916 in his notable survey of higher education among Negroes that no type of education is more eagerly sought after by the colored people than college education, he stated a simple fact (83—55). But behind this fact is the group's unique experience, and this experience has been recognized in a general way by all who have been acquainted with the ideals and objectives operating within the Negro group.

To explain in the large how the Negro's drive for education arose and why it operates even today with such force is no matter for profound research. We need only to remember that there was a time when education was denied to black folk, and that this denial early placed a premium on it; to consider the harsh toil they endured in order to understand how escape through the door of education came to be the great hope, remembering, too, that to a greater or lesser degree the same hope stirred the hearts of all our native poor and the recent immigrant; to realize that freedom and opportunity of the sort the Negro was given could permit a moneyed aristocracy no growth, and to understand, therefore, that the aristocracy of the educated took its place. To this should be added the impetus given by the churches in their desire to educate the Negro, and also the national and international fame that individual Negroes received—Booker T. Washington, W. E. B. DuBois, Mary Church Terrell, John Hope, Mary McLeod Bethune, and others —because of their intellectual achievements or their efforts on behalf of the education of their people.

Having tasted of this desired fruit—education—what is the nature of that salvation which has come to the Negro?

A recent report on economic security in this country states that "it is tragically evident that education and training are not a guarantee against dependency and destitution" (20—47) in any group. This fact is the first to strike the attention of the person looking about in the Negro world and pondering upon the kind and quantity of education found in it. Considering everything, a fairly large percentage of the Negro group now receives

14

high school and college training, but the prejudice that asserts that Negroes are suited only for unskilled work keeps 67 per cent of them in unskilled work as over against 22 per cent of native white and 29 per cent of foreign-born whites (31—356). Moreover, this unskilled work, when it is available, pays poorly.

It is from the middle and lower classes, economically speaking, that a large percentage of Negro college students comes. Typical of the kind of income of the families of Negro college students is that described in Caliver's *Background Study of Negro Students*. The families of all of the two thousand students studied had a median monthly income of $94.72. "That Negro students, whose parents have an economic background represented by so low a range of monthly income as $63.50 to $161.41, manage to enroll and remain in college is one of the enigmas in the Negro's progress" (16.—78-9).

A comparison of the situation of the average Negro college student with that of college students of the total population is appropriate here:

> Those from families with higher incomes get to college; those from families with lower incomes find it much harder. Among the 5,000,000 young persons of college age from families with incomes of $1,700 up, one out of every five was in college; but among those 6,500,000 young persons from families below this level, only one out of every 26 was able to attend college (90—49).

In this world of the poor where a large group of families of low income manage to keep just one step ahead of destitution itself, Negro men and women still believe in the potency of education to help clear away the bad elements in the situation and they toil prodigiously to send their sons and their daughters to college.

Johnson notes a striking increase in Negro women college students in recent years, especially since they began sharing higher education freely with men (46—57). In the whole group of 5512 graduates in the Johnson study, 1994 (36.2 per cent) are

15

women. From all indications this is the present ratio (46–56). The increase in Negro women college students has caused alarm in some quarters. Caliver points out the existence of a genuinely serious situation because of the disproportionate number of girls compared with boys ready for the freshman year of college.[6]

With this great increase in the number of Negro college women it is still true, however, that more men than women are college graduates, for it is more possible for men to take the initiative about their education, even though family groups usually rally to the aid of the ambitious boy or boys in the family. Caliver found that 30 per cent of men as contrasted with less than 10 per cent of women anticipated earning all of their support in college; that over 55 per cent of men as contrasted with about 25 per cent of women anticipated earning at least half of their support; while less than 20 per cent of men as contrasted with over 50 per cent of women anticipated earning none of their own support (16–41). Doubtless, also, the nature of the masculine drive in a masculine-dominated civilization operates to send men to college.

The willingness today on the part of Negro families to send daughters to college can largely be explained by the facts of the social situation which confronts the Negro people living in the United States.

The foremost fact in this social situation is that the work open to all educated Negroes is in fields where women as a whole have their best work opportunities. For all men in the country the chief occupations are manufacturing, agriculture, and trade; for all women in the country they are domestic and personal service, clerical occupations, manufacturing, and professional work. Pidgeon says: "In their five major occupation

[6] "Negro schools and colleges are not making the most of the masculine resources of the race.

"Although, as is shown by a recent study, the enrollment of Negro boys in the first two grades surpassed that for girls, by the time the freshman year of college is reached the ratio has changed in favor of the girls. . . . Without disparaging what is being done for girls, the continued progress of the race and its future welfare dictate that a larger proportion of our boys and young men be given the opportunity of a higher education." (Caliver, *op. cit.*, pp. 100-107.)

16

groups, women outnumber men only in domestic and personal service, though they almost equal men in clerical work and are not far behind them in professional service, the last mentioned being due in a large measure to the number of women who are teachers (65—19)." Figures for the 1940 Census show that women now actually outnumber men in professional and related services. Now, among the Negro people agriculture and domestic and personal service afford employment to 65 per cent of their workers. Among Negroes in the occupational groups having smaller percentages there is a heavy concentration in teaching, a field where women in general have their best professional opportunity; and while the proportions of Negroes in social work and clerical occupations are still small—fields where women in general have some of their best opportunities for work—these are among the best work opportunities for Negroes after teaching (86—90).

Pidgeon also believes that "From the advancement in the education of women it was a logical result that they should be able to take up the kinds of work that led to their great increase as school teachers, social workers, stenographers, typists, and other clerical workers; . . ." (65—17). The Negro family knows that the girl has a chance for a job as a teacher or in some form of social service, and while the reasoning is not close, it knows also that when the economic situation becomes strained, women—paid nearly everywhere a lower wage than men (65—6) for the same work undercut men for available work in these fields. Johnson says concerning a study of unemployment among Negroes in New Jersey in 1932: "The per cent of Negro male college graduates unemployed was 5.4 and of female college graduates 2.6" (46—110).

Closely related, of course, to economic opportunity is economic responsibility. Quite aside from the heritage of the disorganized family life—before freedom, the woman had to be the stable element in the family because of the children (37—45)—today also, since there may be better chances of work for the woman than for the man, it seems wise to give the Negro woman

17

that help and training which will enable her to be the family security if needs be.[1]

A second factor in the situation is that the work conditions of a particular family may be such that the young girl can best be spared. This is particularly true if the family is engaged in agriculture, or where there may be supporting jobs in the heavy industries for both the older and the younger men of the family group.

Less obvious factors are also part of the picture. It may be a mark of prestige for a family to send a girl to college; the prestige may arise either from the family's ability to send her or the envisaged hope—not too often realized because of work opportunities away from home, and marriage—that the daughter will return and influence the whole family group with ideas and ways of living obtained at college. Among some families, still another reason is found in the intention to have the girl acquire a higher marriage opportunity and desirability, for education will give her an elevation in class, and, other things being equal, she may have better marriage opportunities. Sometimes, too, college is seen as a means of getting a girl away from undesirable surroundings, and the college, particularly those that follow the early missionary-school traditions, is seen as a safe shelter. And there are also now, of course, a number of family groups having a father or mother, or both, with college background, and in many of these families sending the children to college is taken as a matter of course.

For whatever reasons, we now have a sizable number of Negro college women. The Johnson study listed 1994 graduates out of more than 2000 Negro women graduates for the period 1870–1932. The acceleration in the rate of graduation for Negro

[1] The education of Negro women for the support of the family does not present a unique situation in the development of education for women. In a reference to the education of Sarah Pierce, Woody points this out for early days: "Her brother, knowing she must help support the family, early conceived the idea of sending her to New York to be educated . . ." (Woody, op. cit., Vol. I, p. 340.) The particular aspect applying to Negro women is the numbers for whom higher education is made a possibility for such a reason.

18

women from colleges began in the early nineteen twenties and has continued upward to the present time. These women were graduated from colleges in both the North and the South, with an increasing number coming from northern institutions.

This study will be largely concerned with attempting to learn something of the attitudes of a group of Negro women toward the college experience, something of the satisfactions and dissatisfactions they have with regard to it, how they see themselves functioning in a number of ways in our society and the contribution of the college education to that functioning.

Before, however, taking up the opinions and interpretations of the respondents to the questionnaire, which has already been noted as the basis for the study, we shall need to see the general picture that the group presents.

19

Problems in Black Women's College Education

F[lemmie] P. Kittrell, "Current Problems and Programs in the
Higher Education of Negro Women"
(Quarterly Review of Higher Education, 12 (January, 1944), 13–15)

Current Problems and Programs in the Higher Education of Negro Women

By F. P. KITTRELL

Any country at war finds the role of its women shifted considerably. In fact, it can be said that war affects women more fundamentally than it does men. All of our major wars have changed the status of women for better or for worse. Russia, after the Revolution, attempted the absolute equality of men and women. The apparent emancipation of German women under the Republic following the first world war is a great contrast to her return to home duties under the Hitler Regime.

In any discussion of the higher education of women, we will remember that there are many problems in common with those of men. Her formal education, however, is much younger—for the most part under one-hundred years' old. We find that there are many fundamental problems based on tradition, sanctions and restrictions. These make it extremely difficult for the intelligent women to fulfill her role effectively.

A great many activity studies have been made of women's work after leaving college. The study conducted by Dr. W. W. Charters for Stephens College is one of the most outstanding. The studies of any note have been conducted in relation to white women. Programs of studies have been developed around the findings—yet the American woman on a whole, has not reached the goals that she knows she can and ought to reach. We will discuss this fact later on in the paper.

What about the Current Problems and Programs of Negro Women today? Our problems are basically the same as all other women—except that we have additional handicaps of race, followed by prejudice and segregation. These facts enter into practically every phase of our life and further warp and cripple our personalities so that they never quite reach fulfillment. That is our background. What are some of the major facts facing us today?

More than a million women graduated from colleges and universities between 1900 and 1930. There were few women graduating from professional schools prior to 1920. In 1900 about 41 per cent of the enrollment of Teacher's colleges consisted of men, while in 1931 only 21 per cent were men. College women including all races—have increased almost 600 per cent from 1900 to 1930. Th number is still on the increase. Prior to 1941, the enrollment of women in Negro colleges far outnumbered men. In a recent sampling of Negro Colleges for this year's enrollment, it was found that more than five times as many women as men are enrolled. This is what was expected of course, due to the lowering of the draft age to eighteen years for men.

If the trend in womens' enrollment in Negro Colleges continues after the duration as before, there will be very definite problems that we will have to face. The traditional cultural pattern will, no doubt change. Negro women will, as other women, change their concept concerning their own personal role in groups, their attitude toward the home and family, religious outlook, marriage, their participation in civic life and public welfare, their economic responsibility to society and their point of view toward war.

Does our present program help them to face and meet these problems adequately? Pearl Buck thinks not—we can only answer these questions partially from the studies that are available, and studies now in the making.[1] Let us cite briefly the role of the average Negro College woman graduate now working in Civil Service jobs in Washington. On her job she performs her skills well—but is almost totally lacking in those social attitudes which makes her liked by people. She is loud in manner, not careful in dress, not tactful in dealing with people and on a whole does not present a co-operative attitude in working with the group. Of course the pressure of Washington these days makes a difference in people's behavior, but should our education fit us for just such pressures as these—to see and work toward our purposeful goals no matter what the difficulty.

Other studies of Negro college women show that a great majority of them are able to find employment in their chosen field, but there is little correlation between their general education and their ability to function satisfactorily as a member of the family. Her health habits are poorer when she leaves college than when she entered—not withstanding that health and physical education are required of all students.[2] She finds it difficult to live within her income and to manage her resources well, including her time. She has taken a full college program each year—including courses in religion, history, economics and the like, yet her point of view towards life lacks direction. She is confused and there are social and other prejudices, that continue to warp her mind. In marriage there is conflict and much difficulty in adjusting to her marriage role. The care and protection of children—one of her chief roles in life—is strange to her and she starts a new life off on the wrong foot. A knowledge of food—so essential to the welfare of all—is learned only partially after she and her family have had evidence of deficiencies, diseases and low vitality. She is so tied down with home problems that she finds it impossible to participate in community activities for the common good of all. Her knowledge of voting is not adequate. These are some of the many problems that we face in our Negro College women graduates today. Not all of them in any one graduate—but a combination of two or more in a great many. And may I add here that our Negro Colleges are turning out some excellent women graduates who are able to take their place in the world with dignity and make their adequate contribution to the general welfare.

There are other problems in relation to employment in industry. Mr. Heningburg now of the Urban League will have some information on this point, which he is now preparing for this study.

War jobs and the Women's Army Corps have taken many young women from the College campus. What the effect will be of this move, we do not know—time will tell. We know, of course, that Negro women have not been given the opportunity to participate in the WAVES and SPARS.

Some attempts have been made by Colleges whereby women are participating more fully in the war effort—courses in health, foods, first aid, child care, home nursing, auto mechanics, physics, mathematics, agriculture, foreign languages and the like have been added to the program. Accelerated programs are tried by many colleges.

All of these efforts are good as far as they go, but they do not go far enough. They continue to make piecemeals out of education, rather than working them into a total pattern for living. We still do not help our women to

1 Information gathered of College Women employed in Washington and living in the government homes. L. M. Jetton.
2 A sampling of a few outstanding Negro Colleges.

see life as a whole—nor do we help them to sense the responsibility of carrying their full load in working for the democratic way of life. This will include helping to remove barriers to living, doing away with restrictions and outworn customs and traditions that warp the mind and make it impossible for women to reach their full status and do the work they know they can and should do.

Pearl Buck in her book, *Of Men and Women* has this to say:
"The whole nation would be better off if all women would do the work waiting for them to do, not only because these women themselves would be happier, but because their relations with men would be more satisfying than they are now."—They would and should be pulling their full load.

The Negro Colleges have a big job facing them now and after the duration, as to its women students. What shall be their future role in our society?

The Effect of World War II on Black College Women, 1944

Excerpt from minutes of the Fifteenth Annual Conference of the National Association of Deans of Women and Advisers to Girls in Negro Schools
(North Carolina State College for Negroes, April 6–8, 1944, 232–239)

Fifteenth Annual Conference of the

National Association of Deans of Women and Advisers To Girls in Negro Schools

Women Students in Today's and Tomorrow's World
April 6 - 8, 1944 North Carolina State College for Negroes
Durham, North Carolina

OFFICERS

President:
Flemmie P. Kittrell
Dean of Women
Hampton Institute
Hampton, Virginia

Vice-President:
T. Ruth Brett
Dean of Students
Bennett College
Greensboro, North Carolina

Recording Secretary:
LeRosa Hampton
Dormitory Recreation Director
Lincoln University
Jefferson City, Missouri

Corresponding Secretary:
Louise Latham
Assistant Dean of Women
Howard University
Washington, D. C.

Treasurer:
Josephine Dibble Murphy
Fort Valley State College
Fort Valley, Georgia

Committee Chairmen:
Hilda A. Davis
Executive Committee
Member-at-Large
Dean of Women
Talladega College
Talladega, Alabama
Virginia Simmons Nabongo
Program
429 N. Park Street
Madison, Wisconsin
E. Estelle Thomas
Research
Washington, D. C.

Local Hostesses:

Miss Ruth G. Rush, Dean of Women
North Carolina State College of
Negroes, Chairman
Mrs. Ernestine Hopps
Mrs. Lottie Kimble
Mrs. Nan Jones
Mrs. Annee P. Washington
Mrs. Reba R. Borders

OPENING SESSION
April 6, 1944

The fifteenth annual conference of the National Association of Deans of Women and Advisers to Girls in Negro Schools was opened in a most inspirational manner by the president, Dean Flemmie P. Kittrell. The thirteenth Chapter of the Corinthians read by the president, and the Lord's Prayer repeated by the entire group gave the conference spiritual strength and courage for tasks that were ahead. An expression of appreciation to North Carolina State for giving the association the privilege of "coming to such a successful college," was made by Miss Kittrell. She also commended "the spirit of the deans in braving travel" to attend the annual conference.

Dean Ruth G. Rush, local chairman of arrangements and Dean of Women at North Carolina State, extended a cordial welcome to the group and expressed regret that the President of the college, Dr. James E. Shepard, found it impossible to attend the first session. She assured the group, however, that the entire college family was happy to entertain the association.

All persons present then introduced themselves to the assemblage.

At the conclusion of this informal acquaintance period the president steered the thinking toward the discussions for the morning. The first topic, "Meeting the Social Needs of Students" by Dean Jessie P. Guzeman of Tuskegee Institute provoked much thought and discussion." The problem of meeting students' social needs has always been a serious one with most colleges even before the war began because of the difference between what students seemed to desire and what the college offered," she began. Dean Guzeman explained that various types of colleges had different problems. The denominational college, the smaller institution the larger institution, the women's college—all of necessity required different social programs. She stated that at Tuskegee Institute the problem consisted of obtaining a balanced program, so that neither the formal nor the informal aspects of the scheduled program would be too top heavy. With the beginning of the war, the work that had been done toward the solution of the problem was forced to take on a new outlook. The leaving of many Tuskegee students, the campus becoming the training center for cadets, and the college detachment, and the establishment of an army flying school only seven miles from the campus—all colored the program that must be devised.

Tuskegee has carried on their regular program with modifications. The army units on the campus participate in somewhat the same way as the regularly enrolled men students do. In addition to this they have integrated their program with that of the Army Flying School, the College Training Detachment, and the local U. S. O. Club.

They have found that the problem of how large a share the students should have in their own self direction must be faced. The work of the Institute Council on Campus Life, the Women's Council, and the Leaders Conference was described.

Dean Guzeman emphasized the fact that the social needs of students change with changed conditions. The dean of women must do her share in meeting these needs.

Discussion

Question: Is it wise that the college plan to invite service men to the campus for social activities?

Answer: It was agreed that the inviting of service men to college social affairs is a way that the college can do its part for the war effort. However, the group was just as certain that some definite control must be had over these guests. The dean's office should make an effort to interpret to officers in charge the standard that the college desires to uphold at each institutional activity. Once having conveyed this philosophy, there should be continuous efforts to gain the co-operation of these officials in the supervision of the service men while on the campus.

Question: What provision has been made for the social needs of students who are now in college?

Answer: Dean Ruth Brett explained the program that Bennett College has found it wise to foster: Each Sunday night some activity is sponsored for soldiers who may visit the campus and for the students as well. During the week, at the end of the study hour, all students may assemble at a designated place and engage in some planned activity. Miss LeRose Hampton also stated that at Lincoln University it was considered an urgent need to plan for students some activity to substitute for the many activities that were no longer possible because of the changes brought by the war. At Lincoln in one of the dormitory recreation rooms, Monday through Friday, from six-thirty to nine in the evening, some activity is planned and supervised. Students who have "time on their hands" find it possible to learn new games or to participate in those that they already know. Most of the games are those that can be played in limited space and with a minimum of hilarity and confusion.

Question: Is there a responsibility to the soldiers who may feel ill-at-ease because he is not on the educational level of the students?

Answer: Dean Emma Gray, Dean Murphy and others believed that the college girl can do much to "ease" the situation. Girls may try to teach the men games, do their best to be good conversationalists, and to see that they are introduced to the girls present.

Question: What kind of relationship should exist between college girls who act as hostesses at the camp entertainments and the city girls who go as hostesses also?

Answer: Dean Bolton and Dean Foster expressed the belief that the problem must be worked through co-activities in the community, and mostly by exhibiting the humanitarian spirit. Good feeling must be created for a successful program.

* * *

The third topic discussed was "Problems with High School Girls" by Miss Fannie Clay, Dean of Girls, Austin High School, Knoxville, Tennessee, who was introduced to the audience. Many problems have made their appearance because so many of the high school girls are now defense workers, Dean Clay stated. These girls have learned much and think they know more. Consequently they are hard to control. There is little, anyway, that can be done to punish a high school student, the dean felt.

Because men are rampant in the community the dean found that the problem of the high school girl becoming interested in this element was great.
The most regrettable fact, she believed, was "the feeling on the part of many high school girls that school is not so necessary now."

* * *

The last presentation for the morning was given by Mrs. Pauline Butler, representative of National Nursing Council for War Service. She outlined the opportunity that is being given the Negro girl through the United States Cadet Nursing Program. She was confident that the dean of women can do much toward guiding the type of student into nursing who will be a real credit to the profession. The speaker pointed out that the Cadet Nursing Program not only provides one with training, but also it gives the girl a means of earning a respectable living.

BUSINESS MEETING

President Kittrell asked that each member read the minutes of last years' meeting and be prepared to vote on them at the Friday morning session . She also announced that committees would be appointed at that same time.

The death of President J. R. E. Lee of Florida A. and M. College was announced. Dean Kittrell expressed sympathy on behalf of the association to Dean K. E. Whitehurst, dean of women at Florida A. and M. Dean Whitehurst accepted gratefully the expressions. Dean Kittrell also asked that a telegram of sympathy be sent to the Lee family for the association.

Through Dean Kittrell's suggestion, it was agreed that flowers be sent to Mrs. James E. Shepard, who has been confined to bed for sometime.

A telegram of greeting to the National Association of College Women, in session at New York City was deemed appropriate.

SECOND SESSION

2:00 P. M.

Miss T. Ruth Brett, who presided at the afternoon meeting, introduced to the association Dr. Paul Cornely, Executive Director of the National Student Health Association. He presented his topic. "What is an adequate Health Program for Students?" Because Negroes die more rapidly, because there are certain diseases that ravage Negroes—every intelligent, thinking race group must find itself interested in health, Dr. Cornely declared. There were discussed by the speaker the general principles of the ideal health service. He mentioned that it was very necessary that personnel deans become familiar with these principles. A brief outline of Dr. Cornely's discussion follows:

What Is An Adequate Health Program for Students?

DR. PAUL CORNELY.

I. ADMINISTRATION

    A. President's Conviction that there is a need for the service.

    B. Departments in set-up.
        1. Department of health
        2. Department of physical education
        3. Department of Medical service

    C. Faculty Health Council
        1. Dean of Women
        2. Dean of Men
        3. Superintendent of Hospital
        4. Nutritionist
        5. Others

II. FACILITIES

    A. Separate Building
        1. Waiting Room
        2. Examining Room
        3. Consultation Room

    B. Infirmary
        1. Women's Building
        2. Men's
        3. 10-12 beds per 1,000 students

Following Mrs. Smith's address, the annual message of the president of the association was delivered. Dean Kittrell spoke from the subject "Women and War." She began by saying that all wars have changed the status of women, and further stated the belief that there is more opportunity extended women to serve during the time of war than at any other time. Very clearly did Miss Kittrell review the heroism and progress of the women of Russia, Germany, England, and France. In all of these countries and in our own, women have shouldered the added responsibilities and have done a creditable job with these new privileges and greater burdens.

Mention was made of the many new fields that were heretofore believed too difficult and too intricate for the "weaker sex." It was obvious, from the president's interesting account of the many records that have been made all over the world by women, that women have proven their capability.

Dean Kittrell advised that the urgent need at present is that women settle in their minds and hearts just what it is they want. This settlement must come before women will be able to reach their ultimate goal. In conclusion Miss Kittrell said, "If we are smart, we can learn lessons, even during war."

The final number by the choir was the spiritual, "I can tell the World About this."

* * *

Immediately following the public meeting, the association was entertained in the lobby of McLean Hall. The entertainment was given by the Durham Branch of the National Association of College Women.

* * *

FOURTH SESSION
Friday, April 7, 10:00 A. M.

Dean Mayme U. Foster, presiding at the first session of the morning, announced that Mr. George L. Weaver, Race Relations Officer for the CIO, could not attend the conference because of illness. The first speaker, therefore, was Dean Rebekah Jeffries. Her topic, "Counselling College students during these times" was begun as she remarked, "I am impressed with the idea that we must turn to God for guidance." She expressed the fact that youth has not changed, and also admonished those who counsel young women to remember this: the youth which they counsel now are the products of War I. The inheritance of youth has been such factors as the repulsive technique of the flapper, the misconception that it was smart to get something for nothing, dislocation in American industry, and the tempter-prohibition.

Dean Jeffries stated that there were two pertinent problems facing the dean for counsel: the problem of education and the problem of personal adjustment. The major emphasis in the solving of the former problem will be upon keeping young women in school. The second problem will find a less difficult path if the dean can encourage women to set a real example of religion.

* * *

Dean Foster then presented the second speaker, Mrs. Gladys H. Groves, Director of the Marriage and Family Council, Inc., Chapel Hill, North Carolina. The subject from which she spoke was "Family and Marital Status during War Times." This all important problem, Mrs. Graves explained, faces its difficulties just as any other problem must meet greater difficulties and tests during the tension of war.

245

In the very beginning, the speaker clearified her answer to the question, "Is marriage during wartime wise?" In her opinion, the answer depended upon individual circumstances and could not be answered by stating generalities.

She divided her discussion into the consideration of the problem of family and marital status from angles of three distinct types of individuals: Those who have recently married during the war, those who are in college and are thinking about marriage, and those who are not yet facing the problem.

Those persons who have recently married face the question of whether they should have children. In order to answer this question well, the couple must avoid hasty conclusions. Factors regarding sterility, at what age it is wisest to have children, and answers to similiar questions must be considered. They must face such questions as these: Will we want to adopt children if we are unable to have our own? Would we be happy without children? Helpful material for this group can be secured from the National Council of Family Relations.

One of the greatest services that the dean of women can render the second group, those who are in college and are considering marriage, is to help them find answers to their questions. This group should be made to realize and understand these facts: (1) Each person who wants to marry affects the person he intends to marry and vice versa. (2) The simple choosing of a mate does not settle all problems. Marriage is a new undertaking, a way of life.

The third group, those who are not yet facing the question, present the less difficult problem. These young people are in the "truly romantic mood." At this point in their lives they should be made to realize the difference between the ideals of marriage and the reality of it. The dean must aid these students in discovering their own personalities, and show them the value of being a real person.

Discussion

The question, "What should the dean do to have young married women students realize that they are married," seemed an important outgrowth of Mrs. Graves topic. Dean Foster mentioned that these young married women could work on marital problems at community centers. They may also be housed in separate quarters, and be granted senior privileges.

• • •

At the end of the discussion a brief business session was held. Dean Kittrell announced the following committees:

Nominations

Dean I. Bolton, chairman
Dean E. Gibson
Dean I. Jenkins

Time and Place

Dean P. E. Thigpen, chairman
Dean J. Fairfax
Dean I. Preyer

The Double Barrier of Race and Sex: A Voice from the 1940s

Willa B. Player, "The Negro College and Women's Education"
(*Association of American Colleges Bulletin,* 33 (2), May, 1947, 364–365)

THE NEGRO COLLEGE AND WOMEN'S EDUCATION

WILLA B. PLAYER

REGISTRAR, BENNETT COLLEGE

WHILE education to achieve its true value should be pursued in a mixed environment, there are certain aspects in the training of Negro women which would be neglected if left to chance attention in the white college of today. Advanced education should prepare every young woman to earn a living; it should help her to become an efficient homemaker; and it should train her for leadership and worthy citizenship in the community in which she lives and in the larger world community. In preparing for a career it is important to make careful surveys of occupations to determine the vocations where women have the largest opportunities. To be truly realistic, however, in planning the education of Negro women, the task must extend itself to an investigation of the job opportunities open to Negro women It is not only unsound but also unjust to prepare a young woman for a profession from which she is barred at the start; unless she is the unusual person who gears herself to fight to the end to achieve her purpose. Because of this situation, it is highly important for a Negro woman to have broad preparation in related areas which will fit her for jobs that lie outside of her specialized field. The danger that she may lose out in the struggle for employment because of her racial identity is a very real one.

In the area of homemaking, special attention must be given to problems of diet and disease. The Negro woman homemaker will have two major handicaps in her environment to confront She will have far less money to spend. She will live in the poorest sections of the community under inadequate housing conditions. She must be equipped to combat disease, to care for illness in the family and to plan for adequate feeding on low income diets. As the mother in the home, she must be as creative as possible where her children are concerned in order to help them to develop an objectivity on the race question as early as possible, and to resolve the social conflicts which threaten to disorganize their personalities before they reach maturity.

364

Perhaps it is in the area of community leadership where the responsibilities of the Negro college woman are largest. Certainly the problems are more intensified and more difficult to solve. In most instances she will be the only trained person in the local environment—the number of college women will exceed the number of trained men—so that she will be almost totally responsible for intelligent community leadership. It is up to the woman to help modify race attitudes, to teach techniques of social action and to help create and maintain unity and integrity within the group. She must know how to deal with race prejudice in a very real sense because in her position as a member of a minority group she is a target for race prejudice on every hand.

The Negro college woman finds herself in a peculiar position in society. She is hardly accorded the courtesy which other women receive. If she lives in the South, she is treated as rudely as a man and no matter how superior she is in intellect or in economic status, she is seldom if ever accorded the title of "Miss" or "Mrs.," which she appropriately deserves. This world of prejudice is capable of robbing her of the belief in her own innate capacities, of shattering her ambition and destroying her self-confidence. This is a constant threat to her security and often taxes her stamina to such a degree that she tends to develop attitudes of dependence and inferiority. Somewhere in her college experience she must have an opportunity to develop poise, to increase her self-esteem and to establish a sense of her worth and dignity as an individual. She must experience peace and beauty in her environment and she must be accorded the respect and courtesy which is so lacking in her life on the outside. The education of the Negro woman should give her an opportunity to exhaust to the fullest her powers of expression and creativity. Her only barriers must lie in the area of her own limitations as an individual, not as a Negro. She must meet daily the challenge to achieve thorough scholarship to the end that she may destroy by her own strength the unseen chains and the unwritten laws which threaten to undermine her possibilities for becoming a number one citizen in America's envisioned democracy.

Spelman in the 1950s

Excerpts from an interview with a 1956 Spelman graduate
(Interview conducted by Elizabeth L. Ihle, March, 1987)

INTERVIEW WITH A 1956 SPELMAN COLLEGE GRADUATE

Elizabeth Ihle interviewed this 1956 Spelman graduate in March, 1987. She is referred to in the interview as SCG, Spelman College Graduate.

SCG: I had been greatly influenced by a Spelman grad who was a high school teacher, and it was really my desire to go to school so after one year at Florida A&M, I was able to get Masonic loan since my father had been a mason and they paid for the rest of my education at Spelman College, the tuition and room and board. So then I was able to do three years at Spelman College. I think the reason that I went there, I can just sum up and say, was because of that Spelman graduate that I was so impressed with, and I was impressed with the stories that she used to tell about Spelman. She carried herself in a manner that made me want to go there and be as much like her as I could.

ELI: Was she a high school teacher?

SCG: She was a high school teacher; she taught government and political science, I guess you would call it now. She was just one of the most articulate, just effervescent persons I think that I had met and one of the most well qualified ones on that high school staff. She talked about Spelman everyday; she was able to get in something; she was a good recruiter and that was before recruiting became popular but she was very influential in persuading some of the girls to go.

ELI: What were some of the contrasts between Florida A&M and Spelman?

SCG: Oh, size number one. Flordia A&M had at that time around four or five thousand. Spelman had four hundred. So the classes were different. At Spelman the classes were very small, twenty at the most. you got individualized, specialized treatment.

ELI: How did it compare academically?

SCG: Academically it was much harder at Spelman than at Florida A&M, although I think I got a good basic background at Florida A&M. I'm not selling them short. With the individual treatment that students were able to get, that one is able to get at Spelman, you ended up much more confident and self-assured when you left there.

ELI: You said that you were more confident and more self-assured. Does part of that relate to the fact that this was a women's college?

2

SCG: I think so. They jokingly sometimes tell us that we are
     pushy. I hate to think that but maybe we are. I have a
     feeling that getting an education in an all-female or
     all-male setting has its advantages in that if you tend not
     to be self-confident and if you tend to be intimidated by the
     opposite sex, then that's one way for you to gain some
     confidence. We were all leaders. If you have a setting with
     males and females, usually you tend to let the males take the
     lead. But we developed and we knew that were just as good.
     We could be presidents and vice presidents. We might not
     have gotten that opportunity in a male and female setting.

ELI: Did you have much interaction with male students, like at
     Morehouse?

SCG: Very much. When I was in school, and its different now, the
     fellas came to classes. We've always had classes. We've
     always been allowed to take classes throughout the center.
     They came over to campus to take classes with us so that
     we had that interaction. Our visiting hours were limited,
     but we could have company for all of a whole hour, 5-6
     o'clock and on Sundays it was a little longer; I think two
     hours. Then they would have to clear the grounds.

ELI: You are telling me that that was all; you couldn't go out on a
     date?

SCG: You could go out on a date, but I'm saying for them to come
over
          and sit and be with they had to clear the grounds except
          for those times.

ELI: Spelman's grounds were sacred and no men were allowed?

SCG: If they were not in class, they could not stay. If they were
     attending class they would go home after class. We just
     didn't have that much interaction except for visiting
     hours and then the campus would be just crowded.

ELI: What about the faculty members, were they male or female?

SCG: They were male and female. It has always been male and
          female, black and white. Coming to Spelman was my first
          association with having white faculty members and most of
          them were from the eastern part of the country. People
          who were very dedicated to teaching and they just had a
          dedication and a loyalty to teaching. You learned for
          learning's sake, and they wanted you to be all that you
          could be, and they were going to pull it out of you if it
          was in you. We got a very good thorough background. I
          think that nobody back in '56 wanted a C; it was just not
          something that you aspired for, you wanted to have A's or
          B's if you possibly could. It was very competitive thing;
          however, the honor roll was not the kinds of honor rolls

that I see in the school now. The honor roll used to be,
I think for the whole 400 of us we would have about 20 or
25, but you knew that those 25 people were the cream of
the crop. We worked very hard to try to see if we could
do our very best.

Autherine Lucy and the University of Alabama, 1956

Nora Sayre, "Barred at the Schoolhouse Door"
(*The Progressive,* 48 (July, 1984), 15–19, reprinted by permission)

Barred at the Schoolhouse Door

Autherine Lucy's case mirrored the black experience

BY NORA SAYRE

In the 1950s, the Democratic ballot in Alabama still bore the slogan WHITE SUPREMACY. In Birmingham, a city ordinance forbade black citizens from riding in elevators or taxicabs with whites, or from playing checkers with them. The signs on the doors of public toilets read "Ladies," "Gentlemen," and "Colored," revealing that both sexes had to share the last of these. Since many whites considered blacks unclean, the races rarely ate at the same table, though most white meals were cooked by black hands.

The Supreme Court's 1954 *Brown* decision, which outlawed segregation in public schools, brought a reaction that revitalized the Ku Klux Klan, and White Citizens Councils were formed in direct response to the Court's ruling. Council members—mostly male—often tried to dissociate themselves from the Klan: Many wore neckties, not hoods, and they felt themselves to be of a higher social class than the Klansmen, but a number of them funded the Klan, and some were willing to resort to violence.

Klansmen and Citizens Council members were united in the belief that the NAACP was dominated by communists. The label was appropriate to the Cold War 1950s, of course, but some of the older segregationists still remembered the efforts of the Communist Party to organize black workers in the South during the Great Depression. "Outsiders" who came South "to agitate the Negroes" were suspected, therefore, of being Soviet instruments. Those who wished to join the Central Alabama Citizens Council, the largest in the state, signed a membership application that asserted, "I pledge myself to help defeat the NAACP, integration, mongrelism, socialism, Communist ideologies, FEPC [the proposed Fair Employment Practices Commission], and one world government."

Perhaps there is one event that occurs early in many Americans' lifetimes that educates them about the nature of their country. For me, that event was the Autherine Lucy case of 1956, which I followed closely at the time. I was raised in several states, moving between New York and California and New England, but I knew all too little about lethal racial passions until I read about the experiences of the first black student at the University of Alabama in Tuscaloosa. No other black had ever attended a white school or college in that state.

Autherine Lucy, twenty-six, was admitted to the University after a three-year lawsuit sponsored by the NAACP Legal Defense and Education Fund, Inc. The youngest of ten children of a tenant farmer, she had graduated from Miles College, a black Methodist school in Birmingham. She had then taught high school English and Sunday school, and she was eager to earn a degree in library science. In 1952, her friend Polly Anne Myers, who had been prominent in the student chapter of the NAACP at Miles, suggested that they apply to the state university for graduate work in fields that black colleges did not provide.

Myers, a mettlesome, enterprising young woman, was the initiator; Lucy, a retiring and modest person, has said she was not an activist. It was not against state law for blacks to attend the University, which had no written policy that denied admission on racial grounds, but black applicants were always advised to go elsewhere. After the two were rejected, they consulted Arthur D. Shores, Birmingham's most eminent black lawyer and the NAACP Fund's counsel in Alabama. Shores filed their suit in conjunction with Thurgood Marshall, then chief counsel for the NAACP, and Constance Baker Motley.

In the wake of the *Brown* decision, Federal District Judge Hobart H. Grooms ruled that the University could not disobey the law and that both women had to be enrolled. (The Supreme Court had also established that the ban on segregation applied to tax-supported colleges and universities.) The case was brought as a class-action suit, meaning that other qualified blacks could enter the University in the future.

In those days, the state retained detectives to investigate the personal backgrounds of plaintiffs in desegregation suits—in hopes of disqualifying them. (Such plaintiffs were also apt to lose their jobs with white employers, or to be deprived of their home mortgages at local banks.) It was learned that when Polly Anne Myers applied to the University, she had been pregnant by a man convicted of burglary; her baby was born six months after her marriage. The University excluded her for her "conduct and marital record." But Autherine Lucy's dossier was impeccable, and she became the sole candidate.

When she registered for her courses in February 1956, the Montgomery bus boycott led by Martin Luther King Jr. was two months old. The timing

This innocent country set you down in a ghetto in which, in fact, it intended that you should perish. Let me spell out precisely what I mean by that, for the heart of the matter is here and the crux of my dispute with my country. You were born where you were born and faced the future that you faced because you were black and for no other reason. The limits to your ambition were thus expected to be settled. You were born into a society which spelled out with brutal clarity and in as many ways as possible that you were a worthless human being. You were not expected to aspire to excellence. You were expected to make peace with mediocrity.

*James Baldwin
1962*

Nora Sayre, the author of "Running Time: Films of the Cold War" and "Sixties Going on Seventies," is now at work on a book about the 1950s.

was significant; some thought the boycott heightened the fury that greeted the desegregation order. Segregationists were discovering that black Southerners were ready to defy the status quo; there was no need for Northern agitators to animate them. The Autherine Lucy case became a symbolic battlefield for those who were determined to maintain segregation and those who had resolved to abolish it. The issue was not the presence of one black woman on a single university campus; the quiet, diffident individual was the representative of millions whose adversaries had begun to realize that they were confronting a social revolution.

All through the summer of 1955, Lucy's friends in the NAACP advised her on how to conduct herself on campus. She was told to wear her best dresses, to ignore all insults, to hold her head high. Local papers, such as The Birmingham Post-Herald, reported that her clothes were too "fashionable," that she was "hustled ahead" of white students waiting in the registration line, and that she paid for her tuition with "a crisp $100 bill."

She was refused a room in a dormitory and barred from the dining halls. She was informed that the University's board of trustees had specifically ordered that she should not be assigned a room because "it might endanger the safety or result in the sociological disadvantage of the students." Hence she had to commute to her classes every day from Birmingham, a distance of sixty miles in each direction.

Some whites surmised that blacks who were not destitute must have acquired money by illicit means. If they appeared to be more than solvent, they might possess shady connections. Segregationists were often outraged by intimations of black prosperity. Lucy's carefully chosen wardrobe, the $100 bill, and the fact that she once arrived in Tuscaloosa in a Cadillac excited so much hostile comment that Constance Baker Motley compiled a "fact sheet."

It explained that Lucy had been allotted a scholarship by a New York foundation, but the University had returned the money because she was not yet registered. "A citizens' committee in Alabama had raised funds" for some of her expenses; "therefore, on the morning ... when she needed money to pay her tuition until the scholarship matter could be straightened out, the chairman of the committee hurriedly withdrew $100 from the bank and handed it to [her], so that there would be no question of her having completed registration on time." She had been "escorted" to the front of the registration line "by anxious university personnel"—who had not foreseen how much that gesture would be resented. She was driven daily from Birmingham by black volunteers: On the first day, she was delivered "by a man who happened to own a Buick"; on the second day, in a Ford; on the third, in an Oldsmobile; on the fourth, "by a man who happened to own a Cadillac."

Later, when Thurgood Marshall asked University trustee John Caddell, in court if Lucy had done "anything unlawful when she came to the University," Caddell replied, "She came in a Cadillac automobile and she had a chauffeur, and waited in a way as to be obnoxious and objectionable and disagreeable." Caddell implied that "the actions" of Lucy and her companions had generated the violence that ensued: "All the publicity was calculated to cause rioting and they knew it."

Tuscaloosa had twice as many whites as blacks, but many of the whites thought of themselves as a minority. The city's first White Citizens Council was organized right after Autherine Lucy put in an appearance there. Its temporary chairman, Leonard Wilson, a sophomore at the University, told the membership, "We will control every public office from the lowest county peanut politician to the Governor's mansion."

At subsequent meetings, State Senator Walter Givhan declared that communists were advocating desegregation "because they know that the South is one of the few places in which pure Anglo-Saxon blood exists." He said the NAACP was scheming "to get a Negro elected Vice President, and then to take over the country by assassinating the President." The number of Councils in Alabama expanded rapidly in the next few weeks.

Much of the press depicted Tuscaloosa as a place where blacks and whites enjoyed harmonious relations—until the advent of Autherine Lucy. The New York Times reported, "Race relations in Tuscaloosa had been so happy that, as the Lucy affair was coming to a head, Negroes only gathered to watch and laugh when a fiery cross was burned on the edge of a Negro high school campus." But soon Lucy was known as "the controversial colored girl" (Newsweek) who had infused a whole city with hatred.

The Klan took credit for gasoline-soaked crosses that were set ablaze at and near the University. Bomb threats were frequent. Racist leaflets were distributed on campus by Robert Chambliss, who would be convicted many years later for the 1963 bombing that killed four young black girls in a Baptist church in Birmingham. But Lucy went through two days of classes without incident, and some students even told her that they wished her well.

While she was away over the weekend, though, mobs assembled on the grounds. After a protest rally, they paraded through the neighborhood and vandalized a post office, where they splashed ink on the American flag—a symbol of the Supreme Court and its desegregation ruling. Amid yells of "Keep 'Bama white!" and the waving of Confederate flags, University President O.C. Carmichael was showered with gravel and firecrackers when he tried to address the jeering demonstrators, who had also damaged the vehicles of several black townsmen.

Leonard Wilson had told a large crowd that Lucy deserved "a greeting she would never forget." When she arrived on Monday, her black driver barely escaped injury. Bottles were thrown. The University chaplain, who attempted to pacify the rioters, was kneed in the groin. Several University officials would later testify that the mob of about 2,000 seemed ready to commit murder; some pursued Lucy with shouts of "Let's kill her! Kill her!" as she was driven from one class to another. They also chanted outside her classroom, "Hey, hey, ho, where in the hell did Autherine go? Hey, hey, ho, where in the hell did that nigger go?"

As Jefferson Bennett, the assistant to the President, and Sarah Healy, Dean of Women, risked their lives in protecting her. The windows of Dean Healy's car were shattered. Lying on the floor of a highway patrol car, Lucy was finally driven away from the bellowing throng. The next day, she was suspended

"for her own protection" by the trustees. In the Alabama Senate, Senator Albert Davis praised the demonstrators and said, "Yesterday was a great day for Alabama."

T he Lucy case was the first occasion when a black student's admission to a Southern university was so savagely opposed. Some other blacks had entered all-white Southern universities without encountering resistance, so neither the University nor Lucy's lawyers had anticipated the tumult at Tuscaloosa. The mobs that had menaced her had included some undergraduates, but many of the men were rubber workers from the nearby Goodrich plant or employees of a steel foundry. The NAACP heard that people from other parts of Alabama and even from other states had come to swell the hordes. The national press did not allude to the Klan, but the local papers and University officials did—at length and often.

The case made headlines all over the world, and it was given detailed coverage in the Soviet press. Columnists censured the University for capitulating to mob rule. One of the few white politicians who displayed a strong reaction was Governor Av-

erell Harriman of New York, who demanded "vigorous" Federal action against those who were preventing Lucy from continuing her education.

Adlai Stevenson said the "situation" merited "the prompt attention of the President," but suggested the topic of segregation should be avoided in the upcoming Presidential campaign. When pressed, he called segregation a local matter, and he suggested that 1965 might be a possible target date "for a gradual settlement of the school racial crisis." President Eisenhower, who had been cool to the *Brown* decision, "deplored" the rioting, said Federal "interference" was undesirable, recommended "moderation," and subsequently remarked, "Let's don't try to think of this as a tremendous fight that is going to separate Americans and get ourselves into a nasty mess." He then managed to shun the subject until it was necessary to send Federal troops to defend the new black students at the Little Rock Central High School in Arkansas in 1957.

Some blamed Governor James Folsom of Alabama because the state National Guard had not been summoned after President Carmichael sent a request through the mayor of Tuscaloosa. (Folsom was absent from his office and his staff did not act

The attitude of fear is such that when a Southern newspaper editor, a known liberal, was chided for remaining silent amid the madness, he said quite seriously: "I think we're courageous not to take a stand now. We risk all we have simply by not whooping it up for segregation every day of the week."

Stan Opotowsky
1957

on the request.) Folsom, who had been regarded as quite enlightened about civil rights—to the extent that some Citizens Council members had demanded his impeachment—then made some highly ambiguous remarks about desegregation.

In March, the University trustees found a legal pretext to expel Autherine Lucy. Her lawyers had filed an affidavit accusing the trustees of conspiring with the mob. The charge of collusion could not be proved in court, and Lucy was expelled for "libelous allegations against the Board and the President." Leonard Wilson was expelled soon after for the same reason; not only had he "fomented" the crowds, but he had called for the dismissal of President Carmichael. It was stressed that students of both races had been disciplined.

Immediately after the Lucy case, the zeal of the segregationists intensified: At a Citizens Council meeting in Montgomery, Attorney General Eugene Cook of Georgia referred to desegregation as "racial suicide." The Alabama House of Representatives passed a resolution to determine whether the NAACP was "directed or controlled by Communists," and Lucy was subpoenaed to appear as the first witness. (She had already left the state, and the hearings did not take place.) The Councils sent questionnaires to candidates in Alabama's next Democratic primary, asking whether they were committed to segregation, and it was understood that the replies would be made public.

A resolution in the Alabama legislature requested Federal funds to relocate black Alabamians in Northern and Western states, where they "are wanted and can be assimilated." Representative Charles McKay of Talladega said he thought "most white Southerners" would be "glad to cancel out any debts" owed by blacks if they would leave the state; he recommended that they be convicted of felony if they returned. Bills were introduced to terminate grants to black colleges such as the Tuskegee Institute if a single black student were allowed to remain at a white state college. A House resolution was also passed requiring President Carmichael to supply the names of some 200 students (out of 7,000) who had signed petitions in support of Autherine Lucy.

The NAACP in Alabama was shut down for eight years, and some members believed the injunction issued against their organization was a direct consequence of the Lucy case. Huge fines were imposed on the NAACP when it declined to reveal its membership list to the state authorities.

Segregationists felt they had won a great victory, but some of their opponents also had a sense of achievement: Autherine Lucy and her lawyers had opened the University to black students, though none actually attended until 1963, when George Wallace "stood in the schoolhouse door" and performed his charade of resistance until he was instructed to step aside on the orders of President Kennedy. Ample Federal troops were on hand, and the University had prepared for weeks for the registration of two black students; even the soft drink machines on campus were emptied or sealed up, so that no one could use a bottle as a weapon. In the same year, the city of Birmingham repealed all its segregation laws.

In April 1984, I took a bus from Birmingham to Opelika to visit Autherine Lucy Foster, bringing her regards from Arthur Shores, Judge Grooms, and others. She does not dwell on the past—the case was one chapter in a very full life, and she doesn't want to be defined by it. An extremely private person, she has no love for interviews, but she feels an obligation to share the history that claimed her. She never chose to be a public figure, but she seems at ease with the vanished decades. She laughs freely, sometimes at unexpected moments, and she is quick to challenge a question, though she pauses and grows pensive when she explores her memories.

Following her expulsion, she married her long-time fiancé, Hugh Lawrence Foster, who soon became a Baptist minister. Since he has been assigned to many parishes, they have moved often. They have four children. Autherine Foster has taught in public schools in Texas, Louisiana, and Alabama, and now works as a substitute teacher. The publicity the case received probably cost her some jobs in the early 1960s. One school superintendent said her association with the NAACP made her unacceptable: "To him, I was ... the infamous Miss Lucy." Others who didn't hire her were not so frank, but she sensed their awareness of the case. The NAACP provided some lecture dates, and since the 1970s, she has been invited to address several American history classes at the University of Alabama.

We spoke of the day in 1956 when the mob raced after her up the steps of the library, yelling "Let's kill her!" I asked what had sustained her at the time. She was and is a deeply religious person, and it's clear that part of her resilience springs from spirituality. She told me she had sat and prayed inside a locked room while she heard the voices outside chanting "Hey, hey, ho. . . ."

She recalled, "I asked the Lord to give me the strength—if I must give my life—to give it freely. And if I were to give my life, to let someone else take over where I left off. And that if it were mine to see it through, to give me the courage to go through with it."

Although that morning was terrifying, she said she was rarely frightened on other occasions. While she stayed with her sister in Birmingham, her brother-in-law and his cousin guarded their home with guns because their phone was throbbing with death threats. But the butt of all that hatred did not lose sleep or her appetite. She continued to expect a more rational and humane world than the one she inhabited.

She does not think she was particularly brave—"I can't take credit because so many other people went through much"—and she referred to the many times that Arthur Shores's house was dynamited while he worked on one desegregation case after another: "And he just wouldn't be stopped." She talked about others who were beaten, bombed, and lynched during the struggle for equal rights, and she said she was fortunate that she wasn't harmed.

Naturally, it had been hard to approach the University alone, after Polly Anne Myers was excluded. But, after praying for guidance, "I decided that it was just something that I must do. That I felt it was my task to do. That I couldn't stop until I felt that I had gone as far as I could." When I inquired whether those days on campus had made her wary of whites or had affected her opinion of human nature, she said no, but it had taught her that "there are some people in all races who may not accept

you," and that some blacks did not favor desegregation or the part she played in it.

I asked Autherine Foster for her thoughts on how life has and has not changed for black Americans. She spoke with pleasure about riding in any seat on the bus, staying in any motel, eating in any restaurant. But she remarked on the scarcity of black teachers in the schools she knows, the disadvantages of black students in integrated classrooms, the overwhelming majority of white school administrators and trustees.

She described "segregation within integration": the "isolation" in housing (she lives in an almost entirely black neighborhood), the gulf between black and white churches even though "we say that we worship the same God," the undergraduates who sit with their own races in the lecture halls. She mentioned the young men and women who do have interracial friendships: "They have found that there can be good blacks and good whites, there can be bad blacks and had whites."

She is glad everyone receives the same education at the University of Alabama—which now has the highest percentage of black students of any of the once-white universities in the South. But she regrets

that they belong to separate organizations. She says she is devoted to her state, delighted to be living there once more, and "proud of Alabama." She still wishes she were a graduate of the University. Yet even though she was expelled, "even though things may not work out as you would have wished," she is heartened by the numbers of black students there and hopes the races will profit from mutual exposure—even though "they are separate." She added, "I'm still benefiting, though, if others are benefiting."

In retrospect, the Autherine Lucy case and its consequences seem to mirror much of the black experience in this country. A new generation can hardly believe that universities and lunch counters and apartment houses were once closed to their parents.

But if we are still appalled by what happened in Tuscaloosa in 1956 and wish to think that no mob could wield such power today, we're forced to witness the most recent furor in response to busing, or the crosses that were burned on someone's lawn last month, last week. The case is a continual reminder of race and hasn't altered in America—in any city, in any town, or state. ∎

Voluntary action does not obviate the need for strong legislation. Law can go a long way toward making most men act right, and law can be decisive in building the legal foundations of integration and providing Negroes with the peaceful weapons they need to fight their way to the freedom they were promised a century ago.

Editorial
1963

Black College Women's Education in the 1950s: a Survey

Jeanne L. Noble, "Negro Women Today and Their Education"
(*The Journal of Negro Education,* 26(1):15–21, 1957)

Negro Women Today and Their Education

JEANNE L. NOBLE

The City College of New York

The first two words of this article taken separately might at first glance cause some people to exclaim: "Oh no! Not another article on that subject!"

It is true that volumes have been written about women. In the Teachers College Library, Columbia, the card catalogue has one and one-half drawers full of cards measuring 23 inches in thickness that deal with every subject that could possibly relate to womanhood: their nature, their motivation, their jobs and the like. On the other hand cards concerning books about men measure three-fourths of one inch and have such vague and general titles as "Of Mice and Men" and "Man the Unknown." Likewise, there have been many volumes written about Negroes. The titles deal with very much the same subject-matter as that pertaining to women. They measure about 16 inches in thickness in the card catalogue. Interestingly, only a few cards refer to the subject of white people and they mostly deal with a topic concerning relationships with Negroes.

The subject is not confined to books, nor lacking in current interest. The latest bound copy of *Readers Guide to Periodical Literature* (March 1955 to February 1956) indicates that there were approximately 3 pages of articles written about women, 3½ inches of one page about men, 3½ pages on the subject of Negroes and not one single article concerning white people. The topics, therefore, are still currently researchable and of great interest.

But, despite the fact that Negro women have a close affinity with women and Negroes, the reader has had to rely on footnotes and postscripts concerning them. And unfortunately, many of the statistical studies, such as the Kinsey report, carry the following kind of statement of reservation: "There were not enough Negro women in the sample from which to draw generalizations." To be sure, few books (a negligible dozen or so) and fewer articles, have been written on Negro women. Among this number still fewer have been devoted to the subject of Negro college women. Certainly the findings and generalizations about Negroes and women have implications for the guidance and education of Negro women. But, there is much in their own history and present position that is both fascinating and unique and very much researchable and worthy of study. The study reported in this article deals with one area of this field of research.

Negro women college graduates from six geographical sections of the country who have had an opportunity to test out in life the results of their education were asked to participate in a questionnaire survey. All types of colleges were represented. An effort

---

[1]The content of this article is based upon a book by the writer entitled: *The Negro Woman's College Education.* New York: Teachers College Bureau of Publications, 1956.

15

was made to find out what these women wanted out of college, what college did for them and what college failed to do as they now see it in retrospect. Through the interviewing method, an attempt was made to probe into deeper levels of responses. Therefore, ten Negro women, most of them nationally known leaders, and all of them outstanding in their professions, were interviewed in order to furnish insights into the findings of the questionnaire study. Finally, effort was made to interpret and evaluate what was said about college education in the light of a historic and philosophical review of higher education for Negroes and women in general and Negro women in particular. The study was limited to sorority members who now reside in large cities and who had been out of college at least 5 years at the time the data were collected.

A LOOK AT THE PAST

Any current exploration of the education of Negro women must necessarily be grounded in history. As we plan for the future it is well to ask: What are the echoes of history that resound today in the current attitudes toward the education of women. Or, indeed, perhaps reflected in their education today?

A backward look at the education of women and Negroes is like viewing two streams winding down a mountain path. At some points they seem to merge, and at other times they are miles apart. And yet, they are headed in the same direction--toward the great body of water. The tempestuous journey of all groups, while heading toward the great body of knowledge—college education

—has echoed in the education of Negro women.

Furthermore, two distinguishing features have made the Negro woman situation unique among women. The first had to do with the general conception of the Negro woman's role and sphere. Woody indicates that the South generally believed the white woman's place was in the home, and that men appreciated "the nobleness the purity, the gentleness of woman and accorded her the unstinted and sincere homage she deserved."[1] Certainly there were white women in the lower classes that did not evoke such attitudes of concern. But, on the plantation the contrast was apparent. For there the Negro woman was a slave and, therefore, not considered delicate or worthy of homage. Her's was a disorganized and unstable life, and the role that she often fulfilled as concubine did not add to her dignity.

Though her role in the white world was undignified and subservient, there is a second distinguishing factor. In her racial group the social role of the Negro woman was equal if not superior to that of the Negro man. E. Franklin Frazier states that:

> Neither economic necessity nor tradition has instilled in her the spirit of subordination to masculine authority. Emancipation only tended to confirm in many cases the spirit of self-sufficiency which slavery had taught.[2]

There is no evidence to support the idea that white women assumed a sim-

[1] Thomas Woody, *A History of Women's Education in the United States.* New York: The Science Press. Vol. I. p. 96.

[2] E. Franklin Frazier, *The Negro Family in the United States.* New York: the Dryden Press, 1948, p. 102.

flar role. Indeed, the picture was quite the contrary.

So, by and large, there were these distinguishing factors: the degradation of Negro womanhood as contrasted to the elevation of white womanhood in the plantation system, and the development of a Negro matriarchal family system as contrasted to a white patriarchal family system.

Consistent with the idea concerning woman's role as being in the home, education for white women, prior to the Civil War, sought to make them agreeable embellishments of society. The suffragettes fought to discredit this education-for-adornment idea and prove that women should be educated like men to do similar professional jobs. Though one school, Myrtilla Miner's School in Washington, D. C., had been started in 1857[1], and one woman, Mary Jane Patterson,[2] had graduated from Oberlin, neither Myrtilla Miner, nor Miss Patterson viewed education as an adornment enterprise. Miss Miner stated that she trained her students to teach, and Mary Jane Patterson taught school soon after receiving her degree.

Emancipation created problems of adjustment that demanded trained leadership of any and all available Negroes --men and women. Catapulted into a society that placed them at a most disadvantaged economic position, Negro women had neither the economic security nor the traditional desire to stay home. They continued their working and laboring role. This time, how-

ever, they entered college along with Negro men to receive an education in order to do the job that had to be done. One job was teaching. Interestingly, few founders of colleges felt it necessary to build separate colleges for men and women. Most of the colleges from the earliest founding were coeducational. To be sure, Negro women were entering college at a time when there was great controversy concerning the abilities and mental fitness of Negroes' and women'. Arguments held that both groups were inferior mentally and that it was therefore useless to educate them in the higher arts. Amidst this controversy many argued that colleges for Negroes and women were too imitative of the prevailing education for white men. This point of view held that the peculiar needs of women and Negroes should be considered in their separate curricula. Some of the criticism concerning how various groups in the culture should be educated was directed at education for Negro women. Some critics held that it was most necessary that their education be grounded in moralistic and character training. Interestingly, none went so far as to say "her place is in the home." But this attention to their moral education seemed to arise from feelings of unresolved guilt concerning the sexual status of women during slavery[3]. The moral education, however, was usually religious in nature and was enforced through rigid rules and regu-

[1]Carter G. Woodson, *Education of the Negro Prior to 1861*. New York: G. P. Putnam's Son, 1915, p. 268.
[2]Robert Fletcher, *A History of Oberlin College*. Oberlin, Ohio: Oberlin College, Vol. II.

[1]George Oscar Ferguson, *The Psychology of the Negro*. New York: The Science Press, 1916, p. 126.
[2]Wooly, *op cit.*, p. 154.
[3]Jack Thorne, "A Plea for Social Justice for the Negro Woman." Occasional Papers No 2, Negro Society of Historial Research, Yonkers, New York: Lincoln Press Association, pp. 2 6, 1912.

lations designed to govern the lives of women. Other than this, little difference has appeared in the education of Negro women and men.

A LOOK AT THE PRESENT

Indeed, spurred by the need for trained leaders and accompanied, perhaps, by the inherited self-sufficiency (as described by Frazier) thousands of Negro women have availed themselves of a college education. Though at first more Negro men than women received college education; by 1930, four out of every ten graduates were women, and from 1940 to the present more Negro women than Negro men have received college degrees. Today 1.6 per cent of all Negro men in the population 14 years of age and over have completed four-years-or-more of college as compared to 2.1 per cent of Negro women. In the white group, the figures are 6.0 and 4.4 respectively.[*]

As one would expect because of their working history, a larger proportion of Negro women than white women is gainfully employed. Negro women, however, comprise 58 per cent of all Negro professional workers and white women comprise about 85 per cent of the white professional group.[**]

The women in the present study reflect in many ways the general picture of Negro women in society. The majority of the graduates are in the teaching profession, which has traditionally been the main occupation for Negroes and women. It should be stated however, that among the youngest graduates, over 60 per cent are engaged in occupations other than teaching Optimistically this reflects the expanding opportunities for Negroes.

The majority of the graduates are married. Slightly over 10 per cent of the women are childless, and 38 per cent have only one child. Havemann and West[ ] in a study of college women also found a low incidence of childbearing among college women in general. A fact to keep in mind, however, is that only 6 per cent of the women in this sample are housewives. The rest are gainfully employed, this accounting in some way for small families.

More than 73 per cent of the graduates have studied beyond the baccalaureate degree. Approximately 48 per cent of the graduates have earned M.A. degrees. In the majority of cases their husbands have not had as much education as they, nor are they employed in as many "middle class" jobs.

The majority of the women are graduates of Negro coeducational colleges, with the next largest number having graduated from white coeducational colleges. The number of graduates of women's colleges, Negro and white, was small.

The graduates were asked to react to certain issues and concerns in the education of women. Among them was the issue concerning the desirability of a curriculum for women different from

[*]United States Department of Health, Education and Welfare, Office of Education, "Earned Degrees Conferred by Higher Educational Institutions, 1952-53," *Circular* No. 380, December 1953, p. 7.

[**]United States Department of Labor, Women's Bureau, 1952. "Handbook of Facts on Women Workers," *Bulletin* No. 242, pp. 24-25.

[ ]Ernest Havemann, and Patricia West, *They Went to College.* New York: Harcourt Brace and Co., 1952, p. 87.

that of men, as advocated by some educators. The overwhelming majority of the graduates expressed the feeling that college education for women should not differ at all from the ideal education for men. Those who indicated that it should be different expressed the feeling that education should prepare women for both a career and marriage.

When other college women in society have been asked to indicate values they believe to be most important in a college education, they have invariably chosen a cultural, liberal arts value as most important. They have deemphasized the vocational aspects of education." The majority of the graduates of this study chose the following items as those important for college to give a Negro woman: (1) training for a particular occupation and profession, (2) the desire—and the ability—to be a more useful citizen, and (3) preparation for marriage and family life. They chose the following as least important: (1) a better chance to get ahead in the world, (2) development of good moral character, and (3) education for international cooperation and participation.

There is some difference between graduates of Negro and white colleges as to the choice of what is important and unimportant to get out of college. The graduates of white colleges are less utilitarian and more liberal-arts minded than are graduates of Negro colleges. They included, for example,

"See: American Association of University Women. "AAUW Members Look At College Education." An Interim Report. Washington: The Association, 1944. Also: Robert Shostech. "Five thousand College Women Report." Washington: B'nai B'rith Vocational Service Bureau, 1953.

one of the three most important values to get out of college: "A sharper, better trained mind for dealing with all sorts of problems." This was rated considerably lower by women graduates of Negro colleges.

With the exception of preparation for marriage and family life the graduates indicated that college had made an appreciable contribution to preparation for a vocation, and citizenship education. Over 50 per cent of the graduates of all types of colleges indicated that college gave too little attention to preparation for marriage and family life.

A Look at the Future

There is a relationship between what graduates feel important to get out of college and what college emphasizes. When we consider what the women in this study wanted and what they received we might conclude: "They got mostly what they wanted." Yet, the graduates rejected important values while at the same time indicating that their colleges had given these values too little attention. This is certainly true in the area of "education for international understanding and cooperation." This was chosen as one of the least important values to get out of college and over 52 per cent of them felt their colleges had had no particular effect or a negative effect on their education in this area.

Conversely, there is knowledge displayed by these graduates concerning the probable life roles Negro women generally lead beyond college, and a desire to be educated to fulfill them. On the other hand, the knowledge that most Negro college women will enter occupations may have prompted those who graduate from white colleges to recognize that their colleges did not give enough attention to preparing them for a job.

It would seem, then, that colleges might consider (1) the probable life roles of their students and (2) the needs of their students.

What will be the probable social and psychological life roles of Negro college graduates? Certainly the majority of these women will work. White college women may or may not plan to work, but tend to pursue a college education as a kind of preparation that they might fall back on in case of an emergency." This is somewhat unreal for Negro women. The economic status of the Negro is such that fathers cannot afford to have their daughters "waste a college education" and if married, the majority of their husbands cannot maintain middle class status without the combined paychecks of husband and wife. One finding of this study is that an overwhelming majority of Negro women contribute toward the financial responsibility of their family.

If it is possible to generalize from this study, we can say that a college education will not seriously hinder a Negro woman from marrying. It may mean that she will marry someone with less education than she, since there are fewer college educated Negro men. But most of them will plan to marry and have children. There have been those who have disliked the fact that the

Negro woman is unable to stay at h[...] and take care of her children. A[...] some have said that a man's prid[...] hurt because his wife works and [...] plays independence. It has yet to [...] established that children of stay-[...]home mothers are less secure t[...] children of working mothers. It [...] the quality of the contacts with ch[...] dren, not the quantity that usua[...] counts in the long run. Furthermo[...] the cause of the Negro male's h[...] pride, if this is the case, is comple[...] and psychological in nature. To [...] sure, hurt pride will not vanish by t[...] woman surrendering her independen[...] —her right to work. This must [...] dealt with as a psychological prob[...] lem of the marriage partner who fee[...] the threat.

Interestingly, preparation for ma[...] riage and family life seemed to be t[...] area in most need of attention in co[...] leges. Perhaps this grows out of th[...] vagueness and ambiguity concernin[...] women's roles in general. As long [...] teachers and counselors are confuse[...] about "why women work" and off[...] complex excuses for women who utili[...] their abilities and capacities outsid[...] the home; or guide them into jobs, lik[...] teaching. that seem to offer the be[...] time for combining homework and a[...] occupation, there will still be expres[...] sions of dissatisfaction from graduate[...] Colleges must educate and guide me[...] and women toward a concept of equal[...] ity in marriage. One psychiatrist state[...]

We must recognize the right o[...] women as well as men to becom[...] friends on a basis of equality as per[...] sons and reorganize our social con[...] ditions to make this possible. W[...] must grant them the right to work[...] with men toward mutual ends, ph[...]

"Jane B. Berry, "Life Plans of Freshmen and Sophomore College Women." Unpublished Doctor of Education Project. New York: Teachers College, Columbia University, p. 84.

marriage on the basis of equality, with each partner contributing to the full extent of his or her potentiality in whatever area these potentialities lie—social, financial, intellectual, etc."

Another probable role expectation of Negro women is that they will be called upon to give leadership and support in citizenship responsibilities. The ten leaders who were interviewed had had much experience in this area. These leaders expressed appreciation for the fact that Negro women chose citizenship education as an important value though they believed the choice limited to domestic issues, and unrelated to international citizenship. As a matter of fact the graduates of the study indicated that education for international cooperation was least important for college to provide. Surely, colleges should be encouraged to create the kinds of experiences that expand the student's interest beyond the problems that have been traditionally faced by Negroes in a white society to include education for international understanding and cooperation.

It was stated that education should also meet the psychological needs of students as well as prepare them for their probable life roles. These needs are not always apparent in expressions of what is important to get out of college. For example, training for the practicalities of life took precedence over the aspects of education that relate closely to the personal development of women. The ultimate test of any education, nevertheless, is its effec-

tiveness in developing a person's capacity to know herself, accept herself, and realize self fulfillment. The overall picture of the graduates' choice of important values in education indicates that they did not place much importance in this concept of education. The question is raised: Does the hard earthy need of holding a job and contributing to the family budget subjugate learning for full creative expression to a lesser sphere? Maybe the concept of self-fulfillment seems a luxury to those who are facing many practicalities in their lives. Yet it appears that the more doggedly they see themselves as breadwinners rather than women who have a right to develop their personal interests and abilities, the more apparent is the need to encourage them to develop themselves as persons.

As the college—white or Negro, coeducational or women's—draws upon the experiences and opinions from former students such as the graduates in this study, it must seek to push toward a common denominator that cuts deep into the heart of college education—deeper than the mere addition of courses to the curriculum. Such a college might strive to understand the human needs that underlie job adjustment, family relationships and citizen participation. Prominent among these needs, it would seem, are the attitudes concerned with self-acceptance. A college should seek ways of cultivating the seeds of self-reliance, self-expression and of human warmth and understanding. In other words, college education should, above all else, help a person to know herself, accept herself and reach self fulfillment.

"Joan Harte, "Modern Attitudes Toward Women." (Lecture, ACAAP, Auxiliary Council to the Associates for the Development of Psychoanalysis, West 98th Street, New York, 1953.

Breaking Away: Higher Education in the 60s and Beyond

Angela Davis at Brandeis, 1961–1964

Angela Davis, excerpt from *Angela Davis: An Autobiography*.
(New York: Random House, 1974, 117–136, reprinted by permission of the author)

*P*erched on an enormous boulder protruding from a grassy knoll on the outskirts of Waltham, Massachusetts, is a brass sculpture of Justice Louis Brandeis, his arms outstretched, winglike, as if he were about to take flight—as if there were nowhere else to go.

I had come to assume that in order to safeguard its unorthodoxy, Elisabeth Irwin had spun a cocoon around itself. During those two years in New York I never quite overcame the sense of being out of place, of being an outsider who had penetrated that cocoon by accident. Nevertheless, I confronted it head on. And when the atmosphere became too close, too oppressive, I could always tear away a piece of the wall and slip out to other worlds—my childhood friends, Margaret and Claudia, Mary Lou Patterson, Phyllis Strong; politi-

cal work in Advance; my Black and Puerto Rican friends at
the Youth Center run by Mrs. Melish in Brooklyn.

Brandeis University was different. There were no roads
leading outside.

Its physical and spiritual isolation were mutually reinforc-
ing. There was nothing in Waltham but a clock factory, and
Cambridge and Boston were unreachable for those of us who
couldn't afford a car.

I searched the crowds of freshmen for others who were
Black. Just knowing they were there would have made me feel
a little more comfortable. But the full scholarship Brandeis
had bestowed upon me was apparently a guilt-motivated attempt to increase their Black freshman population of two. We
three were all female. I was glad that one of them, Alice, lived
on the same floor as I.

Although Alice and I struck up a friendship immediately,
it did not essentially alter my attitude toward the college. I
felt alienated, angry, alone and would have left the campus if
I had had the courage and had known where to go. Since I
was there—to stay, it seemed—I lived with this alienation and
began to cultivate it in a romantic sort of way. If I felt alone, I
refused to feel sorry for myself and refused to fight it by
actively seeking friends; I would *be* alone, aloof, and would
appear to enjoy it. It didn't help the situation that I had gotten
very much involved in the writings of the so-called Existential-
ists. Camus. Sartre. I retreated into myself and rejected practically everything outside.

Only in the artificial surroundings of an isolated, virtually
all-white college campus could I have allowed myself to cultivate this nihilistic attitude. It was as if in order to fight off the
unreal quality of my environment, I leaped desperately into
another equally unreal mode of living.

During that first semester, I didn't study very much. I
told myself that the courses I was compelled to take were
irrelevant anyway. I stayed out of the social life of the school,
or would wander into a formal dance in the blue jeans I wore

all the time—just for the sake of making a point. I called myself a communist, but refused to be drawn into the small campus movement because I felt that the politicos had approached me in an obviously patronizing manner. It seemed as if they were determined to help the "poor, wretched Negroes" become equal to them, and I simply didn't think they were worth becoming equal to.

The one thing that did excite me during that freshman year was the news that James Baldwin was scheduled to deliver a series of lectures on literature. Since I had first discovered *Go Tell It on the Mountain*, I read all of Baldwin's writings I could find. When he came to Brandeis, I made sure I captured a front seat. But he had hardly gotten into his lecturing when the news broke that the world was teetering on the edge of the abyss of World War III. The Cuban Missile Crisis had erupted.

James Baldwin announced that he could not continue his lectures without contradicting his moral conscience and abdicating his political responsibilities. In the meantime, a campus-wide rally was being pulled together, while students roamed the campus, either in a silent daze or else screaming out their fear that the world was about to be consumed in a nuclear holocaust.

Some of them got into cars and took off in a panic, saying they were on their way to Canada. What was so striking about the students' response to the crisis was its strongly selfish quality. They were not interested in the fact that the people of Cuba were in terrible jeopardy—or even that millions of innocent people elsewhere might be destroyed if a nuclear conflict broke out. They were interested in themselves, in saving their own lives. Girl friends and boyfriends went off together to get in their last little bit of love.

By the time the rally took place, large numbers of students had gone off by themselves and they were not able to hear the powerful speeches given by James Baldwin, Herbert Marcuse (this was the first time I heard him) and several other professors and graduate students. The point of their speeches was not to be frightened, not to despair, but to put pressure on the government to withdraw its threat.

It was good to feel part of a movement and once again be participating in rallies, teach-ins, demonstrations. But when the crisis was over, things settled back into their old grooves. During the brief period of protest, I was drawn toward the people with whom I felt I had most in common—the foreign students. I became friends with an Indian man, who was very gentle and had a keen sense of what was happening around us. It was my friendship with Lalit more than anything else, I suppose, that helped me understand concretely the interconnectedness of the freedom struggles of peoples throughout the world. I was profoundly moved when he talked about the incredible misery of his people in India. As he spoke I found myself constantly thinking about my people in Birmingham, my people in Harlem.

I also became friends with Melanie, a young woman from the Philippines, and Mac, a South Vietnamese woman about to be deported because she was opposed to Diem. Around the same time, I entered into a close friendship with Lani,' probably because we both felt so outside things at Brandeis.

Flo Mason, one of my friends from Elisabeth Irwin, and I corresponded regularly. I don't remember who initially conceived the idea, but we both decided to attend the Eighth World Festival for Youth and Students in Helsinki, Finland, the following summer. I was eager to meet revolutionary youth from other parts of the world, but my decision to make this trip was also motivated by a simple desire to leave the country in order to get a better perspective on things. It seemed that the farther I became removed from my home, my roots, the more restricted I felt and the farther I wanted to go.

The rest of the year I worked to earn money for the trip. I refiled books in the library stacks, filed cards in the Biology Department, and worked in Chomondeleys, the campus coffee shop. And I found a job in a two-bit soda parlor in Waltham. Having gotten back into the habit of studying, between my jobs and my books I didn't have very much time to do anything else. Even my social life—I was seeing a German student, Manfred Clemenz, around this time—consisted mostly of coffee in the cafeteria after an evening of studying.

Then it was June. My festival scholarship called for doing some volunteer work at the Festival Committee Headquarters in New York: typing, mimeographing, mailings. The Brandeis charter plane took us to London, where I wandered alone about the city for a day or two before my train left for Paris. My friend Harriet Jackson was going to meet me at the Gare du Nord, but a strike threw all the schedules awry, and there I was in Paris alone, knowing no one and without the slightest idea of how to find Harriet.

After a few days in a dirty hotel in the Latin Quarter exploring the city, and reading with horror the racist slogans scratched on walls throughout the city threatening death to the Algerians, I finally made contact with my friend. She had left a note at American Express in hopes that I would think of going there. By the time Flo arrived, we had moved into a tiny room on the top floor of an apartment building in the Sixteenth Arrondissement so close to the Eiffel Tower that from the one-foot-square window pane, you could see the elevator rising and falling. The *chambre. de bonne* had been rented by one of Harriet's friends who was studying in Paris and had agreed to let us use it while she was away.

One of ten such rooms, it could only be reached by climbing six flights of a rusty fire-escape type stairway. Like all the others, it had no plumbing, only a filthy toilet bowl and a cold-water hydrant at the end of the corridor. There was just enough space for a bed, a small closet, a table, and floor room for an air mattress and a pallet. Flo, Harriet and I took turns sleeping on the bed, the air mattress and the floor. We thought it was crowded in our room until we became acquainted with the people across the hall—a frail woman from Martinique trying to live in the same amount of space with her four robust daughters, ranging in age from about fourteen to twenty. Having just arrived from the Caribbean, they all left each day in search of work. Each evening they returned with nothing to show for their day but tired bodies, a little less money and, frequently, horror stories of being mistaken for Algerian women.

The three of us rushed around Paris being tourists, doing the things that cost the least and gave discounts to students: the Louvre, the Rodin Museum, Molière at La Comédie Française (which cost one franc for students). Hanging around the crowded cafés along the Boulevard St. Michel, we met people with interesting and exciting stories to tell— especially when it came to their distaste for the French. They were Africans, Haitians, other Antillais and Algerians. We were introduced to working-class Algerian eating places, hidden in the network of back streets in the Latin Quarter.

To be an Algerian living in Paris in 1962 was to be a hunted human being. While the Algerians were fighting the French army in their mountains and in the Europeanized cities of Algiers and Oran, paramilitary terrorist groups were falling indiscriminately upon men and women in the colonialist capital because they were, or looked like, Algerians.

In Paris, bombs were exploding in cafés frequented by North Africans, bloody bodies were discovered in dark side streets and anti-Algerian graffiti marred the sides of buildings and the walls of métro stations. One afternoon I attended a demonstration for the Algerian people in the square in front of the Sorbonne. When the *flics* broke it up with their high-power water hoses, they were as vicious as the redneck cops in Birmingham who met the Freedom Riders with their dogs and hoses.

The new places, the new experiences I had expected to discover through travel turned out to be the same old places, the same old experiences with a common message of struggle.

After Harriet left for the Soviet Union, Flo and I decided spontaneously to board a train for Geneva, but ended up trying to hitch-hike with a Swiss student just back from the University of Wisconsin. It was typical of our luck that it happened to be July 14—anniversary of the storming of the

Bastille—and thus virtually impossible to catch a ride. We got as far as Orly Airport, just on the outskirts of the city, pitched the Swiss student's tent in a field, ate dinner at the airport and bedded down for the night, with him outside guarding the tent. Not doing very much better the next morning, we caught buses and trains till we reached Lausanne, where the student's mother put us up for a few days.

With its quaint little houses built on ascending levels on the slopes of hills, Lausanne was the cleanest, most beautiful city I had seen. Now I understood why the wealthy sent their children to Switzerland.

From Lausanne, it was Geneva, back to Paris and on to Finland for the festival. The drab, monotonous postwar architecture of Helsinki concealed the tremendous vibrancy of the youth who were gathering there from all over the world.

In the brief two weeks of the festival, there were spectacular cultural programs, mass political rallies and countless seminars on the struggle in Africa, Latin America, Asia, the Middle East. The most exciting dimension of the festival, in my own opinion, came from the bilateral delegation meetings, because they were occasions for more intimate contact with the youth of other lands.

The cultural presentation given by the Cuban delegation was the most impressive event of the festival. Not that they performed in the most polished, sophisticated manner, but because their performance conveyed a fiercely compelling spirit of revolution. They were the youth of a revolution that was not yet three years old. With the U.S. delegation as audience, the Cubans satirized the way wealthy American capitalists had invaded their country and robbed them of all traces of sovereignty. They presented their attack on the invaders in plays, songs and dances. During those days, long before women's liberation had been placed on the agenda, we watched the Cuban militia women zealously defending their people's victory.

It is not easy to describe the strength and enthusiasm of the Cubans. One event however illustrates their infectious dynamism and the impact they had on us all. At the end of their show, the Cubans did not simply let the curtain fall. Their "performance," after all, had been much more than a mere show. It had been life and reality. Had they drawn the curtain and bowed to applause, it would have been as if their commitment was simply "art." The Cubans continued their dancing, doing a spirited conga right off the stage and into the audience. Those of us openly enthralled by the Cubans, their revolution and the triumphant beat of the drums rose spontaneously to join their conga line. And the rest—the timid ones, perhaps even the agents—were pulled bodily by the Cubans into the dance. Before we knew it we were doing this dance—a dance brought into Cuban culture by slaves dancing in a line of chains—all through the building and on into the streets. Puzzled Finns looked on in disbelief at hundreds of young people of all colors, oblivious to traffic, flowing down the streets of Helsinki.

Though it was the dominant theme, camaraderie was not the whole story of the festival. In keeping with the dictates of the Cold War, the CIA had planted its agents and informers in all the strategic areas of the festival, including the delegation from the United States. (A fact later admitted by the Agency). Provocations were frequent and assumed varied forms. Members of the delegation from the German Democratic Republic were kidnapped, for example, tear-gas bombs were set off in crowds during mass events and Hell's-Angels types picked fistfights with delegates in the streets of downtown Helsinki.

After saying good-bye to my new friends, and spending some time visiting my German friend, Manfred, I returned to the States to find an FBI investigator awaiting me.

"What were you doing at that Communist Youth Festival this summer?" the agent wanted to know. "Don't you know how we feel about Communists? Don't you know what we do to Communists?"

• • •

The experiences of the summer still very much alive, I felt older and more confident as I entered my second year at Brandeis. Meeting people from all over the world had taught me how important it was to be able to tear down the superficial barriers which separated us. Language was one of those barriers which could be removed easily. I decided to major in French. That year I immersed myself totally in my work: Flaubert, Balzac, Baudelaire, Rimbaud and the thousands of pages of Proust's *A La Recherche du Temps Perdu*. My interest in Sartre was still quite keen—every spare moment I could find, I worked my way through his writings: *La Nausée, Les Mains Sales, Les Séquestres d'Altona*, and the rest of the earlier and later plays, and the novels comprising the sequence *Les Chemins de la Liberté*. I read some of his philosophical and political essays and even tried my hand at *L'Etre et le Néant*. Since I had to contend with the isolation of the campus in one way or another, I decided to make constructive use of it by spending most of my waking hours in the library or in some hidden place with my books.

At first I roomed with Lani, but since we both preferred to live alone, she moved into a single when one became available. Tina, a Swedish friend, who wanted to live off-campus with a friend, pretended to move into my room, thus leaving me with the privacy I desired.

Gwen and Woody, graduate students at the university, were in charge of the Ridgewood men's dormitories. The fact that we were Black and had common friends in Birmingham made us feel close even before we got to know each other. If they wanted to go out on evenings and weekends, they could always count on me to stay with their baby boy while I studied. And whenever I felt like talking, they were ready to listen and give advice.

It was a quiet, subdued year on the campus—until the smug sense of comfort which reigned over this white liberal college was abruptly shattered by the appearance of Malcolm X. In the largest auditorium on campus, Gwen, Woody and I sat one-third of the way back, engulfed, it seemed, by the white crowd waiting breathlessly to hear this man who was the spokesman for the prophet Elijah Mohammed. Elijah Mohammed called himself the messenger of the Islamic God, Allah, chosen to reveal Allah's message to Black people in the United States.

Years before, at Parker High School, one of our classmates had been arrested for selling a "Black Muslim" newspaper. He was a gentle-looking, soft-spoken boy who kept to himself. Several times I had tried unsuccessfully to talk to him. On the day following his arrest, I learned for the first time that there was a nationwide organization of "Black Muslims" and, not questioning the prevailing propaganda, I thought they were a strange sect of people ranting and raving about Allah's future destruction of all white people—a group essentially unable to help solve the problem of racism. For a long time it bothered me that this classmate of mine was a member of the Muslims. I could not reconcile my own stereotyped notion of the Muslims with his sensitivity. I waited for him to get out of jail and return to school so I could ask him who the Muslims really were. But I never saw him again.

Finally Malcolm strode in, immaculately dressed, encircled by conservatively dressed, clean-shaven men, and women in long flowing robes. From their manner of carrying themselves I could feel the pride emanating from them. Quietly they took their seats in the first three rows. Malcolm, accompanied by several of the men, walked onstage.

Malcolm X began his speech with a subdued eloquence, telling about the religion of Islam and its relevance to Black people in the United States. I was fascinated by his description of the way Black people had internalized the racial inferiority thrust upon us by a white supremacist society. Mesmerized by his words, I was shocked to hear him say, speaking directly to his audience, "I'm talking about you! You! You and your ancestors, for centuries, have raped and murdered my people!" He was addressing himself to an all-white crowd and I wondered whether Gwen, Woody and the four or five other Black people in the audience felt, from that moment on, as outrageously misplaced as I did. Malcolm was addressing himself to white people, chastising them, informing them of their sins, warning them of the Armageddon to come, in which they would all be destroyed. Although I experienced a kind of morbid satisfaction listening to Malcolm reduce white people to virtually nothing, not being a Muslim, it was impossible for me to identify with his religious perspective. I kept thinking that it must be a tremendous experience to hear him speaking to a Black audience. For the white people, listening to Malcolm had been disorienting and disturbing. It was interesting that most of them were so bent on defending themselves and on distinguishing themselves from the slave master and the Southern segregationist it never struck them that they themselves could begin to do something concrete to fight racism.

Earlier in the year I had applied for a place in the Hamilton College Junior Year in France Program. After receiving the news of my acceptance, I fought hard with the Brandeis scholarship office, until they finally agreed to do the unprecedented by extending my regular scholarship to cover my third-year studies in France.

By the time the two busloads of us arrived from Paris, the resort of Biarritz, on the Bay of Biscay, near the border of Spain, had already been abandoned by the wealthy tourists. This was where we were to have our preparatory language courses. Deserted, the gaudy beachside casinos seemed even more decadent than if they had been teeming with voracious vacationing gamblers. The countless trinket shops lining the arcade-covered streets had a ravaged appearance that was exaggerated by the absence of customers. The shopkeepers looked desperate, as if they were wondering how to survive the next months without the tourists' money, and at the same time relieved that they had managed to survive the summer onslaught.

Walking through the streets of Biarritz, I felt like someone wandering into a place where a long drunken party had just broken up. The last staggering guests had already gone home, but no one had gotten around to cleaning up the mess. The traces of the summer orgy were embarrassing—like dirty underwear inadvertently left behind—and at the same time infuriating. I could see them squandering enormous wealth without the vaguest feeling of compassion for those whose slavery had created that wealth.

Not long after our arrival, a curious thing happened in the abandoned city: there was a sudden, massive flea invasion, the likes of which the working people of Biarritz had never seen before. For days, it was impossible to find a single patch of land or air uninfested by fleas. In our classrooms, the teacher could hardly be heard over the constant scratching. People scratched in cafés, movie theaters, bookstores, and they scratched just walking down the street. People with sensitive skin were beginning to look like lepers, their arms and legs covered with infected bites. Like everyone else's, my sheet was covered with little spots of blood.

If Ingmar Bergman had done a movie on the oppressive, parasitical tourists who come to Biarritz, and had included the flea invasion in his script, critics would have written that his symbolism was too blatant. In this city in its odd position of trying to recuperate from tourists and fleas—in this group of typically American students which without my presence would have been lily-white—my old familiar feelings of disorientation were rekindled.

SEPTEMBER 16, 1963

After class I asked the three or four students with whom I was walking to wait a moment while I bought a *Herald Tribune*. My attention divided between walking and listening to the conversation, just skimming the paper, I saw a headline about four girls and a church bombing. At first I was only vaguely aware of the words. Then it hit me! It came crashing down all around me. Birmingham. 16th Street Baptist Church.

The names. I closed my eyes, squeezing my lids into wrinkles as if I could squeeze what I had just read out of my head. When I opened my eyes again, the words were still there, the names traced out in stark black print.

"Carole," I said, "Cynthia. They killed them."

My companions were looking at me with puzzled expressions. Unable to say anything more, I pointed to the article and gave the newspaper to an outstretched hand.

"I know them. They're my friends . . ." I was spluttering.

As if she were repeating lines she had rehearsed, one of them said, "I'm sorry. It's too bad that it had to happen."

Before she spoke I was on the verge of pouring out all the feelings that had been unleashed in me by the news of the bomb which had ripped through four young Black girls in my hometown. But the faces around me were closed. They knew nothing of racism and the only way they knew how to relate to me at that moment was to console me as if friends had just been killed in a plane crash.

"What a terrible thing," one of them said. I left them abruptly, unwilling to let them have anything to do with my grief.

I kept staring at the names. Carole Robertson. Cynthia Wesley. Addie Mae Collins. Denise McNair. Carole—her family and my family had been close as long as I could remember. Carole, plump, with long wavy braids and a sweet face, was one of my sister's best friends. She and Fania were about the same age. They had played together, gone to dancing lessons together, attended little parties together. Carole's older sister and I had constantly had to deal with our younger sisters' wanting to tag along when we went places with our friends. Mother told me later that when Mrs. Robertson heard that the church had been bombed, she called to ask Mother to drive her downtown to pick up Carole. She didn't find out, Mother said, until they saw pieces of her body scattered about.

The Wesleys had been among the Black people to move to the west side of Center Street. Our house was on Eleventh

291

Court; theirs was on Eleventh Avenue. From our back door to their back door was just a few hundred feet across a gravel driveway that cut the block in two. The Wesleys were childless, and from the way they played with us it was obvious that they loved children. I remembered when Cynthia, just a few years old, first came to stay with the Wesleys. Cynthia's own family was large and suffered from the worst poverty. Cynthia would stay with the Wesleys for a while, then return to her family— this went on until the stretches of time she spent with the Wesleys grew longer and her stays at home grew shorter. Finally, with the approval of her family, the Wesleys officially adopted her. She was always immaculate, her face had a freshly scrubbed look about it, her dresses were always starched and her little pocketbook always matched her newly shined shoes. When my sister Fania came into the house looking grubby and bedraggled, my mother would often ask her why she couldn't keep herself clean like Cynthia. She was a thin, very sensitive child and even though I was five years older, I thought she had an understanding of things that was far more mature than mine. When she came to the house, she seemed to enjoy talking to my mother more than playing with Fania.

Denise McNair. Addie Mae Collins. My mother had taught Denise when she was in first grade and Addie Mae, although we didn't know her personally, could have been any Black child in my neighborhood.

When the lives of these four girls were so ruthlessly wiped out, my pain was deeply personal. But when the initial hurt and rage had subsided enough for me to think a little more clearly, I was struck by the objective significance of these murders.

This act was not an aberration. It was not something sparked by a few extremists gone mad. On the contrary, it was logical, inevitable. The people who planted the bomb in the girls' restroom in the basement of 16th Street Baptist Church were not pathological, but rather the normal products of their surroundings. And it was this spectacular, violent event, the savage dismembering of four little girls, which had burst out of the daily, sometimes even dull, routine of racist oppression.

No matter how much I talked, the people around me were simply incapable of grasping it. They could not understand why the whole society was guilty of this murder—why their beloved Kennedy was also to blame, why the whole ruling stratum in their country, by being guilty of racism, was also guilty of this murder.

Those bomb-wielding racists, of course, did not plan specifically the deaths of Carole, Cynthia, Addie Mae and Denise. They may not have even consciously taken into account the possibility of someone's death. They wanted to terrorize Birmingham's Black population, which had been stirred out of its slumber into active involvement in the struggle for Black liberation. They wanted to destroy this movement before it became too deeply rooted in our minds and our lives. This is what they wanted to do and they didn't care if someone happened to get killed. It didn't matter to them one way or the other. The broken bodies of Cynthia, Carole, Addie Mae and Denise were incidental to the main thing—which was precisely why the murders were even more abominable than if they had been deliberately planned.

In November our group moved to Paris. I was assigned to the Lamotte family at 13 bis rue Duret, a little ways from the Arc de Triomphe. Two other women from the Hamilton program lived there too. Jane was on the third floor with M. and Mme. Lamotte and their three children. Christie and I shared one of the two bedrooms in the smaller second-floor apartment of M. Lamotte's mother. Each morning she brought us a big wooden tray with two large bowls of café au lait, pieces of a freshly baked *baguette,* and two hunks of butter. In the evening we had dinner with the family upstairs. We walked through the old cobblestone courtyard to the métro station around the corner, and traveled underground on the old red trains to the Latin Quarter to attend our classes. Most of mine were at the section of the Sorbonne called the Institut de Préparation et de Perfectionnement de Professeurs de Français à L'Etranger.

In the Sorbonne, I always felt as if I were in church—it was centuries old, with tremendous pillars holding up uncommonly high ceilings which displayed faded old paintings. The sacredness exuded by the place forced thousands of students inside to observe the silence. My business there seemed incongruous with the surroundings. My studies were devoted almost entirely to contemporary literature—one course on contemporary French novels, another on plays, one on poetry and one on Ideas. The only other course I took was organized by the Hamilton program itself and required attending the theater each week and discussing and writing about the plays we had seen. By the time the year was up, I had the feeling I had seen most of what was interesting on the stage in Paris—including the Peking Opera and the Ballet Africaine from Guinea.

When the news broke in Paris that Kennedy had been shot, everyone rushed down to the U.S. Embassy. Kennedy's assassination was certainly no source of joy to me. Though his hands were far from clean (I kept remembering the Bay of Pigs), killing him was not going to solve any problems. Besides, the Vice President from Texas and his cronies in the oil monopolies would probably only make things worse for my people. Nevertheless, I felt out of place at the Embassy, surrounded by crowds of "Americans in Paris" and it was difficult to identify with their weeping. I wondered how many of them had shed tears—or had truly felt saddened—when they read the *Herald Tribune* story about the murders of Carole, Cynthia, Addie Mae and Denise.

Later on in the year, I accompanied a friend who had been invited to attend the Vietnamese Tet celebration. That night, two New Year's programs were taking place—one organized and attended by the South Vietnamese who remained loyal to Diem and the other organized and attended by the North Vietnamese, together with the socialist and other op-

position forces in the South. We attended the North Vietnamese celebration. Held in a gigantic stadium in a working-
class district of Paris, it was a grand seven-hour spectacle
consisting of songs, comedy acts, acrobatic numbers and skits,
all full of the vigor of their struggle and conveying a message
that did not require an understanding of Vietnamese. Like the
thousands of Vietnamese sitting around the stadium, I was
enchanted. But I was shocked back to the brutal realities of
their experiences by the recurring satires directed against the
U.S. government and its military. The longest and most vehe-
ment applause and laughter were always at the appearance of
an actor dressed up like a U.S. GI, who was the butt of jokes
or, in more serious episodes, fell in defeat.

Although I was on the verge of receiving a degree in
French Literature, what I really wanted to study was philosophy. I was interested in Marx, his predecessors and his successors. Over the last years, whenever I could find the time, I
read philosophy on the side. I didn't really know what I was
doing, except that it gave me a feeling of security and comfort
to read what people had to say about such formidable things
as the universe, history, human beings, knowledge.

During my second year at Brandeis, I had picked up *Eros
and Civilization* by Herbert Marcuse and had struggled with
it from beginning to end. That year he was teaching at the
Sorbonne. When I arrived in Paris the following year, he was
already back at Brandeis, but people were still raving about
his fantastic courses. When I returned to Brandeis, the first
semester of my senior year was so crowded with required
French courses that I could not officially enroll in Marcuse's
lecture series on European political thought since the French
Revolution. Nevertheless, I attended each session, rushing in
to capture a seat in the front of the hall. Arranged around the
room on progressively higher levels, the desks were in the style
of the UN General Assembly room. When Marcuse walked
onto the platform, situated at the lowest level of the hall, his

presence dominated everything. There was something imposing about him which evoked total silence and attention when
he appeared, without his having to pronounce a single word.
The students had a rare respect for him. Their concentration
was not only total during the entire hour as he paced back and
forth while he lectured, but if at the sound of the bell Marcuse
had not finished, the rattling of papers would not begin until
he had formally closed the lecture.

One day, shortly after the semester began, I mustered up
enough courage to put in a request for an interview with
Marcuse. I had decided to ask him to help me draw up a
bibliography on basic works in philosophy. Having assumed I
would have to wait for weeks to see him, I was surprised when
I was told he would be free that very afternoon.

From afar, Marcuse seemed unapproachable. I imagine
the combination of his stature, his white hair, the heavy ac-
cent, his extraordinary air of confidence, and his wealth of
knowledge made him seem ageless and the epitome of a philosopher. Up close, he was a man with inquisitive sparkling
eyes and a fresh, very down-to-earth smile.

Trying to explain my reasons for the appointment, I told
him that I intended to study philosophy in graduate school,
perhaps at the university in Frankfurt, but that my independent reading in philosophy had been unsystematic—without
regard for any national or historical relations. What I wanted
from him—if it was not too much of an imposition—was a list
of works in the sequence in which I ought to read them. And
if he gave me permission, I wanted to enroll in his graduate
seminar on Kant's *Critique of Pure Reason*.

"Do you really want to study philosophy?" Professor
Marcuse asked, slowly and placing emphasis on each word.
He made it sound so serious and so profound—like an initia-
tion into some secret society which, once you join, you can
never leave. I was afraid that a mere "yes" would ring hollow
and inane.

"At least, I want to see if I am able," was about the only
thing I could think of to answer.

"Then you should begin with the Pre-Socratics, then Plato and Aristotle. Come back again next week and we will discuss the Pre-Socratics.

I had no idea that my little request would develop into stimulating weekly discussions on the philosophers he suggested, discussions which gave me a far more exciting and vivid picture of the history of philosophy than would have emerged from a dry introduction-to-philosophy course.

Shortly after the Nazi seizure of power in Germany, Marcuse had emigrated to the United States, along with a group of intellectuals who had established the Institut für Sozialforschung. Among them were Theodor Adorno and Max Horkheimer. They had continued their work for a number of years in this country, but after the defeat of the fascists, they reestablished the Institute as a part of the regular university in Frankfurt. I had first become acquainted with the work of the Institute through Manfred Clemenz, the German student I had met my first year at Brandeis. During the summer after my studies in France, I had spent several weeks in Frankfurt attending a few of Adorno's lectures, and getting to know some of the students there. At that time, my knowledge of German was minimal, but the people around me translated the essential points of the lectures into English or French. Later I read all of Adorno's and Horkheimer's works that had been translated into English or French, in addition to Marcuse's writings. In this way I had acquainted myself with their thought, which was collectively known as Critical Theory.

During that last year at Brandeis, I made up my mind to apply for a scholarship to study philosophy at the university in Frankfurt. Marcuse confirmed my conviction that this was the best place to study, given my interest in Kant, Hegel and Marx. The remaining months of the school year were consumed by intensive preparation in philosophy, German language and the final requirements for my B.A. degree, including a year-long honors project on the Phenomenological Attitude, which I thought I had discovered in the works of the contemporary French novelist Robbe-Grillet. The most challenging and fulfilling course was the graduate seminar that Marcuse conducted on the *Critique of Pure Reason*. Poring over a seemingly incomprehensible passage for hours, then suddenly grasping its meaning gave me a sense of satisfaction I had never experienced before.

My parents were not overjoyed at the idea of my leaving the country again, particularly since I had not yet decided how long I wanted to remain in Germany. Nevertheless, they were extremely proud to attend the graduation ceremony, where they heard my name called among the Phi Beta Kappas and magna cum laudes. I gave my mother the diplomas, certificates and medals and we packed up the things I had accumulated over the last four years, dropped off my friend Celeste in Providence and headed down the highway for Birmingham.

Nikki Giovanni at Fisk, 1959–1967

Nikki Giovanni, excerpt from *Gemini: An Extended Autobiographical Statement on My First Twenty-five Years of Being a Black Poet.*
(Indianapolis: Bobbs-Merrill, 1971, p. 7, reprinted by permission of the author)

Nikki Giovannl: Her Years at Fisk in Retrospect
(Interview with Nikki Giovanni by Elizabeth L. Ihle, November, 1989)

You always think the ones you love will always be there to love you. I went on to my grandfather's alma mater and got kicked out and would have disgraced the family but I had enough style for it not to be considered disgraceful. I could not/did not adjust to the Fisk social life and it could not/did not adjust to my intellect, so Thanksgiving I rushed home to Grandmother's without the bitchy dean of women's permission and that dean put me on social probation. Which would have worked but I was very much in love and not about to consider her punishment as anything real I should deal with. And the funny thing about that Thanksgiving was that I knew everything would go down just as it did. But I still wouldn't have changed it because Grandmother and Grandpapa would have had dinner alone and I would have had dinner alone and the next Thanksgiving we wouldn't even have him and Grandmother and I would both be alone by ourselves, and the only change would have been that Fisk considered me an ideal student, which means little on a life scale. My grandparents were surprised to see me in my brown slacks and beige sweater nervously chain-smoking and being so glad to touch base again. And she, who knew everything, never once asked me about school. And he was old so I lied to him. And I went to Mount Zion Baptist with them that Sunday and saw he was going to die. He just had to. And I didn't want that. Because I didn't know what to do about Louvenia, who had never been alone in her life.

I left Sunday night and saw the dean Monday morning. She asked where I had been. I said home. She asked if I had permission. I said I didn't need her permission to go home. She said, "Miss Giovanni," in a way I've been hearing all my life, in a way I've heard so long I know I'm on the right track when I hear it, and shook her head. I was "released from the school" February 1 because my "attitudes did not fit those of a Fisk woman." Grandpapa died in April and I was glad it was warm because he hated the cold so badly

NIKKI GIOVANNI: HER YEARS AT FISK IN RETROSPECT

Elizabeth Ihle interviewed Nikki Giovanni in November, 1989, about the latter's experiences at Fisk as recorded in <u>Gemini</u> and her subsequent career there. The following are excerpts from that interview:

ELI: Evidently, you eventually went back to Fisk and graduated. You must have gone to Fisk at a very young age--sixteen?

NG: I was an early entry. I'm not sure we still have that option. The Ford Foundation sponsored a program through which you could take your SAT's in your sophomore or junior year. There were twenty-one of us early entrants at Fisk when I was there. What we did was simply skip our senior year and go to Fisk. My classmate Tanya Garland was fifteen because she had skipped both her junior and senior high school years. She was a math whiz. Sherman Green was a part of that program. Sherman lives in New York now, I know that both Morehouse and Spelman had similar programs.

ELI: In retrospect, do you think that early entry was a good idea?

NG: Why not? If you are going to blow a year, you might as well blow it at college as to blow it at high school. I'm not a math person, for example, so I missed trigonometry because that is a senior level course, but it wasn't going to affect me any. My classmate Tanya, who was a whiz, had already done it anyway. Yes, I think it is a good program. I think in all fairness to Fisk, the others, and me, I must say that Sherman Green was the only one of the twenty-one of us who graduated on time.

But, now looking back on our experiences, I think Fisk needed more sensitivity to the situations--I don't even want to say problems--that you might face going from high school, for example, into a college. Going from being under your parents to actually living on your own, I don't think the school was capable then and--of course we didn't know as much as we do now--of being as aware as you probably need to be to that group of youngsters.

ELI: Were you all integrated into the regular program?

NG: Yes.

ELI: Were your identities known to the other freshmen?

NG: I think so. If I recall correctly, I think probably everybody pretty much knew who we were because we tested

302

out of the freshman classes anyway. We didn't have to take
freshman English; we were in honors programs. I tested
into humanities, because I had done all the reading. That
was going to be my field anyway.

ELI: So you knew going into college, you were going to be a writer
or just in the humanities or...?

NG: All I was interested in books, but vocationally I didn't
begin to choose until I actually graduated from college. I
knew writing was what I really liked, but in terms of what
I was interested in I knew I wasn't going to be a doctor or
a chem major. I didn't have a background in it, and my
interest in science is theoretical. What I had read was
Alfred North Whitehead because the guy I used to date was a
math whiz, and so I did a lot of theoretical reading, even
Einstein. My interest though was not in solving these
problems; it was in applications. How do we take what we
know about the universe and apply it?

ELI: In your book you say that you evidently came home for
Thanksgiving without permission. This must have been about
1960.

NG: I suppose it was. I haven't reread Gemini.

ELI: Fisk students had been active in the Civil Rights Movement
in the late 50's. Was Diane Nash [a Fisk student and a
leader in the Civil Rights movement] there?

NG: Yes, Diane was there. They were all there. Jim Lawson was
there. Of course, I am sure Diane doesn't remember me from
Fisk because I was an early entry, and she certainly was a
big figure on campus. All freshmen knew who Diane Nash
was. Fisk was involved in the sit-ins.

Just to set the record straight with you, the Tennessee State
students started the Nashville sit-ins, and because they
were in a state college they got a lot of pressure to
desist. They ran the risk of being kicked out because
State was heavily dependent on the Tennessee legislature
for funds. Fisk was a private, liberal arts school, and we
had an intellectual reputation. DuBois was one of our
graduates; we had James Weldon Johnson as one of our
presidents. Fisk students took up the movement after the
TSU students were being expelled, suspended, or just being
heavily pressured. The Fisk attitude was, and I think
rightly so, that students are independent human beings and
have a right to demonstrate. We got a lot of support too
from our French professor, Joseph Cottin, and Roger Askew
was especially supportive of the students. The
administration didn't much care for our activism.

I think the students in my generation were absolutely right to put schools on the line. What's the point of an education if you can't utilize it, can't be a normal human being?

ELI: During that first semester that you were there, were you politically active?

NG: Nearly everybody sat-in. One of the things that made Fisk exciting was to sit-in because you felt an obligation.

ELI: Did you every think about going to any other place besides Fisk?

NG: I never did. I only applied to one school. Grandpoppa was going to Philadelphia because he has a daughter, my aunt, who lives in Philadelphia, and asked if I would like to go. So I went to Philadelphia. Grandmother called when I was up there and said I needed to come back because we had gotten this telegram from Fisk that I had to take this test and that if I did well I probably would be accepted. I took the train back and took the test and was accepted. I never had a reason to apply any place else.

ELI: So you got in some trouble when you went AWOL from Fisk at Thanksgiving?

NG: A lot of it, and a lot of it was not the fault of the institution; some of it purely belonged to me. First of all, we were young, and we were intellectually capable. We literally had the dean of students, Anne Cheatham, in a position of kicking out of school dean's list students. Not a good thing to do, but there were a lot of real struggles going on too. Probably we lost in one respect really good students who got in a struggle with Anne Cheatham who got to kick us out, but on the other hand she was allowed to resign at the end of the year. It was probably a tit-for-tat. I think Fisk probably just didn't deal with the fact that we were going to be individuals and certainly someone like myself, who had strong feelings about what I should and shouldn't ask people to do, who didn't--and still don't-- recognize anybody's right to tell me when I can and can't go home. Probably Cheatham wasn't used to someone saying to her, "I don't recognize your authority." It was that kind of a struggle of wills if you can see a 16-year old saying to a dean of students, "I simply don't concede to your authority; I think you are wrong." It bothered my mother because she and my grandmother came down and said things like, "You are going to get kicked out!" And I said, "Well , if she can do that more power to her." But actually she could and she did. So I had to rethink how do you approach changes that you want to make.

ELI: According to _Gemini_, you got invited to leave after the first semester because of your attitudes weren't in accord with those of Fisk woman.

4

NG: That's a catch all-phrase they use all the time. I don't know
    that Fisk kicks people out these days. I'm sure they do
    probably for good reason, but that was a catch-all phrase.
    But they were right--I wasn't doing a lot of bending, and I
    think it's important. I don't know if I said in _Gemini_, but
    I have said it a lot since: if you are not getting something
    you want, it's important to rethink. So, when I got
    kicked out, I really did have to rethink, and I traveled for
    a while before returning to Fisk and graduating. I could
    have graduated from some place else. But I thought that I
    don't want this to stand because it represented a failure to
    me.

    I went back in 1964. In the meantime, a woman who died two
    years ago--I dedicated my latest book to her--named Jackie
    Cowan had become the Dean of Students, and Jackie and I
    became friends.

ELI: How was Fisk different the second time?

NG: Well, the fit was little bit different. First of all, Cowan
    was a MSW, and I have a lot of respect for Master Social
    Work because they approach people. We also had a new
    president, James Lawson, and Fisk was much more student
    oriented. But, then I was older. Also, I had learned a lot
    about how one goes about getting things done. You just
    can't walk in and say, "I'm smart and wonderful. You have
    to put up with me no matter what I do." I think there is a
    maturing process.

ELI: You evidently brought the campus chapter of S.N.C.C.
    [Student Nonviolent Coordinating Committee] back into being.

NG: Well, S.N.C.C. had been and always will be radical. It just
    didn't seem fair at all. I am an older student first of all,
    and I was working with the school newspaper. We started a
    literary magazine. What was that called? I saw it briefly
    when I was going through some of my papers. We had a new
    honors lounge, which was really nice, in Jubilee Hall which
    is our flagship.

    So the kids who used to hang in the honors center decided to
    start a magazine. What does it take to start a magazine?
    You need a room with paper, and so we were doing things like
    that. The thing about S.N.C.C. came about because somebody
    wanted to hear Stokely Carmichael, and someone had to invite
    him. At Fisk, like most small schools that I'm familiar
    with, fraternities and sororities had the power, and they
    ran the campus. It seemed to me that S.N.C.C. was no
    different from any other group. S.N.C.C. had lost its
    charter some time ago not for cause, but because it annoyed
    people. We held a rally, and I spoke. We took some kids
    over to the student council.

ELI: At this point you are one of the student leaders? you
     had graduated to leadership status?

NG: Yeah, it seemed like the reasonable thing to do, and
    it seemed that the student council wasn't thinking. I mean
    why wouldn't you grant a charter to S.N.C.C.?

ELI: So, it wasn't an administrative decision; it was a student
     decision.

NG: Oh, it was an administrative decision, but it was
    administered through the students. Never misunderstand that
    if the administration didn't want something they would let
    the students know they didn't want it. The students, of
    course, enjoyed the power that they had, so they would act
    for the administration. I think that happens on your campus,
    it happens on mine, and so it was a question of taking it
    back to the student council. Instead of saying you are a
    bunch of lackeys for the administration, which we could have
    done and have engendered poor feelings, we said why don't we
    talk about this because there is no appreciable difference
    between S.N.C.C. and Kappa or Delta or any of the other
    sororities or fraternities. What we are saying is these
    people have a right; we as students have a right to associate
    in a non-violent manner. We have a right to have part of the
    student funds to bring in speakers that we want to bring in.
    So it was a reasonable request.

ELI: So you got the charter. Did you invite Stokely Carmichael?

NG: Yes, and he came, and I was responsible for Carmichael's
    first visit because I was head of S.N.N.C., and we controlled
    it very well. The police used to trail Stokely around, and
    what you didn't want was inciting [to riot]. We absolutely
    did not want Carmichael on the campus inciting. And it is
    not that Carmichael incited, but he could. So what we wanted
    was a speech in the chapel. You know, "Put you suit on,
    Stokely, and give a speech in the chapel." And the second
    time he came was a problem, but I had graduated.

    I finished in February. Dean Redd, who was our academic dean,
    stopped me, I was walking across campus one day and said,
    "Did you realize that you have not fulfilled all your
    requirements?" And I said no. What I had forgotten to do was
    to take freshman history, which as a history major I was
    required to take. I absolutely had forgotten it, and nobody
    had flagged it. So, I'm a history major graduating with
    honors and he says, "Well, you know you forgot to do that."
    And I said, "Well I'll just come back,." because I was like
    any other kid, I had no plans. So I said I'll just come back
    in September," because it was only offered in September. He
    said, "Well, I was thinking of waiving it and letting you go
    on." Because at this point all I'm really doing is kind of

    organizing the campus.

ELI: Maybe they were kind of glad to let you leave.

NG: I'm sure they were very happy. I mean what am I going to make
    on world history? I'm going to make an A, right? So, why
    make me come back to take one course? I mean it didn't make
    sense, and it was again what I would call the New Fisk
    because I think five years previous to that they would have
    said no. So Dean Redd said "No, you can actually leave!" You
    can go on now, and you can come back and march if you want
    to, but you are finished here."

Women and Men: the Balance of Power on College Campuses

Yvonne R. Chappelle, "The Black Woman on the Negro College Campus"

(*The Black Scholar,* January–February, 1970, 36–39, reprinted by permission)

THE BLACK WOMAN ON THE NEGRO COLLEGE CAMPUS

by YVONNE R. CHAPPELLE

THE BLACK WOMAN is a dominant presence on the Negro college campus. As a student, she is in the majority when one is comparing the number of females versus the number of males. As an employee, she holds more faculty positions and has more of the top administrative jobs than her black male colleagues. In the secretarial and staff jobs (where women are traditionally hired), she outnumbers both her black male and her white co-workers.

This state of affairs is both an asset and a liability to the black revolution. It is an asset because the black woman is in a position to influence developments on the Negro college campus in ways that might be beneficial to the revolution. On the other hand, her position of power itself contradicts a major goal of the revolution: namely, to reverse the matriarchal pattern imposed on black people by years of racism and of political and economic hamstringing of black people. It appears to me, therefore, that the most important task for the black woman on the Negro college campus is to help change there this balance of power and of numbers.

YVONNE CHAPPELLE is Coordinator of Student Life Programs at Wilberforce University. She has been the bi-lingual secretary for the Guinea Student Project Office of the African-American Institute in Washington, and served as Executive Secretary of the High Commission for the Inga Dam Project, Republic of the Congo. She has travelled throughout the Third World and Europe.

Let us first examine the position of the black co-ed. Although the ratio of men to women may have been nearly the same in her freshmen class ,the higher dropout rate for male students means that she is in the majority in the total student population. The danger of this situation is that the male student on Negro campuses may be so overwhelmed by the female presence that he fails to be aggressive in competitive situations.

A FACULTY member recently relayed to me a story which illustrates what being outnumbered by the ladies can do to black males in the classroom. During his first few meetings with his large class in which there were far more women than men, the professor found that discussion dragged. The men in the class said very little, seemed easily intimidated by a female classmate's reply to their comments, and did not refute the arguments advanced by ladies in the class. Finally, the professor decided to divide the class into two sections. One section had women only, and in the other section, the men were in the majority. Right away, he said, there was a noticeable change in the behavior of the men in the class. They began to participate actively in discussions, not fearing to advance controversial arguments and not hesitating to contradict the opinions of their classmates — male or female.

The black female student, then, must assist the revolution by finding ways to encourage aggressiveness on the part of her male fellow-students. It is true that to some extent she is already doing this. For example, she looks to the males on campus for leadership. Thus, although the black co-ed is very active on campus, she is unlikely to be president, vice-president or treasurer of anything other than her sorority (if she belongs to one) or other exclusively female organizations. However, there is some indication that this willingness on the part of distaffers to entrust leadership to the males may not be enough to create more strong, assertive black men in the student body.

On my own campus, for instance, I am beginning to hear complaints that it is "hard to find people to work on committees." Although the complaint is generally expressed in terms of finding "people" or finding "students," it really has to do with a dearth of *males* for these committee assignments. The speaker often implies that he would like, or even expect, to see the spot filled by a male. An implication that lies even deeper beneath the surface is that the women on campus are hesitant to participate in co-education groups that do not have strong male leadership. Yet, the dearth of male leaders for these organizations is a disquieting fact of campus life. The result could be that women will begin to fill the void, thus extending the campus matriarchy instead of helping to eliminate it. The freshmen at Wilberforce this year elected the first female Class President in the recent history of the University. My fear is that this election may be the beginning of a trend, rather than an exception.

In saying this, I am suggesting that there is a need to find new ways of encouraging aggressiveness in the black male student. I don't pretend to have any formulae. However, the alert black co-ed might try: (1) to ask his opinion more often; (2) to express her own views so as to allow for the possibility that he may have different ideas, equally rational or

valid; (3) to praise and support him whenever he does assert himself positively.

The task of getting more black men than women on the Negro college campus is more difficult to deal with with. It may require greater community efforts to encourage black men to remain in high school. It certainly requires improving the method and content of education so that it will be more exciting and more "relevant" to the black male youth of our times. Meanwhile, the black woman must encourage the men in her life to go to college — and to stay there long enough to get their degrees.

The problem of black female dominance over the black male within the faculty and administration at the Negro college is complicated by the presence of large numbers of white men in key positions. I became suddenly aware of the extent of the problem about a year and a half ago. A small group of administrators, faculty members and students had been invited to meet with a similar group at a neighboring, predominantly white college, to explore possibilities for cooperation. Looking around the room as the meeting started, I noticed that there was not a single black male present. My college's representation consisted of approximately equal numbers of black women and white men.

It then occurred to me that there were far too few black males on our college payroll. At that time, there were six full-time faculty members and twelve major administrators among the 104 persons falling in these two categories. One and a half years and two student boycotts later, the situation is but little improved. Seventeen black men have been hired since then. However, ten black men have left the college in that period. Thus, there has been a net gain of only seven black males, all but one in the administration.

Statistics on this group of new employees may provide some answers to the question, "How does the Negro college compete with industry and with the large, well-endowed white college in attracting black males?" First, over half of the black men hired during the period came to accept newly established administrative posts. This meant that the jobs they were accepting were higher paying than the average campus post. It also meant that there was an opportunity for them to develop their own job descriptions, thereby permitting growth according to one's interests and abilities. The importance of this factor will be seen later in the discussion.

A second statistic of interest is that, of thirteen newly employed black men still on the campus, nine are alumni and nine are under 30. It appears, then, that one must look to the graduates of the institution and to the young. For, the young are more likely to really believe in the goals of the revolution, and the alumni are more likely to feel enough concern about the college to consider making some sacrifices in order to be a part of its development. For both the young and the alumnus, it may be an easy way to meet the revolutionary obligation "to return and to relate to the black community."

MEANWHILE, what can and should the black female administrator or faculty member do to overturn the matriarchal rule in the Negro college? First, she should do her part to increase the number of black males on the campus. This requires not only working to bring new talent to the campus, but also working to keep on the campus the talent that is there.

There are several things that the distaff employee can do to help the college recruit black men. For a start, she may take every opportunity to stress to key people on the campus the need for a diligent recruitment campaign. Next, she may encourage talented black men that she knows or encounters to apply for campus openings. It may happen that a talented black woman is offered a post on the Negro college campus because the administration is convinced a qualified black male cannot be found at a price the college is

able to afford. Should this happen, the black woman has an obligation to refuse the position and force the institution to continue the search (even if it means compromising by changing the definition of "qualified," or by raising the price it is willing to pay).

The problem of keeping on the campus the black men who are there is one of considerable proportions. The number of black males who come to the Negro campus only to leave within a year or two is disquietingly high. For example, of the ten black men who left our campus during the past eighteen months, only two had been associated with the college more than two years. Two more had been here for two years. Five had stayed for a year, while one had lasted for only a few months. Of the black men currently employed by the college, only four (including the President) have been here more than eighteen months. If we may judge from past trends, nearly half of these newcomers will have left the college by August 1970.

Only a few of the black men who leave the Negro college campus every year do so so only because of the lure of better opportunities elsewhere. Most leave primarily because they are frustrated in their attempts to be *men* in the college setting. This may be less of a problem where the job description is not rigidly fixed, as with a newly established position. But even the person in the new position shares much of the frustration of other "soul brothers" employed by the college.

THE SOURCES of the frustration of the black male employee are varied. He may feel that his job offers too little opportunity for growth or advancement. He may be unwilling to accept the necessity for approval of his proposals or for control over his program by white administrators. He may feel that these and other abridgements of his autonomy are intended as a subtle judgement by the institution of his capacity to perform competently. He may be impatient with the time consuming methods of the college bureaucracy, especially when he is in a hurry to get done the things that should have been done long before he came on the job. He may feel uncomfortable about the need to cultivate people who wield power and influence not suggested by their job titles.

The black woman staff members has an important role to play in easing this frustration factor. For one thing, she can suggest and support promotion opportunities for her male colleagues. For another thing, she may "run interference" for him by having the patience to wage necessary battles. I note here that the black male is generally unlikely to fight to change the situations and the conditions that he finds frustrating. His impatience to get on with the job is much more likely to make him respond by adding these conditions and situations to the list of reasons why he should leave the campus.

BUT the most important service the black woman can render in seeking to ease the frustration factor is simply to be a friend to her male colleague. There may be times when she may listen to him explode and thereby prevent him from saying something rash in another presence. As a friend, she is in a position to suggest to him more tactful ways of accomplishing his goals. As a friend, she may boost his morale at crucial moments by letting him know that he is needed, wanted and appreciated on the campus.

The second task of the black woman as she seeks to change the balance to favor the black man on the Negro college campus, is to use her position of power and influence to make the black university the kind of place to which a black man would want to come. We must assume here that the black men who are willing to come to the black campus believe it is a good place to be involved in the black revolution. Such men will be looking for a campus where black students are proud to be black. They will be looking for a campus where black students are willing to work hard to acquire the knowledge and skills necessary to assist in the task of improving the lot of black people in the world. They will be looking for a campus where the faculty and administration are progressive, innovative, and supportive of students.

The black woman on the Negro college campus, then, must work hard to make her institution progressive, innovative, and supportive of the goals of black people. She must constantly be aware of the needs and goals of black students. She must continually endeavor to make her colleagues equally attuned to these goals and needs. She must consistently develop and submit proposals for meeting student needs and for assisting the progress of the institution. In short, she must be intensely loyal to the black college and to the black man. By her loyalty and her hard work, she may indeed make the black campus a place where black men will want to be — both as students and as part of the "establishment."

314

The Graduate Experience

Joanne V. Gabbin, "First Fruits: Harvesting the Promise of
Education, 1969–1970"
(Manuscript by Joanne V. Gabbin, James Madison University,
December 1, 1989)

First Fruits: Harvesting the Promise of Education, 1969-1970

In 1969 when I realized that I wanted to go to graduate school, it did not occur to me that there would be any barriers that I could not scale. I did not have money to pay tuition; I had not been accepted into a graduate program; I did not even know where my education would lead me if I accomplished the other steps. However, I was determined to attend and convinced that I would be successful.

Perhaps my confidence issued from the optimism of an age in which idealistic men and women sought to better their society by holding it accountable to its Constitution. Perhaps my determination lay in my awareness that enough people had suffered and sacrificed to allow me and others like me equal access to education. Or maybe my youth convinced me that there was time enough to try this new experiment called graduate school. Whatever my reasons, I proceeded to the office of the secretary of the English department at the University of Chicago and said, "I want to go to school. Could you help me?"

A kind, officious woman by the name of Catherine Ham was on the receiving end of this question. She had worked at the University of Chicago for many years and had rarely encountered a black student in an advanced program in literature and languages. She was aware of the uneasy truce that existed between the University and the black people who lived in the communities bordering Hyde Park. She understood better than most the great psychological distance between those privileged, well-heeled intellectuals at the U of C and the people who resided just across the Midway Pliassance in Woodlawn. Like many other whites from the university, she avoided Woodlawn where burned out buildings and business establishments evidenced the self-destructive fury that was unleashed just a year earlier in the wake of the assassination of Martin Luther King. The Black P Stone Rangers

317

ran Woodlawn; led by Jeff Stone, they controlled their turf just as surely as Richard Daley held reigns over the political and economic affairs of the rest of Chicago. I am not certain that any of this had any bearing on her response to me, but when I left her office I had her assurance that I would be admitted to the M.A. program in English with a full academic scholarship.

When I enrolled at the university in September of 1969, I was eager to learn and even more concerned about proving that what I was doing was relevant. "Relevant" that was an important word in the late sixties because so many of us carried with us the weight of being "firsts" and with that came the uncomfortable realization that we could not betray or forget those blacks who had paid very dearly for the benefits that we were reaping. The Little Rock Nine and Daisy Bates, the Greensboro students who endured the harassment and violence of hostile whites in non-violent sit-ins, the Freedom Riders who rode from Alabama to Mississippi amid the threats of beatings and firebombings were carried with me as I entered those classrooms where I studied Mark Twain with Hamlin Hill and made Shakespeare and George Bernard Shaw a part of my vocabulary because of the incomparable teaching of Elder Olson. My already tortured sense of double consciousness received another jolt when shortly after I began my studies Fred Hampton, Mark Clark and the members of the Black Panthers were brutally murdered in a pre-dawn raid masterminded by the state attorney's police. The realization of these and other sacrifices kept me humble and vigilant.

I soon discovered that some professors did not know what to make of me. After my first semester, one man who acted as my academic adviser asked, "Why aren't you having trouble here?" His question not only registered his curiosity about my better-than-average

2

performance but also his dismay. All that he knew about the superior education boasted by the university, all the assumptions that he harbored about the limited ability of black students from small, historically black institutions were being upset by what he saw as a troubling exception. Unfortunately, his myopia would not allow him to realize that I was not an exception. I had simply gotten a good education at Morgan State College where my professors were excellent teachers and scholars. Nick Aaron Ford who headed the English department at Morgan was a noted critic of Afro-American literature. Waters Turpin, who taught me the poetry of the Romantics, was a respected novelist and chronicled the lives of blacks living on the eastern shore of Maryland. I was also taught by Ulysses Lee who, along with Sterling A. Brown and Arthur P. Davis, edited the groundbreaking anthology Negro Caravan. Eugenia Collier and Ruth Sheffey, challenging teachers, were making names for themselves as critics and scholars in the field of Afro-American literature. This kind of education was outside of his understanding, and it was much easier to dismiss me, as well as my academic background, as a perplexing aberration.

In truth, the university was no less perplexed by the question of what to do with its black faculty. Its temporary answer to the problem of attracting black scholars was to bring one or two in for a semester or year. At the end of their visit these scholars would return to their colleges, and the host department would congratulate itself for having a black on its faculty, without making a long-term commitment to black scholarship. This certainly would have been the case for George E. Kent, the man who became my mentor, had it not been for a fortuitous string of events. George Kent had come to the U of C in 1969 as a visiting scholar from Quinnipiac College in Hamden, Connecticut. His classes on the Harlem Renaissance, Wright, Baldwin and Ellison, Faulkner, the writers of the Black Arts

3

Movement drew students from all over the campus. His strong commitment to Black literature and his insistence that it must be seen in light of its ability to bear the full weight of Western culture and the Black folk tradition encouraged in me a deep respect for the discipline.

Therefore, when I heard that Professor Kent was nearing the end of his stay and realized that no one had offered him the option of remaining at the university, I was disturbed. I demanded to know why this man with impeccable academic credentials was not being considered for a full time position at the university. After talking with the head of the English department, I knew that I was powerless alone to persuade him or the rest of the faculty to offer a position to George Kent. So I organized a petition campaign in which I got signatures from black students all over the campus. It really did not matter that they were not students in English. I convinced students in the medical school, in business, history, religion, and social work that signing the petition would send a message to the administration that blacks demanded a serious commitment to black studies and to a black presence at the university. Needless to say when I met with the English department with petition in hand, we students prevailed. George Kent was offered the position of full professor with tenure. Now there would be a permanent scholar in Afro-American literature, making serious scholarship in the field possible.

This was the real beginning of my education at the University of Chicago. I began to take charge of my own learning. Although there was no black studies curriculum, I decided that I would be the architect of my own. Without the blessing of the English department faculty who suggested that all my courses should be taken in English, I took courses from two outstanding black scholars who taught at the U of C. I had a memorable

4

class with historian John Hope Franklin who taught a class in the Antebellum South. I remember this man, author of the monumental study, From Slavery to Freedom, coming into the class with a stack of legal pad pages. He would sit down and proceed to talk for an hour without one reference to his notes. With the most obscure dates at hand and with an uncanny grasp of the nuances of the psychology of the South, he held us spellbound with his insights. I also took a seminar with theologian Charles Long whose classes were an incredible mix of sermonettes, homiletics, camp meeting drama, and hermeneutics. His witty and challenging style combined with the energy produced by my fellow students made the class a model of what a courageous teacher could do when he or she trusted in the potential that resides in every classroom.

However, without a doubt, George Kent was the greatest influence on my development as a scholar. Under his mentorship I studied Langston Hughes, Zora Neale Hurston, Gwendolyn Brooks, and Sterling A. Brown. He not only encouraged me to read widely in the field of Afro-American literature and folklore, but he also exposed me to the dynamic world of writing and publishing that flourished in Chicago during the late sixties. Through Kent I met Gwendolyn Brooks, the renown poet laureate of Illinois; poet Don L. Lee (Haki Madhubuti), the founder and editor of Third World Press; Hoyt Fuller, the editor of Black World; Lerone Bennett, popular historian and writer for Black World, and poet Margaret Burroughs, then curator for the DuSable Museum. I found myself in the midst of a New Black Renaissance where artists, musicians, poets, and political theorists came together to produce an outpouring of literature that affirmed Black life and culture.

My forays outside the classroom inevitably led me to another kind of school, Operation Breadbasket, now called PUSH. Along with hundreds of other Chicagoans, I

5

went each Saturday morning to a renovated synagogue to hear Jesse L. Jackson, the charismatic leader known as the "Country Preacher." As he intoned his "I Am Somebody" battle cry, those of us in the audience stood a little straighter and believed, at least for that moment, in the vision of this man who knew intimately of black struggle. "I am - black - beautiful - proud - I must be respected - I must be protected - I am - God's child." Whether he made parallels between Moses and Dr. King or talked about the patterns of sacrifice and nurture of black women, each Saturday we were convinced again and again of his extraordinary ability to articulate our most private pain, our fears, and our most expansive hopes and expectations.

It was also during this period that I got my first opportunity to teach . The Civil Rights Movement of the sixties , the martyrdom of King and Medgar Evers and others, the national rage at rights long withheld and promises long unkept had begun to open many doors in the early seventies. One such door was to Roosevelt University. Students there were now clamoring for courses in black literature. I, a newly made M.A. in English, was hired to teach a course called "Revolutionary Self-Conscious Literature." Never having taught before, I found myself in a classroom telling my students, many of whom were older and far wiser than I about the anger that was endemic in the works of Amiri Baraka, the principles of the Black Arts Movement espoused by Ron Karenga, and the works of struggle written by activists from Frederick Douglass to Malcolm X. While teaching at Roosevelt, I invited Gwendolyn Brooks, to read her poetry. It was then that I learned that in 1962 Frank London Brown had tried to get her a teaching position at Roosevelt. Apparently, Roosevelt considered her, had her fill out application papers, and then denied her the position on the grounds that she did not had a degree. Because of this new lesson I

6

realized the power of the time to effect change and the ironies that attend a society still beleaguered by the status quo.

What I learned during my first year as a student at the University of Chicago provided me a lifetime of insights. I was one of the first fruits of the civil rights struggle which opened the nation's universities to black scholarship. Never before, and unfortunately never since, were so many talented black students enrolled in graduate studies. We sensed even then that we were pioneers, that what we learned, what we wrote, what we taught would have great significance. And with the spirits of decades of struggle always with us, we were harvesting the promise of education.

Joanne V. Gabbin
James Madison University
December 1, 1989

A Black Woman on a White Campus: the 1970s Perspective

Daphyne Thomas, "College in the 1970's—Climbing Mountains"
(Manuscript by Daphyne S. Thomas, James Madison University, December 1, 1989)

College in the 1970's - Climbing Mountains
By Daphyne S. Thomas

I was born in Rocky Mount, Virginia, a small town with a population of about 5,000 people. Because my mother, who became a widow before I was three, did not have the opportunity to complete school, she always encouraged my sister and me to be the best that we could be and to go to college.

I attended a segregated elementary school, but attended an integrated middle and high school. By the time I graduated, there was only one high school in the county and everyone attended school together. When I left the segregated elementary school where I had done well and had been provided with strong support, I was scared. I had been told that although the white students were no smarter, they had newer equipment, better books, and better opportunities. So I had to be ready.

And, academically, I was ready. Socially, I was not. But I adjusted. I did well in high school and received numerous offers to attend various colleges and universities throughout the United States. Because of my financial situation, my decision had to be practical. I evaluated the various offers, applied to the better quality schools, and waited. I got accepted at all of the schools; then I had to make a decision. Should I attend a historically black university or should I attend a predominantly white institution? I decided to go with the highest bidder, the school that offered me the best and the most secure scholarship package for four years. I became an academic prostitute.

Thus, I attended Virginia Polytechnic Institute & State University, an institution of about 20,000 students in Blacksburg, located in the southwest mountains of Virginia. Tech, formerly an all male military school, was a university long on tradition and slow to change some of those traditions. It was also an institution in the 1970's with fewer than two percent blacks in the student body and about twenty-five percent women.

Tech proved to be quite a shock! Upon arriving to the campus, the school seemed to be an enormous mountain, like Mt. Everest, and I was just a tiny ant with instructions to climb that mountain. I was all alone. True, I did know about five or six people from my hometown, but I had no way of finding them. So I really was all alone. As my family drove away, I turned and looked at the cold gray buildings and resolved that I could climb this mountain alone.

The first day I spent much of my time unpacking and alone in my room. My white roommate, a dairy science major, seemed nice, but a bit different. Our differences did not stem from race, but from social orientation. She was an introvert who went home every weekend. I sought to interact with others. Fortunately, many of the other students in my dormitory also sought social companionship. By dinner time of the second day I had found a group of friends (white), with whom I could laugh and joke and eat.

I saw several black females in the dormitory as I traveled around with my white friends. They spoke to me and I to them, but we continued to go our separate ways. Eventually, a couple of young black women down the hall approached me and invited me to

attend a party with them. I accepted the invitation, and from that
day on I usually ate my meals with the other black students who
attended Virginia Tech. Despite the fact that most people in
college dining rooms eat with people with whom they have something
in common, many of the white students on campus accused the black
students of being separationist because they always ate together.
And by contrast, black students who ate regularly with their white
peers were accused of being "Uncle Tom's" by many black students.

The lives of Martin Luther King and Robert Kennedy touched us
in many ways. The social consciousness of the student in the
seventies reflected an awareness of social injustice and desire for
change. With youth comes the simplistic philosophy that people
should and will be fair when confronted. Thus student protests
were prevalent. Petitions and protests reflected concerns for
everything from the quality of food on the college campus to the
quality of life around the world.

I wanted to change the world. I attended many meetings with
that objective in mind. One organization formed was the Human
Relations Council. Although the name indicated that the
organization was open to all students, only black students joined.
The group decided to protest the playing of "Dixie" at football
games and homecoming festivities and was met with some resistance
by the administration. The protest took the form of many protests
of the 1960's. The more aggressive students visited the
administration with a list of demands. Many other students carried
banners, sang protest songs, or marched as a group in an effort to
influence the administration. However, things were not so simple.
The football team was reluctant to participate in the protests
because they were afraid they might lose their scholarships.
Likewise, students in the University's Corp of Cadets felt that
they could not jeopardize their scholarships or positions. I took
the middle road and participated in the carrying of banners and the
silent protests at the football games. Both black and white
students turned their backs when the song was played. Many
students felt that the playing of 'Dixie' was simply not an
important enough cause.

Those of us who participated found that the issues were much
more complicated. Alumni who had been supporting the University
with substantial contributions wanted to hear the song and
threatened to cut off contributions. Although many of the minority
students felt insulted by the playing of the song, the University
community, as a whole, did not come to the support of the student
group. Instead of immediately dropping the playing of the song of
the confederacy as the student protesters anticipated the
administration would do, the administration instituted new rules
and enforced old rules that had been not used in years in an effort
to minimize the method and the extent of the protests. Before I
graduated, however, the band had stopped playing the song.

The purpose of the Human Relations Council was to encourage a
coming together of the races. However, more often than not, the
Council was involved in issues dealing primarily with Black student
concerns. By the time I became president of the Human Relations
Council (HRC), the organization's focus had shifted from protesting

the playing of racist songs to working towards recruiting more black faculty and minority students and improving the retention of minority students at predominantly white universities.

Students in the 1970's did not take everything seriously. Athletics, parties, dating, fraternities and school sponsored programs dominated the social scene. Their social life had many similarities to college students of today. The illegal consumption of alcohol was just as prevalent at parties 10-15 years ago as it is at college parties now. However, the drugs of choice then were alcohol and marijuana rather than alcohol and cocaine.

Parties were held almost every weekend, and I attended many of them. For the most part, the parties were segregated. Because of the small number of black students at Virginia Tech, the parties were held either in a dormitory room or in one of the graduate students' trailers. Neither proved an impediment to having a good time. However, partying was not common during the week, rather the students lived for Friday afternoons and the weekend.

If we could not find a ride to the trailer where the party was being held, we would walk. Upon arriving at the trailer, we would be able to hear the music and actually see the trailer moving because of the music and the number of people inside. But, we did not care! Parties given by black students differed from those given by white students. Darkened rooms, strobe lights, lots of music and punch laced with grain alcohol described the typical party held by black students. White students who held parties usually offered bright lights and lots of beer and lots of talking In the town of Blacksburg (with fewer than one percent black), the sight of a large group of black students walking down the street late at night while leaving a party was not well received. Our walks were often monitored by the local police.

The visitation policy in the dormitories affected dating styles. In some dormitories, coed visitation was not permitted except in the lobby. In other dormitories, the door to the student's room was required to stay open at least 12 inches if a member of the opposite sex was present. Still other dorms had a closed door policy. However, all of the dorms required that visitation would end at 2:00 a.m. Consequently, dorm parties had to end by 2:00 a.m.

Most black students attended the parties wearing the latest fashions. Dress styles included the form fitting "hot pants" (very short shorts), large afros (hairdo), multicolored polyester shirts with wide and pointed collars, bell-bottomed pants, dashikis (a type of loose fitting shirt), cornrows (hairdo), and platform shoes (shoes with two inch soles). It's hard to believe that my now overweight body actually went out in public dressed in that fashion.

Then and now, the freshmen women's dormitory was the place to meet folks. The upperclassmen always made it a point to spend a lot of time in that building. The upperclassmen also always made it a point to go to Radford or Hollins College, two nearby all female institutions at that time, to meet coeds. In the mid-seventies, Virginia Tech was only about one fourth female. In terms of dating opportunities, one would think that the female attending Tech would have it made. However, with other schools only a half hour drive away, such was not the case. Road trips, as they were called, knew no color. Both black and white males traveled the distance to meet other females or to attend parties at neighboring schools. The female students were not invited to go along. When we asked if we could join them, we received excuses as to why that would not be possible.

College isolated students. When attending college, the world stops at the end of the campus unless, of course, going home for more food or money or to do the laundry. Students attending college in the mountains of Virginia did not make the Watergate scandal a top priority on their list of world concerns. Students were aware of the resignation of Richard Nixon, but I heard few conversations discussing the implications of such an historic event.

Even the interaction between the university and the town was limited. Because Blacksburg is such a small town, many of the citizens in the area had some connection with University. Citizens of the community tolerated the students' presence. Some students attended the local churches, and some townspeople attended cultural or athletic events on campus, but little more was done to cultivate a positive town and gown relationship. Minority students shopped in the local stores on occasion, but, for the most part, their world did not go far beyond the campus boundaries.

Despite the large student body the surroundings were friendly. Lovers of cultural events had numerous opportunities to see world famous performers in the mountains of Virginia. There was no shortage of athletic events either. Students who desired to meet people and participate in school activities were afforded numerous opportunities. Those who chose to stay to themselves found it easy to do so as well. Unfortunately most of the special events brought to campus did not appeal to the majority of minority students. The University eventually would add one event a year (usually during black history month) with emphasis geared towards the minority student. Although Isaac Hayes and Roberta Flack made appearances on campus, many of the minority students were disappointed in the selection of entertainment. They felt that the school was not attracting the "top" groups.

Richard Pryor made an appearance. He made light of everything from the black man/white woman dating issue, to the issues and concerns faced by parents in dealing with young adults, to the Exorcist, a popular movie in the mid 1970s. And it was good to laugh. Watergate, racial issues, the Vietnam conflict-- none of this seemed so oppressing when we were able to find humor in these most difficult situations.

Fraternities and sororities provided the opportunity to get involved in social and community activities as well as being the most overt symbol of segregation left on the college campuses. Two Greek systems existed, one black and the other white. White students who elected to join black fraternities or black students who elected to join white fraternities were viewed in an unfavorable light. Pledging some of the white fraternities or sororities sometimes required the pledgee to perform racially discriminatory tasks which included mocking or imitating blacks. Pledging some of the black fraternities or sororities required the pledgee to become involved in activities viewed as encouraging the separation of the races, such as marching in line or performing step shows. During a period in American society in which the coming together of the races was encouraged, the Greek systems stood out. Despite the racial awareness, I elected to pledge a black sorority. Although black fraternities and sororities sponsored a number a social functions, as did the white organizations, the sorority I joined also emphasized service to the community. I had been given the privilege of getting an education, and I felt that this was an opportunity to give back to the community. And that we did, through visitations to the elderly and infirm, clothing and food drives, etc.

Black students encountered numerous frustrations. They had to be prepared, bright, alert, and independent just like other students, but if they failed in any of these areas they most likely did not successfully complete the course studies. Many found themselves being told that engineering was not an appropriate course of study or that they could never handle the challenges of the architecture curriculum. Where other students were encouraged to work harder or to try again, some African-American students were told to move on. In some classes I could sense the hesitation of the teachers. Often I found that once I proved that I could handle the work, the tensions eased. But I frequently felt that I, as a minority student, was called upon to prove myself in situations where the white student was not.

I elected to attend Virginia Tech because it is an outstanding academic institution, and it gave me a full academic scholarship. I anticipated that I would encounter numerous challenges and opportunities, and I did. The classroom offered a wealth of opportunities for learning. I found professors who were willing to work with students and encouraged hard work. I also found professors who would not offer a helping hand to students. Classroom size varied from 200 students in a biology lecture to 25 students in a special urban studies course.

In classes dealing with social issues, many of the other minority students, as well as myself, were frequently called upon to be the spokesperson(s) for the entire race. In other classes requiring ground work or work with partners, African-American students regularly paired with other African-American students or did their projects alone. In still other classes, professors sought out minority students to offer words of encouragement or to provide special assistance. Many white students expressed a resentment for minority students and assumed that their presence at the institution could only mean that the school had lowered its standards to let the minority student into the University. Although Virginia Tech provided a relaxed atmosphere in which to live, racial issues created tensions and were not readily confronted. Every year during Black History month, the student newspaper was filled with articles by white students criticizing the black fraternities or the Human Relations Council. The papers were also filled with letters from African-American students criticizing administration policies and responding to the criticisms by white students.

Students from urban areas or large cities found it difficult to adjust to the rural atmosphere in Blacksburg. The social and cultural setting differed significantly from what students in the larger cities encountered. Sometimes, this limitation in lifestyle proved so overwhelming that students did not adjust and would withdraw from the school. Consequently, we saw many inner city black students resigning. Not only did students from the urban areas sometimes have difficulty in adjusting to the University, but white and black students from the rural areas also had problems. The personal attention and individual encouragement that many students needed was often lacking.

The dropout rate and the flunkout rate for these students was extremely high. Virginia Tech had not yet developed any programs to help the students with their transition nor to prepare them for the cultural shock. Students' failure to succeed at an institution like VPI can be attributed to the inability to adjust to a different world.

But many students from rural southwest Virginia did graduate, and I was one of them. Four years after entering Virginia Tech, I had climbed that mountain. Yet, I realized that my journey was not complete--it was just really beginning. There would be many more mountains for me to climb.

Spelman: Riding High in the 1980s

Paula Giddings, "Johnnetta B. Cole, Spelman's 'Sister'
President"
(*Essence,* November, 1987, 34, 125, reprinted by permission)

Ronald Smothers, "President's Door Open For Spelman
Students"
(*The New York Times,* January 20, 1988)

JOHNNETTA B. COLE
SPELMAN'S "SISTER"
PRESIDENT

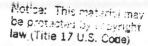
Those who are up early enough on Spelman College's campus may see its new president, Dr. Johnnetta B. Cole, taking her daily 6 a.m. stroll across its tree-lined grounds. Tall and angular, with a penetrating gaze that easily gives way to a warm smile and sense of humor, Cole strikes an imposing figure—though, unlike many college presidents, not an aloof one. "You know, she talks to everyone" is the new campus scuttlebutt. On April 25 of this year, Cole was named the first

Black woman president of Spelman, the historically Black women's liberal-arts institution, with 1,750 students, that is part of the Atlanta University Center. Spelman has an endowment with a current market value of $48 million, second only to Hampton University among Black schools.

Cole, who is 51, grew up in Jacksonville, Florida, and has a sensibility born of an affectionate middle-class family, a supportive Black community and the unforgotten pain of the segregated South of the 1940's. Seeking answers to the double-edged reality of her experience led her to the study of anthropology at Oberlin College in Ohio and Northwestern University in Evanston, Illinois.

Before her appointment to Spelman, Cole was a professor of anthropology and director of the Latin American and Caribbean Studies Program at Hunter College in New York City. She is divorced and the mother of three sons, ages 25, 21 and 17.

ESSENCE: *What kind of impact or difference do you think you will make as Spelman's first Black woman president?*

COLE: You know, sometimes I just let my imagination go, and the other day I imagined inventing a machine whose sole purpose was to measure the impact of Black women presidents. [Laughter]

Seriously, I do think that we have to be careful not to do things differently just for the sake of doing them differently. Spelman has its traditions, and I believe it's possible that doing things in a nontraditional way can take a form that is unproductive. But it's equally possible for the nontraditional to be the only mode that will create needed change. When I look back in history at such women as Ida B. Wells [the journalist who initiated the first antilynching campaign in 1892] or Rosa Parks, I see that they had a traditional approach in much of what they did. But they also changed the course of history by acting in nontraditional ways when they needed to.

ESSENCE: *What would you like to see the graduating students of 1991 doing?*

COLE: I would hope that Spelman students will not only graduate to become great surgeons or corporate executives, but that they will also be among the core of folk who are seeking solutions to such issues as homelessness in America. That they will be engaged in writing the definitive work on the systems of inequality called racism and sexism. There is a saying that solutions to problems are often found by people who can see out of more than one eye. And it is Black women who are able to see out of their Blackness, out of their womanness, often out of their poverty and sometimes out of their privilege. So I believe that it is going to be Black women who will find the answers to many of the problems we face today.

ESSENCE: *But what do you say to those students who are going to college to get skills so they can get a good job, not save the world? I mean, can you teach social responsibility in this age of materialism?*

COLE: You say to them that a good liberal-arts education is the key to getting a good job; that studies show that almost without exception CEO's [chief executive officers] have a strong liberal-arts foundation. That's because it is the kind of education that teaches you to think, to manipulate six different ideas simultaneously, to understand the diversity of the world. This is what executives and CEO's have to be able to do.

And a good liberal-arts education teaches not only skills and information but also a sense of the world in relation to oneself. A Black student isn't well educated if she knows world history and American history but hasn't had a course in Black history. And since that history didn't happen in a vacuum, whites who don't know it aren't well educated, either. An individual who can't relate to the Black community—understand and be understood by her own people—isn't well educated. And I have a strongly held view that a student who only knows theory and never engages in any action isn't well educated. We have to find a means to move away from the sheer language of the classroom to the reality of the community, even if it's only going to the "Y" every Saturday and putting in two hours in a tutoring program. That's that old notion of social responsibility that Black women have always nurtured, socialized, taught and trained, and we have to find a way to bring it back.

ESSENCE: *You may have to do some convincing when it comes to parents...*

COLE: I'm very sensitive to that. I remember telling my grandfather who was a businessman [he started the Afro-American Insurance Company in 1904] that I wanted to be an anthropologist and his laughing at the idea. He said, "How are you ever going to make a living doing something like that?" I burst into tears. But my mother said that he was only concerned that I be able to take care of myself, and that she believed it was also important to find work I loved—otherwise I'd be miserable the rest of my life.

Out of that experience I gained respect for the fact that our education must help us find work, though we must also respect students' passions. If there is a young sister who wants to be a [CONTINUED ON PAGE 125]

335

ESSENCE: *You think of yourself as a teacher as much as as an anthropologist and an administrator, don't you?*

COLE: Yes, a very *serious* teacher; I *love* it. I'm determined to teach at least one class a week at Spelman. My greatest influences were those Black women in education, including my mother. They were our intellectual tradition: the librarians who first got me excited about books, the counselors, the college presidents and so on. And they were the type of people who might not only introduce you to a Claude McKay poem, but could also grab ahold of your pigtails, sit you down, and say, "Girl, if you do that again, I'll knock you into next week!"

I also think of myself as a mother, in the broadest definition of the term—that is, not only in the literal sense. Motherhood to me also means the ability to *socially* reproduce resistance and protest. It is the ultimate social responsibility because it is being an agent of change.

ESSENCE: *What will the Spelman campus be like in the year 2010?*

COLE: There will be a sign at the Atlanta airport that says "This way to the Spelman Center on Black Women's Studies," and there'll be a think tank on one corner of the campus: a place where Black women policymakers—and men, too—come to get the information to deal with important political questions. There will be an archive that houses the papers of distinguished Afro-American women as well as other scholars throughout the world.

Spelman students will look you straight in the eye and present themselves with even more confidence than they have now, because they will have a familiarity with the world. They will know what a young Japanese woman of roughly the same age is about. They will be familiar with what's going on in South America. And they will not be at all surprised to hear someone talking about English-speaking Black people on the Atlantic coast of Nicaragua—they will already know about them. They will have the worldliness that goes beyond the comfort of being Black and a woman, through the curriculum, travel, exchange programs, visiting lecturers and so on.

Of course, we will systematically, creatively, respectfully pursue every one of the traditional money sources to realize these things. But we must also learn to do for self. If there is one thing that anthropologists know, it is that giving establishes, deepens, a relationship. By giving, Black women will make Spelman truly *their* institution. If every Spelman alumna and other individuals—including our scholars—gave just a hundred dollars a year, there are few dreams that we could not begin to realize. Then when the judgment is made about the first Black woman president of Spelman, that judgment will also be made about the hundreds upon hundreds of Black women who helped this presidency succeed. There is a lot at stake, a lot at stake.... —PAULA GIDDINGS

JOHNNETTA B. COLE
● continued from page 34

poet, then we have to help her be a poet. We're not going to spend four years convincing her to be a computer programmer.

President's Door Open For Spelman Students

By RONALD SMOTHERS
Special to The New York Times

ATLANTA, Jan. 19 — Amid the bustle of registration last week for the new semester at Spelman College, several students sat in the high-ceilinged reception area of the president's office.

Their faces were etched with concern about getting transfer credits approved or about the hard realities of paying the semester's bills. A few showed animated enthusiasm about sharing some new idea for enhancing the school's intellectual life.

One by one they were seen by Dr. Johnnetta B. Cole in what has become a weekly ritual in her first year as head of the 1,760-student, private college for black women: the president's open office hours.

As the first black woman to serve as president of the elite 106-year-old school here, it was perhaps predictable that Dr. Cole would start with a ready-made store of good will among

The New York Times/Alan Weiner
Dr. Johnnetta B. Cole

the young women here and the alumnae. Her predecessors were four white women and two black men.

But many here wondered if the new resident role model would be accessible and approachable or a distant beacon lighting the way.

'Visible and Available'

"I didn't expect her to be this accessible," said Lurelia Freeman, an 18-year-old sophomore from Atlanta who was taking advantage of the open office hours for the second time this year. "When you think of a college president you think of someone remote, off being a manager, not talking regularly with students."

"She has a lot to offer and she is always visible and available," said Cecilia Johnson, a freshman from Seattle, who came to bring greetings from a mutual friend and to ask Dr. Cole about Western religions in the African countries in which Spelman's president has worked and studied.

For Dr. Cole, a 50-year-old anthropologist who was a professor at Hunter College in Manhattan before coming to Spelman, the number and variety of contacts with Spelman students have been a pleasant surprise. After years as a teacher who placed a premium on interacting with her students, she said she had expected the daunting task of running a college to bring it all to an end.

She credited the work of her immediate predecessor, Donald M. Stewart, with helping to ease her transition. Mr. Stewart, now president of the College Entrance and Examination Board, built the school's endowment from $9.6 million in 1976 to $48 million now. Dr. Cole said the money allowed her to focus on fundraising "only every other day, rather than every day."

She hesitated to talk about any sweeping changes she might want at Spelman, saying she was still too new for that. But Dr. Cole did say that she wanted to establish endowed chairs, set up a faculty lounge and develop more interdisciplinary studies, such as women's studies and black studies.

She also said she was interested in a program to connect Spelman students with corporate mentors.

But it was the move to open her office to students one afternoon a week that sharpened her awareness of the problems and concerns of Spelman students.

"Teaching is a particular way of going through life, and I basically see myself as teaching in the open office hours," said Dr. Cole. A tall and imposing woman with close-cropped hair and incisive speech, she was named president of Spelman last spring.

Born in Jacksonville, Fla., she studied at Fisk University in Nashville and Oberlin College in Ohio, before receiving her doctorate in anthropology from Northwestern University in Evanston, Ill.

The nearly 100 students who have come to see Dr. Cole's office here have caused her both cheer and frustration.

On one side was the student with a knotty problem in research methodology who came to her for guidance. "It so pleased me because she saw me as a teacher and scholar," Dr. Cole said.

Then there are the concerns that center on the school's old, overcrowded dormitories that need repair or on financial aid problems.

She had listened to the problems and hopes of students before, but, she said, "I never felt it as acutely as I do now, because now the buck stops with me and there is no one else I can turn to."

Balancing such complaints are the times she can personally intervene to solve problems, as she did last week for Tamala Turner. The student met Dr. Cole more than a year ago at a conference on women's studies at Miss Turner's school, the University of Missouri at St. Louis.

Miss Turner was struck by Dr. Cole as "a black woman who was doing what I wanted to do," teach and conduct research in the social sciences.

Miss Turner took a leave of absence in the last semester of her senior year at Missouri to take classes at Spelman. But money was a problem. After a 30-minute meeting the student and the president emerged all smiles with Dr. Cole announcing that the budget allowed her to have a research assistant and that Miss Turner had the job and could now register for classes.

"I just knew she wouldn't forget me," Miss Turner said later.

Dr. Cole seemed excited as well at the prospect of an eager and bright student with whom to work, saying: "She's going to understand what it's like to be a scholar and this is how scholars get made — by hanging out with them."

Black Women's Studies Has Come of Age

Patricia Bell-Scott and Beverly Guy-Sheftall, "The First Five
Years: Looking Backward and Forward"
(*SAGE*, 5 (1), Summer, 1988, p. 2)

THE FIRST FIVE YEARS:
LOOKING BACKWARD AND FORWARD

In memory of Dr. Marion Vera Cuthbert, pioneer in Black Women's Studies, 1896-1989

Five years ago, we began planning this journal after an all-night discussion with our sister, Ruby Sales. Ruby provided, at that moment, the words of wisdom which jolted us into action, and she continues to be one of our most thoughtful and constructive supporter-critics. In the first issue, we outlined a threefold objective for the journal: (1) to provide a forum for critical discussion of issues related to Black women, (2) to promote feminist scholarship, and (3) to disseminate new knowledge about Black women to a broad audience. We also declared the journal to be pro-Black and pro-woman, acknowledging our respect for and commitment to reflect the differences and commonalities among Black women globally. We remain committed to this objective and these principles and hope that our efforts to live up to the challenge are worthy of the faith which so many supporters have placed in the idea of such a journal.

This issue marks the beginning of the second half of a decade for *SAGE: A Scholarly Journal on Black Women*. And, as we reflect upon our brief history, there are five accomplishments of which we are particularly proud. First, we have published thematic issues on the topics of education, mothers and daughters, women writers, health, women as workers, Africa and the diaspora, artists and artisans, as well as a supplement of student writing. The present issue, our first open, non-thematic issue, emanates from the desire of the editorial group and our readers to increase the diversity of topics and perspectives.

Second, the Spelman College Women's Research and Resource Center has become the journal's host site, and we are delighted to have an association with this internationally-renown college for Black women. Third, the journal has developed a subscribers' list of individuals and institutions which covers the 50 U.S. states and 30 foreign countries. Among our individual subscribers and contributors are persons as young as 11 and as old as 92, from all class and racial groups; from all sexual and political orientations; and from inside and outside the academy.

Fourth, to support research and activism in Black Women's Studies, we have established three awards — The Sadie Tanner Mossell Alexander Award for Outstanding Scholarship by a student; The Sue Bailey Thurman Award for Distinguished Service by a student; and the Hilda A. Davis Award for Distinguished Service by a professional. And finally, we fortunately have received financial support for printing, distribution, and related activities from several agencies and institutions, such as the University of Connecticut, The Ford Foundation, The Fulton County Arts Council, The Fund for the Improvement of Post-Secondary Education of the U.S. Department of Education, The Joyce Johnson Fund, the National Endowment for the Humanities, The Pettus-Crowe Foundation, Spelman College, and U.S.A. for Africa Foundation. Moreover, we have been blessed by the financial, moral, and spiritual support of many Black and Women's Studies scholar-activists, without whose support we simply could not have persevered.

This issue is dedicated to the memory of Dr. Marion Vera Cuthbert, early pioneer in Black Women's Studies, who died on May 5, 1989. Her 1942 dissertation entitled *Education and Marginality: A Study of the Negro Woman College Graduate* was among the first to focus on Black women and must be regarded as one of the classics in the field. Cuthbert had a long and rich life which included an appointment at the Burrell Normal School in Florence, Alabama, a Deanship at Talladega College, a staff position at the National Office of the Y.W.C.A., and both faculty and staff positions at Brooklyn College. Though she is best remembered for her academic writings, she was also an accomplished creative writer.

In keeping with the broad interests of Cuthbert, this issue covers a wide range of topics. We are especially pleased by the increased number of non-U.S. themes and contributors, as well as the contributions of students and activists. We have also expanded the book review section; this too is in keeping with the Cuthbert tradition. She maintained an active schedule as a book reviewer for several local clubs well into her eighties.

Finally, in addition to our Cuthbert tribute, we want to honor the invaluable contributions of the editorial collective — Jacqueline Jones Royster and Janet Sims-Woods, who are co-founders; Ann James, Administrative Assistant; and Miriam DeCosta-Willis and Lucie Fultz, Book Review Editor and Associate Editor, respectively. It is with their help, the righteous voice of sister Ruby, and the support of readers/critics/writers from all parts of this planet that we enthusiastically prepare for the next five years of *SAGE*!

Patricia Bell-Scott
Beverly Guy-Sheftall